W9-CPG-758

The Changing Face of Northeast Brazil

THE CHANGING FACE OF NORTHEAST BRAZIL

KEMPTON E. WEBB

COLUMBIA UNIVERSITY PRESS
New York and London 1974

Library of Congress Cataloging in Publication Data

Webb, Kempton Evans.
The changing face of Northeast Brazil.

Bibliography
1. Brazil, Northeast—Description and travel.
2. Brazil, Northeast—Economic conditions. I. Title.
F2583.W42 330.9′81′306 74-1029
ISBN 0-231-03767-8

Printed in the United States of America

To Preston E. James

Inspiring guide to geography
and to Latin America

CONTENTS

MAPS AND FIGURES

PREFACE

As a beginning graduate student twenty years ago, I first became interested in Northeast Brazil through the accounts of the terrible droughts there so vividly portrayed by Euclides da Cunha and others. After writing a master's thesis on the climates of Northeast Brazil in 1955 I was fortunate to spend a first field season in Brazil in 1956–57 studying the geography of food supply in Minas Gerais under the auspices of the National Academy of Sciences and the National Research Council. Two months of food supply research as a technical consultant to the Banco do Nordeste in Fortaleza in 1957 convinced me that I should return for a much longer residence.

A traditional regional approach to all Northeast Brazil was not considered practical or desirable. In discussions with Preston James, I decided to focus upon a line or zone of discontinuity, and to examine the changes in the geography of that zone through time. It was hoped that an understanding of the biopsy or area case study of eastern Pernambuco and Paraíba would have implications for and meaning to the wider area of Northeast Brazil.

Field research support for the 1963–64 season was provided by the Ford Foundation through Columbia's Institute of Latin American Studies. The writing phase in 1968–69 during a sabbatical spent in Portugal was supported by a Fullbright–Hays research grant. The most recent follow-up field trip in May–June of 1973 was partly funded by the American Philosophical Society and the Banco do Nordeste do Brazil.

I am greatly indebted to my American colleagues, Preston James and Charles Wagley, and to my Brazilian colleagues, Speridião Faissol, Pedro Pinchas Geiger, Rubens Costa, José Ajuricaba da Silva, Gilberto Osorio de Andrade, Manuel Correia de Andrade, Ney Strauch, Gerard Prost, and the many others who shared their understanding and hospitality with me and my family. I am grateful for the assistance of the Cartographic Laboratory of the Geography Department in Lisbon, Portugal, and for the cartographic and editorial assistance provided by Mary Virginia Kahl of Columbia University Press and my research assistant, Drew Young.

Kempton E. Webb
July 18, 1974

The Changing Face of Northeast Brazil

Chapter One
INTRODUCTION

Northeast Brazil holds a special fascination for most social scientists who go there to unpack their kit of conceptual tools, hoping to apply them to one or several of the myriad problems found there. It is probably true that more has been written about Northeast Brazil than about any other area of that country, and yet, despite the depth and breadth of interest concerning that distinctive region of contrasts, Northeast Brazil remains today one of the least understood parts of the national territory. Perhaps it is because it has yielded its secrets with great reluctance that social scientists have been drawn back repeatedly to try to fathom the complexities of life and livelihood there throughout more than four hundred years of recorded history.

In the rhetoric that has been delivered over the years, there has always been much talk of moving the Northeast "forward" from a "backward" position, whether this talk has come from Brazilians or from hopeful foreigners who hold altruistic interests in that part of Brazil. Yet with all these references to progress, there has been relatively little discussion of the cause-and-effect relationships of poverty in the Northeast. The history of institutional efforts to deal with the Northeast's problems reaches back to the early years of this century with the founding of IFOCS (Federal Inspectory of Works Against the Droughts) in 1909, followed by DNOCS (National Department of Works Against the Droughts), and later the Banco do Nordeste do Brasil, SUDENE (Development Superintendency of the Northeast), the Alliance for Progress, Food for Peace—and, in more recent years, USAID. The focus of all these efforts has been positive. The word "development," which has been assumed to mean economic development particularly, has become a reflexive expression in the language of Northeast boosters. And yet in the face of such positive thinking and motives, the student of Northeast Brazil who has kept in touch over the past decade or two cannot help but conclude that little has come from all these efforts and that, in many ways, some Northeasterners are worse off today than they were before the development efforts were begun. Two questions loom largely then: What are the negative influences and factors that have held back the greatly desired development? Why are we not able to break the circles of cause and effect that have left the Northeast the largest underdeveloped area of the largest developing country in the entire Western Hemisphere?

One must conclude that the best of motives and the most altruistic of intentions can never substitute for a hard assessment of the realities and the inevitabilities of processes that have discernible causes and consequences.

Northeast Brazil poses to the geographer a particularly inviting challenge in that he is presented with a rich and accessible document to interpret—namely, the earth's surface. The geographer tries to read the landscape, to answer questions that may not be posed in the standard forms, and to locate data that may be found in places unfamiliar to other social scientists. As he reads the landscape of the Northeast, what does he see? The dominant impression is one of grave social, economic, and political problems that are intimately entwined with physical and ecological problems within a long, complex historical fabric. Faced with the wide variations in stages of economic development and degrees of "modernization," we are confronted with the questions of how and why did Northeast Brazil come to its present situation? The cultural and historical geographer is interested in the operation and distribution of processes through time. This involves a careful scrutiny of what the land and livelihood were like in the past. How did the physical habitat and settlement pattern get that way?

While some areas of the Northeast, such as the sugarcane area of the zona da mata (coastal forest region), have been analyzed and discussed in great detail (the most notable study is *The Masters and the Slaves* by Gilberto Freyre), there are many other areas of possibly even greater importance today, such as the agreste (transitional zone), the brejos (moist areas) and serras (mountains), that have been largely neglected. Between the past and the present there must be answers and links that can shed light on the serious and compelling problems of Northeasterners today, and our task is to try to answer some of these questions.

It is the primary aim of this book to set the present landscape of Northeast Brazil in an evolutionary perspective that will throw light on (1) the landscape as it was observed in the 1960s, and (2) the formative interacting processes that have molded it into its present form. A secondary aim is (3) to show how the application of such an evolutionary interpretation can illuminate the very real and urgent problems of Northeast Brazil, and finally (4) to demonstrate a method of geographic investigation that can produce results that can be compared to those of other disciplines.

One conclusion recognizes as essential to regional knowledge an awareness of the interaction between cultural and physical processes through time. This is presented in chapter 2 as the concept of *landscape evolution*. Another conclusion concerns the geographic displacement of regional boundaries: as cattle-ranching moved eastward from the arid sertão (the dry interior), agriculture moved from the humid coast westward to the transitional agreste. Accompanying this, dry conditons ("desertification") moved eastward as culture moved westward. We shall observe how the humid zona da mata in the east and the dry sertão are largely physical regions, whereas the transitional agreste is essentially a cultural or man-made invention of the last hundred years or so. Other conclusions deal with how physical habitats react to different influences and we shall observe the different degrees of sensitivity of the mata, agreste, and sertão zones to the hand of man—or, in other words, the different tolerance levels of the habitat to man's actions. The precariousness of such a region as the sertão cannot really be compared to that of, say, the flat chernozem area of North America.

Finally, we give great importance to the past because the past still exists in the sense that there are parts of Brazil where life is lived today the way it was lived one hundred or even two hundred years ago. This is only one of the reasons that Brazil is so interesting—the fact that there are relict forms of life to be observed.

THE STUDY AREA

Much of the fascination with Northeast Brazil (map 1) stems from its distinction as (1) an arid pocket within the humid subcontinent of Brazil, (2) a large area of widespread poverty, and (3) an area of great potential, if not actual, social and political unrest. These three factors, not to mention others, have heightened the interest in Northeast Brazil on the part of many persons and national and international organiza-

INTRODUCTION

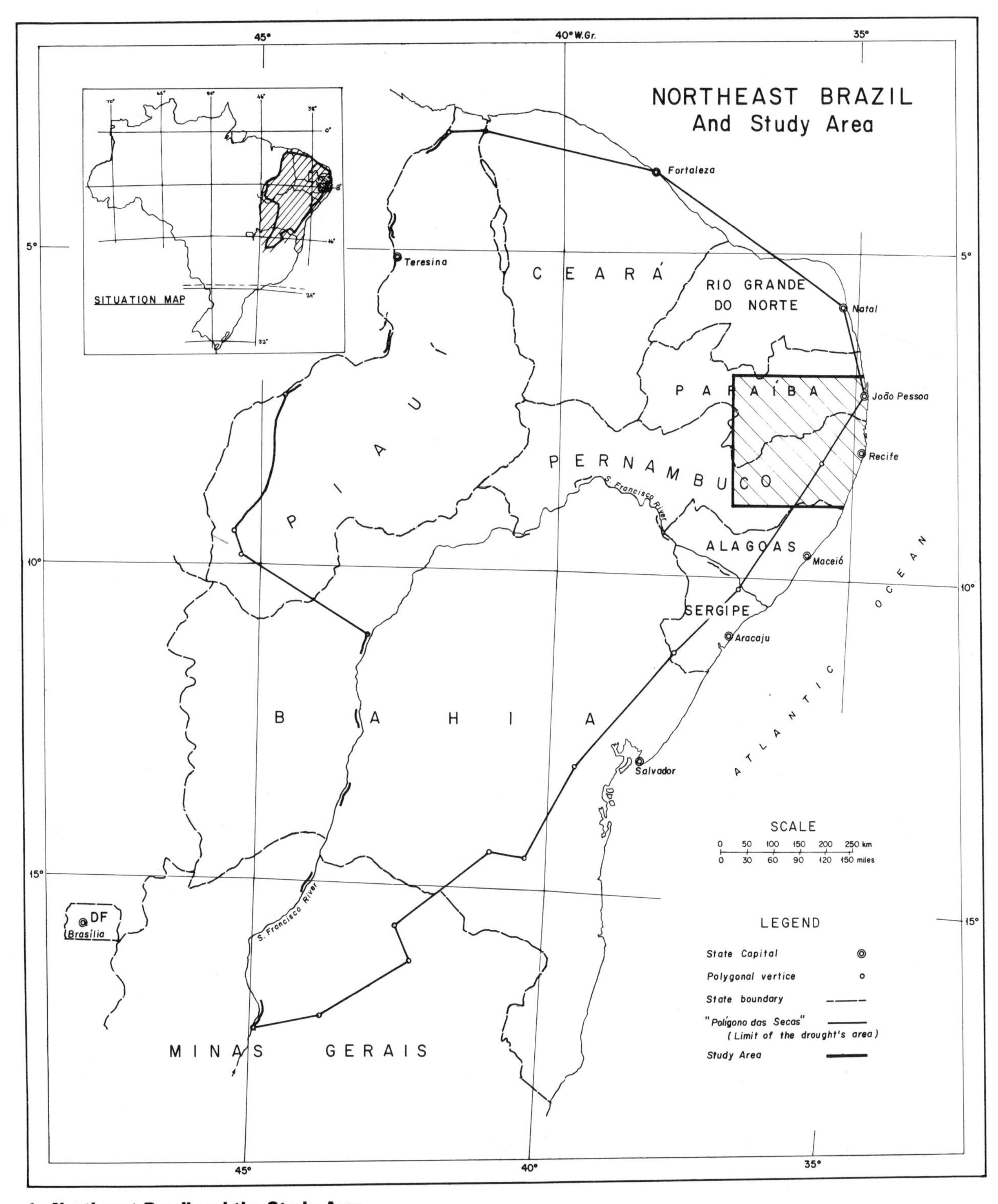

1. **Northeast Brazil and the Study Area**

tions. In the early 1960s, when the *Ligas Camponesas* (Peasant Leagues) were given prominent relief and international attention was focused on them through North America television documentaries and newspapers reports, it seemed to some people that the social problems portrayed there were about to erupt in a leftist revolution and blood bath. Since the rightist military government took over in 1964, the lid has been put on many forms of expression that were heard in the past. The important point is that the basic problems have remained and become intensified, and the fact that we do not hear or read so much about them now does not mean that they have decreased in importance.

One major obstacle to thorough studies on Northeast Brazil has been the lack of basic information, whether this be in the form of large-scale detailed maps or precise census materials on meaningful enumeration areas, which are usable by social scientists. The lack of travel amenities, however, at least as I encountered them in a year's time of traveling over 14,000 kilometers throughout the interior, is more than compensated for by the yield of information and insights.

For the most part, there have been two broad categories of approach to Northeast Brazil. The first is that of general books on the area, which tend to attack broad questions and which are largely unsupported by hard data and field study. The second approach is that of detailed studies of specific areas or topics, such as the community studies done by anthropologists, or the industry-feasibility studies of the economists, or the ground-water studies by engineers. In contrast, the geographer takes as his point of departure the basic document of the earth's surface; that is, the *given*. By using a judiciously selected study area that includes a representative slice of the three dominant ecological zones (the zona da mata, agreste, and sertão of eastern Pernambuco and Paraíba), we will, hopefully, find in it relevance and applicability to other parts of Northeast Brazil. This study, then, will try to be a window through which the reader is introduced to the diversity and problems of Northeast Brazil.

CHANGING PERCEPTIONS OF NORTHEAST BRAZIL

The grand theme of the colonial desbravadors, or bushwhackers, was one of Man Against Nature, and this view of reality has persisted down to present-day Northeast Brazil. While the social scientists have come to acknowledge that the majority of social and economic ills in the Northeast stem ultimately from antiquated production processes and unjust distributions of wealth and the products of work, most Nordestinos still blame a lot of the area's problems on droughts and floods. A discontinuous and erratic enlightenment has accompanied the area's development over the centuries.

First came the brazilwood gatherers who set up their dyewood factories in clearings lost in the dense forest of the humid zona da mata. Then came the sugar planters with their slaves who ultimately transformed the choicest parts of that wild zone into a completely domesticated "man-scape." Let us look briefly at what happened in the dry interior, or sertão, about which José Guimarães Duque has written so authoritatively.[1]

The first invasion by Europeans of the sertão was by vaqueiros (cattlemen and cowboys) who staked out their corrals and proceeded to raise their scrawny cattle on the open range, despite the harsh nature of the contacts between the white man, the hostile-appearing thorn

[1] In addition to his several published books, such as *Solo e Agua no Poligono das Secas* and *O Nordeste e as Lavouras Xerofilas*, Duque's unpublished works dealing with problems of regional development in the Northeast are rich in wisdom and insight born of forty years contact with Northeast Brazil.

forest (caatinga), and the fierce Indians. By furnishing milk, cheese, beef, and leather, the cattle allowed the cattlemen to become fixed in the desert fastnesses. Those early intrepid adventurers taught succeeding generations that those arid areas were suitable for livestock ranching and for the limited cultivation of drought-resistant crops.

Settlement of the interior continued in the following centuries. The dominant figures to emerge, however, were the fazendeiros who became the heads of extended families, the chiefs, the godfathers, the bankers, and the neighborhood counselors for the communities that were formed around them by relatives, friends, neighbors, and workers. It was in this way that the sertão acquired more people, more cattle, more farm plots, and more roads. The habits and ways of living that were inherited and those that were acquired were transmitted from generation to generation until they crystallized into a true patriarchal agrarian society.

The addition of new families, however, seeking other fazendas, inheritances, the enlargement of farms, the clearing and burning of cactus-covered areas, and the multiplying of the herds, signified a biological expansion within a relatively static physical milieu. As a consequence, the xerophytic or drought-resistant vegetation suffered a wastage and setback in its potential as a natural resource. The hand of man, the trampling hooves of cattle, the work of axes and fire, had breached the caatinga and opened the way for the decimation of flora, fauna, and soil with the accompaniment of erosion. The methods developed as the needs were felt because those dispersed societies knew only how to operate with extensive farming methods, using a minimum of effort to take a maximum yield from the land. Those early cattlemen were land-rich and labor-poor.

Toward the end of the nineteenth century, external as well as internal influences of a physical, economic, social, and political nature made themselves felt. The main ones were the periodic droughts, the backland bandits, or cangaceiros, and the feuds and bloody disputes between families and individuals over land, money, and political jobs. On the other hand, and at the same time, educated people were appearing in the area, with leadership in agriculture, commerce, industry, the professions, and politics. New modes of transportation, such as railroad and motor cars, began to make inroads in drawing those backward areas out of the past and into the present. These outside influences of a more enlightened nature were felt, but still the Northeast remained far behind the more progressive areas of the South, to say nothing of foreign countries of the Northern Hemisphere and Europe, upon whose markets Northeast Brazil depended so heavily, especially for sugar and cotton sales.

Nevertheless, the influences of roads, telegraph, radio, airplanes, construction projects of highways and schools, the demographic growth, and the crises of the droughts modified rural life, breaking that hitherto encrusted society. What resulted was that the long-entrenched fazendeiros began to lose their local power, and others assumed it. The money became redistributed and returned to the banks; the people became more mobile and sought other jobs, in many cases in industry in São Paulo and Rio. The new, fabricated novelties and other manufactured items brought in from outside were bought, although the bulk of the population had very little money, and the great poverty of the area was revealed in its nakedness to the rest of Brazil.

In the twentieth century, through the work of various government organizations and programs, efforts were made to relieve the poverty in the Northeast. However, the tremendous disparity between the levels of knowledge of the upper classes and the working classes led the técnicos (those with specialized technical knowledge) and the program directors to believe that any effort at real communication with the working classes was pointless. They (the directors) believed that they should therefore simply introduce their higher level of agricultural technology without even trying to bring about rapport and accommodation with old community customs or preparing the people to receive the technology. As a result, without the human touch much time was lost in the demonstrations of techniques, and without the simplest degree of human understanding and tactfulness much time was lost in the implantation of scientific principles, however true and valid. With rare exceptions, the elites of the political, economic, and cultural groups were incapable of perceiving the true situation and its implications. Yet at the same time, while the upper classes failed in the formulation of an approach to the solution of problems of the Northeast, the common people, for their part, did not even try to cooperate with the government in the use of its facilities.

The phase of institutional intervention began in the early years of this century with IFOCS (1909), the Fomento Agrícola (Agricultural Development), the Institutos Oficiais (Official Institutes), experimental stations, schools of agronomy, and the installation of meteorological stations by means of which attention was focused on water, climate, soils, and plants. More recently, other organizations, such as DNEF, DNER, CVSF, DNPRC, DNOS, BNB, DNERO (all known by their initials), as well as private institutes and universities, afforded valuable collaboration, but the pity is that much of the valuable and painstaking research that has been done, some of which will be cited in this study, has not been used or acted upon by any state or municipal government or other implementing institution. Great expectations were raised, and if great social and economic benefits did not flow from these projects, it was because of administrative independence, the low level of coordination of efforts, and, with few exceptions, the incomplete understanding of human factors involved. In general, the technical and administrative organizations that operate in the Northeast did not make themselves aware of the responsibilities and consequences of their interventions in the general processes of the evolution of the area. And this is as true today, if not truer—in view of the massive foreign aid to Brazil and the Northeast through USAID—as it was in the 1920s with IFOCS when it was building simple reservoirs.

As we anticipate delving into the compelling and complex themes of man and land, we should remind ourselves that the natural resources of an area are not in themselves the decisive elements in the progress of an area, but are rather the mere indications of the extreme possibilities attainable by the collective energies, intellects, and people available. Climatic or physical failures or problems would not be totally invincible by the most carefully prepared human being. If droughts are inevitable, they are, nonetheless, correctable. There has never been a total drought, only partial. Furthermore, it can be pointed out that the rainy state of Maranhão is much less developed than the dry interiors of Pernambuco or Paraiba.

Having thus glimpsed the sharp discontinuities that have existed in Northeast Brazil throughout space and recorded time, we shall pass on to a discussion of the tools and concepts upon which this study is based—the methodology involving the concept of landscape evolution, and the background against which these tools have been applied (chapter 2). Chapter 3 concerns the physical habitat of the Northeast, particularly the eastern halves of Paraíba and Pernambuco where most of the fieldwork was done. Chapter 4 describes the spread of people into and within the Northeast, and their patterns of land use. This historical-geographical orientation is essential to understanding the present situation in Northeast Brazil.

Thus having treated two topics—physical

habitat and settlement—from a regional point of view, we shall pass on to a fairly detailed view of the three major regions: the humid zona da mata (chapter 5), the dry sertão (chapter 6), and the transitional agreste zone (chapter 7). These distinctive zones are examined historically to see how both their internal characteristics and their boundaries have become modified through time. In other words, the regions are examined systematically or topically. Chapter 8 deals with the specific exceptions to the zones, namely the wet spots (the brejos and the serras) that interrupt and otherwise punctuate the landscape of Northeast Brazil with agriculturally attractive conditions. Chapter 9 presents some key factors and processes, institutional and otherwise, that affect man-land relationships within Northeast Brazil. Here, some of the indeterminate as well as determinate factors are treated, and the cultural fabric of the area is given prominence. Chapter 10 summarizes the most important findings, tries to point to the areas that hold the most promise for future research, and provides some guidelines in terms of area-planning programs and evaluation of development proposals.

Chapter Two
THE METHODOLOGY OF LANDSCAPE EVOLUTION

Northeast Brazil is an ideal laboratory for students of man-land relationships and problems. As we noted before, this area has the dubious distinction of being the largest underdeveloped area of the largest developing country of the entire Western Hemisphere.

The purpose of this chapter is not to relate the long history of droughts, crippling poverty, and famine that has been the unfortunate lot of the Northeast, but rather to propose a way of examining the whole complex of man-land relations there which may illuminate its component parts and processes. In short, we propose that a valid approach to the study of population pressure on resources is the analysis of the processes of landscape change.

The main contribution of this methodological chapter is a *concept of landscape evolution,* which can be stated as follows. *The cultural and physical processes that shape any landscape interact continuously, in varying degrees of intensity, with each other, and also with the earth's surface; this surface then becomes altered, thereby presenting a continuously changing base upon which subsequent interactions occur.*

One implication of this concept is that, rather than seeking simple explanations, it embraces a comprehensive yet dynamic view of the earth's surface by considering orders of priority and dominance within the often bewildering complexity of area content and processes.

Because the stimulus of this idea came directly from field experience in Northeast Brazil, it may be useful to present it against the regional setting in which it was conceived. Northeast Brazil is portrayed, then, not as a unique situation but rather as simply one social scientist's laboratory of population pressure on resources in which the concept of landscape evolution may be applied.

Fieldwork was carried on in Northeast Brazil from September 1963 to June 1964 and in May–June 1973. An initial research objective was to formulate physical and cultural definitions to distinguish the warm humid zona da mata (forest zone) from the low dry sertão of the interior and the transitional agreste zone. A second objective was to find how each of these zones had shifted geographically with time.

The original proposal underwent several changes as a result of the first few months of reconnaissance and background work. The most drastic reorientation stemmed from the nature of the primary sources. A comparison of about 400 aerial photographs taken during World War II with 430 recent photographs of the same areas gave a trustworthy and indelible document of observable change in each of the above-mentioned zones. From over 150 interviews with local residents in all zones it was possible to become familiar with the functional processes that produced the images recorded on both sets of photos, and even to become

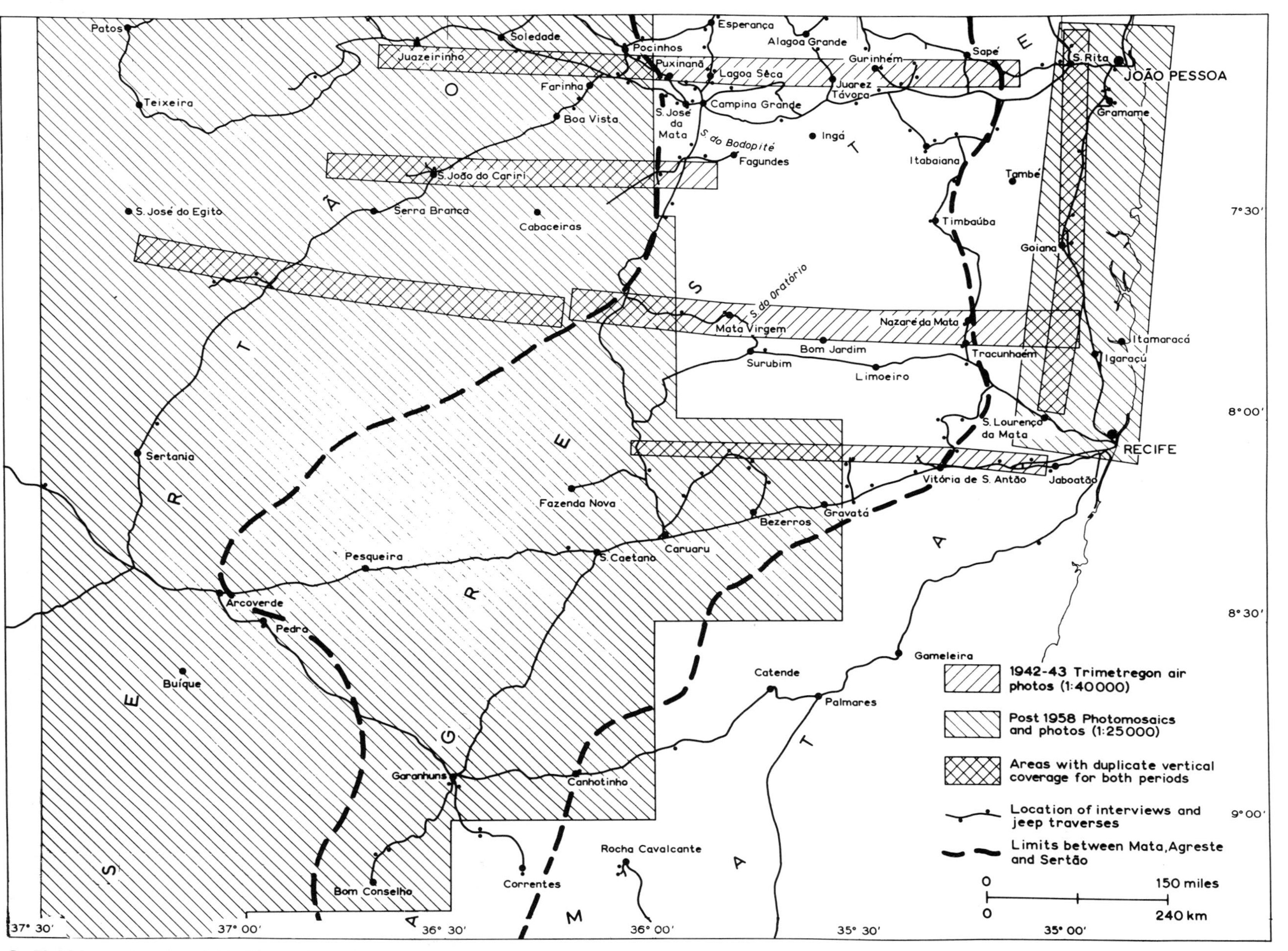

2. Field Interviews and Air Photo Coverage

conversant regarding the earlier geography. Old farmers recalled clearly what habitat and life were like back to the earliest years of this century. (See map 2.)

Such excellent primary source materials impressed me more and more with the processes of landscape alteration *within* each zone, however defined, than with any supposed areal shifts *of* the zones. The theme, borne out by field study on a topographic scale, became a recurrent one: landscape characteristics differed from place to place in different periods for different reasons. These reasons were invariably founded in a unique mix of cultural and physical factors in any given place. Time and again, the analytical mind of the rural Brazilian informant identified the interwoven threads of a complex fabric of areally expressed facts, processes, and institutions that made sense of the old photos as well as the present landscape.

Strange and unfamiliar patterns began to emerge. For example, rainfall amounts and slope variations seemed to assume less importance as explainers of land use; on the other hand, inheritance laws and rural land-tax structures appeared to assume more.

The actual observable land use could be only partly explained by correlating it with cut-and-dried rational assessments of the physical resource base. Frequently, the fundamental decision making with regard to land use had its origins more deeply rooted in such things as traditional use of land, folk beliefs about certain qualities or attributes of areas or activities, or a rigid feudal system of sharecropping. In short, the experience of doing a field study dealing with man-land relations in a small area over a period of several decades proved most illuminating. The experience was valuable for the knowledge gained about the study area itself, but even more valuable for the insights it provided into the more universal subject of man-land relations in general.

NORTHEAST BRAZIL AS A LABORATORY OF CULTURAL AND PHYSICAL CHANGE

Geographers have their laboratories in the field where theories and techniques can be tested and applied. A judicious selection of categories of definition, of scale of analysis, and of the test area itself can do much to aid the geographer in his "laboratory" work. Northeast Brazil lends itself to being such a laboratory, particularly in its eastern parts of Paraíba and Pernambuco where, in a small-scale view, sharp gradients of physical and cultural features are observed in space and through time.

Well-defined geographic regions

A traverse of 180 kilometers westward from the coasts of Paraíba and Pernambuco takes the traveler rapidly from the warm humid lowlands of the zona da mata into the agreste, up onto the Borborema highlands, and then down into the warm, dry sertão. Maps of a scale of 1:5,000,000 and smaller show the alignment of these three zones approximately parallel to the coast. Even their names—zona da mata, agreste, sertão—have specific physical connotations as well as less specific cultural connotations as used by the local people. These zones are discussed below and are shown on map 3.

Zona da mata. This name, meaning forest zone, refers to the contiguous area bordering the coast which was originally covered by a tall, dense, evergreen, semideciduous forest. This former forest and its present-day remnants thrived—and thrive now—on most soils derived from crystalline rocks less than 200 meters in elevation and receiving over 1,200 millimeters of rainfall yearly. The width of this north-south zone varies from 30 to 70 kilometers. Exceptions to these conditions are the broad, flat, sedimentary interfluves, called tabuleiros, whose sandy soils are more conducive to savanna

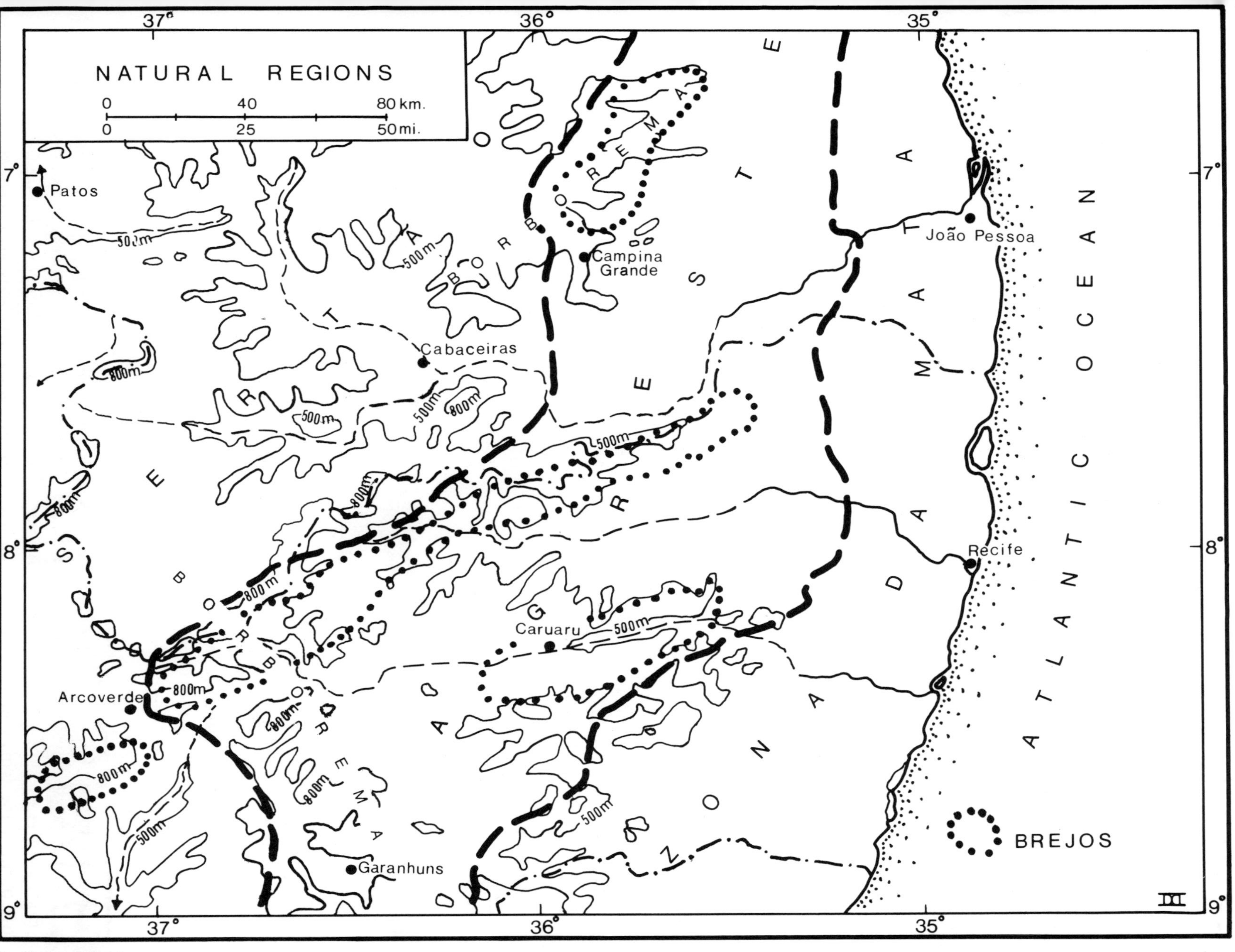

3. Natural Regions

than to a thick forest growth. The cultural connotation of the zona da mata is "land fit for sugarcane," which has been the traditional use of the richer valley soils.

Agreste. The word agreste connotes agressive, rustic, or hard to farm. That is how the agreste must have appeared to the early settlers approaching it from the more humid and verdant zona da mata to the east. The agreste receives only 800 to 1,200 millimeters of rainfall each year, has thinner, sandier soils, and originally had a natural vegetation of something between a dry forest and a dense tropical thorn forest (caatinga). It is found at both higher elevations over 500 meters and at lower elevations in the rain shadows of low mountains and tabuleiro tablelands. A common cultural definition is that the agreste is land suited to the growing of manioc, which is the main food staple of the Northeast's interior. It is commonly called the transition zone between the zona da mata and the sertão. Calling it simply a transition zone, however, does not illuminate the myriad interesting aspects that give it its distinctive character.

Sertão. The sertão is the famous hot, dry, low backlands area characteristic of most of the Northeast's interior. Its characteristic features include an average rainfall of 270 to 800 millimeters which varies widely from one year to the next; shallow, sandy, stony soils; and caatinga vegetation. The cultural connotations of the sertão are extensive cattle raising, subsistence and cash crops grown only with the first autumn rains (if they come that year), and sporadic floodplain (vazante) farming.

Well-defined physical processes and patterns

The range of physical processes that has produced the varied habitats in the Northeast, discounting the works of man, is best shown by the extremes of the zona da mata and the sertão. In the zona da mata, high temperature, high humidity, and rainfall give chemical weathering the upper hand in shaping the particular character of landforms and soils. The depth to sound bedrock in the crystalline areas of the zona da mata is often many meters and is the result of dominantly chemical weathering of soils *in situ*. These soils are high in clay content and are given the local name of barro. They are generally good for agriculture. Landforms in the crystalline areas of the zona da mata are rounded, which is also partly the product of a thick soil-and-vegetation mantle that holds moisture against the underlying bedrock and weathers it to a gently undulating terrain.

The sertão experiences a completely different action of the elements. There, mechanical processes of weathering and erosion dominate. Not only are the amounts of rainfall there much less than in the zona da mata, but there is a long, pronounced, dry season. The general régime of rainfall is one of autumn rains separated by seven or eight months of practically no rain. Accordingly, the natural vegetation has to be drought resistant. The soils of the sertão are shallow, owing to the shortage of water and the sparseness of the vegetation cover that would otherwise hold moisture against bedrock and produce a more deeply weathered soil mantle. In the majority of areas the depth of soils is less than half a meter, and in some places bedrock is actually exposed. The general aspect of landforms there reflects dry-cycle weathering and erosion processes, with their accompanying angular forms. Inselbergs, pediplains, and dry-cycle colluvial and alluvial surfaces abound.

Between the zona da mata and the sertão is the agreste, which is truly transitional in terms of physical processes but which owes most of its distinguishing landscape character to cultural processes. Because of its higher elevation, the upper surfaces of the Borborema highlands are considerably cooler, thus decreasing the temperature component of the rate of chemical decomposition of soils. The serras, or small mountain ranges comprising the eastern outliers of the Borborema, and the actual eastern escarpment of the Borborema, are truly classic orographic barriers to the constant humid easterly winds. There, a multiple effect of high elevation, exposure, and high moisture produces denser vegetation cover and deeper soils where they have not been greatly disturbed by man.

In short, if one looks at this part of Northeast Brazil on a small scale, the physical processes that have shaped the distinctive habitats are fairly well defined. Naturally, any detailed, large-scaled analysis reveals a much higher degree of areal differentiation and the need for greater qualification in each of the zones and their variants.

Well-defined cultural processes and patterns

The laboratory aspect of Northeast Brazil, with its definable physical divisions and processes, is further enhanced by a comparable categorization of cultural patterns and processes. The sequence and patterns of occupance can be related partly to economic and historical factors and partly to the character of the habitat. One consideration to remember while viewing the evolution of settlement and land-use patterns is the changing ratio of available manpower to the definitions of economically or socially justifiable activities of land exploitation. In space and time, the cultural processes and features expressed by land use in the study area exhibit the following divisions.

In its extent and intensity, the brazilwood cycle was the earliest yet the least permanent form of exploitation. The cutting down of randomly located brazilwood trees was carried on most energetically throughout the first fifty years or so of Brazil's history (about 1500 to 1550)—principally in the zona da mata. This random cutting resulted in practically no permanent settlements and very few changes in the habitat.

From about 1550 to 1700, the sugarcane cycle was the outstanding economic and social influence in the zona da mata. Even today, sugarcane is the chief source of income in the rural sectors although there is higher population density and greater economic diversification.

The vast sertão, on the other hand, was, from the beginnings of Brazil's colonial period, very definitely regarded as land suited for open-range cattle raising. The cattle were raised in the sertão to supply the needs of the growing population in the zona da mata for meat, hides, and draft animals. A classic symbiotic relationship evolved and still persists to a certain degree.

Throughout the colonial period and well into the nineteenth century, the agreste was left by default as being ideally suited neither to sugarcane nor exclusively to grazing, considering the limited available manpower. The people who eventually settled the agreste came from both the sertão and the zona da mata. They fled toward the humid east from the periodic droughts that destroyed crops and decimated the herds pasturing in the sertão. Upon reaching the agreste, which was a more well-watered area where subsistance crops could be grown with little fear of droughts, these refugees took root. People also migrated to the agreste from the zona da mata where most of the best land had already been titled to the landholding elite and, therefore, offered few possibilities for anyone getting started in agriculture.

The year 1930 marked the beginnings of an industrial revolution and its uneven impact in Northeast Brazil. From then on, the three zones began, in varying degrees, to become more integrated into both the economically effective territory of the Northeast, and that of Brazil as a nation. The crucial transportation links with city and export markets tended to valorize areas hitherto untouched and still subject to a feudal or subsistence way of life.

One cultural process that affected all areas in one way or another was the generally underrated activity of deforestation. In the zona da mata and the agreste, men cut the forests to clear for crops. In the sertão they cut to a lesser extent for the same reason, and to a greater extent for firewood, house construction materials, and more recently for locomotive fuel and charcoal making for the urban markets of today. The caatinga underwent this gradual but relentless process of desertification in which only the most worthless species were spared the woodsman's ax. And even many of the short, scrubby, worthless species can be made into charcoal.

In summary, one can regard this part of Northeast Brazil as a test area characterized by marked physical contrasts, cultural contrasts, and identifiable turning points in its historical development where each zone was evolving within its own boundaries and, at the same time, stimulated by outside influences.

ANALYTICAL FACTORS

By way of introduction, several factors and assumptions underlying the concept of landscape evolution should be stated.

The notion of the shifting dominant

One valuable and interesting guide in the search for enlightement on man-land relations is stated in Robert Braidwood and Gordon Willey's *Courses toward Urban Life.* Their book is a historical-anthropological analysis of the kinds of conditions out of which cities emerged in different parts of the world in different epochs. In essence, the authors look at the growth spurts for population clusters as they became cities in the generally accepted definition of what a city is. They cite, among other conditions, basic requirements of water, food supply, a viable economic or other base, and a system of individual and group productivity which, through sound administration, enables a greater diversification of tasks and responsibilities. It is the diversification and specialization of occupations and roles which mainly distinguish urban from rural culture.

Braidwood and Willey's analysis suggests that the degree to which the natural habitat or man's works dominate an area depends upon the scale of elaboration of the culture occupying it. This line of reasoning further implies that the habitat would influence indirectly the *loci* or limits of land use and the human activities in a place occupied by people with a low level of cultural evolution and technology. Preston E. James speaks to the same problem when he defines the significance of the habitat in terms of culture: "The significance of the land is determined by the attitudes, objectives, and technical abilities of the people" who occupy it.[1]

What is suggested here is that a carefully qualified extension of the cultural-determinist point of view would lead us back to environmental influences, but *indirect* influences of a very different nature from those cited by the environmentalists themselves. The reasoning is as follows:

1. It is man's culture that gives meaning to the habitat.

2. In any one culture area, the habitat has a specified significance. For example, in the sertão the habitat has the following meaning to local inhabitants:

a. Forest lands are desirable for crops.

b. Dry areas as well as moist are to be planted with humid-land crops such as maize and beans.

[1] *Latin America,* p. 41.

c. Steeply sloping areas are to be planted with crops whose rows will run up and down the slope, not on the contour.
d. The end of the dry season is the signal to cut over and burn areas for crops.

3. The environmental influence is therefore *indirect*, not direct, as in classic environmental determinism. In other words, by his cultural makeup and predispositions, man unconsciously endows his habitat with an imaginary influence or control over his activities.

4. As with so many things related to human nature, it is not necessarily the measurable fact or the scientifically defined reality that men take to be the baseline of their actions. Rather, it is man's personal, and often irrational, perception of what he sees and feels that forms his particular reality as well as the basis of his actions. In this sense, the habitat can be said to exercise an indirect influence on human activities insofar as man's culture imbues that habitat with a quasi deterministic role.

It must be remembered, moreover, that neither the habitat nor the culture of a place are static. Both evolve at varying rates of speed and in interaction with each other, with the local landscape, and with outside influences.

The distinction may appear to be fine, but it merits emphasis: Instead of stating the significance of the land mainly in terms of man's culture, let us recognize indirect or imagined environmental influence as a part of the functional reality, especially where the level of cultural elaboration is low. In other words, the relative dominance, direct or indirect, of the natural habitat or of man's culture on the landscape varies with the stage of cultural elaboration existing there.

The study of processes on a topographic scale

One thesis of this study is that area study on a functional level in general, and landscape interpretation in particular, are most effectively pursued by the detailed study of processes on a topographic scale. Naturally, there is no substitute for an overview of an area's gross features or of reconnaissance to give first impressions and to elicit meaningful questions that may be the focus of later detailed studies. However, a familiarity with the actual functioning reality is gained only by observing and mapping the individual features of the landscape and by probing, through extensive interviews with local inhabitants, the day-to-day and year-to-year details of their activities as they throw light upon man-land relationships. Time spent studying in detail an area representative of a larger zone is more efficiently invested than the same time spent trying to cover the whole zone.

The topographic-scale approach enables one to examine at close range physical processes, cultural processes, and even, by talking with elderly people, historical processes over as much as half a century. The scarcity of published documentary material on certain areas or on certain subjects need not hinder the fieldworker who, if he is an adept interviewer, can tap the riches of information of an almost limitless number of local experts.

The optimum scale for any area analysis would appear to vary within the general category of topographic scale and with the nature of the area itself, the size of the discreet features of land use, the size of land-use associations, the nature and location of land-use decision making, the degree of complexity of economic relationships (market versus subsistence economy), the rate and directions of areal change, the degree to which land-use patterns are representative over a wider area, and the incidence of extraneous features.

Over a period of time, the geographer should be able to acquire a feeling for, and an identification with, the processes of local decision making as they affect people's use of the land in a particular place.

Decision making and local land use

A basic block to sound area analysis is an incomplete awareness of the many stages that exist between the observable fact revealed to the fieldworker's eye or on an air photo and the published map or statistics. There are also many stages of processes of a material and a nonmaterial nature of which the image on the air photo is simply the final product. Sometimes investigators try to infer or deduce the actions and motivations of the man on the land from an inspection of gross data in the form of inadequate maps and figures, and with no functional knowledge of the processes that are only dimly reflected by the maps and figures.

A more time consuming but sounder approach is the reconstruction of the fabric of daily and seasonal activities and relationships observed in the context of land-use patterns. One valid analysis in depth of functional relationships in a representative area may then be extrapolated and, with limitations, applied to a wider area. Thus, the time spent by anthropologists on community studies (such as Marvin Harris, in *Town and Country in Brazil*) and by geographers on regional studies that probe universal themes (such as Gene Martin, in *Land Division in Central Chile*), as opposed to narrowly local studies, appears to be well invested. The approach is inductive, from the specific to the general.

Figure 1 is an attempt, based on field experience, to approach the complexities underlying the rural landscape and to understand how it came to assume its particular aspect. An explanation of the figure follows.

The components (A) of the locale, physical and cultural, material and nonmaterial, are the raw materials that undergo their own individual processes of transformation and that, in greater or lesser degree, interact with other components. Some examples would be overcropping resulting in loss of top soil by erosion, the introduction of new domesticated plants or animals into an agricultural setting, or the impact on a traditional farming system by governmental expropriation of large properties.

The several processes of interaction are then filtered and refracted through man's mind (B) and, depending upon his individual and collective view of himself and of the world about him, he takes overt action by engaging himself physically with the earth's surface. His overt action, which may have been underlain by one or more different motivations (C), produces an observable pattern of land use (D). The sequence of stimuli continues with a certain amount of feedback from the actual land use and its consequences (for example, minifundio, sheet erosion from overgrazing, larger and more productive economic units, blights) to each of the original components. In time, this feedback may alter some aspects of the individual components and may even change man's view of himself and of his place in the world.

The balance between available manpower, exploitable resources, technology, and market

An awareness of the above-mentioned factors and how they vary in space and time in a particular area is most helpful in regional analysis of man-land relationships and problems. Preoccupation not only with the observable, mappable features but also with the reasons for their existence and how they are evolving illuminates the more general concern with processes in an area and gives substance to regional interpretation.

To cite an example, extensive cattle raising occupies by far the greater area of the sertão. Some students therefore mistakenly conclude that cattle raising is the chief source of income there. This is not true. Today, agriculture, carried out in a small fraction of the sertão, accounts for more than half the income of the entire area studied. Others infer that the sertão must be well suited to cattle raising. On the contrary, it is poor when compared to the rest of the world's grazing lands. The fact is that

1. A Functional View of the Determinants of Land Use

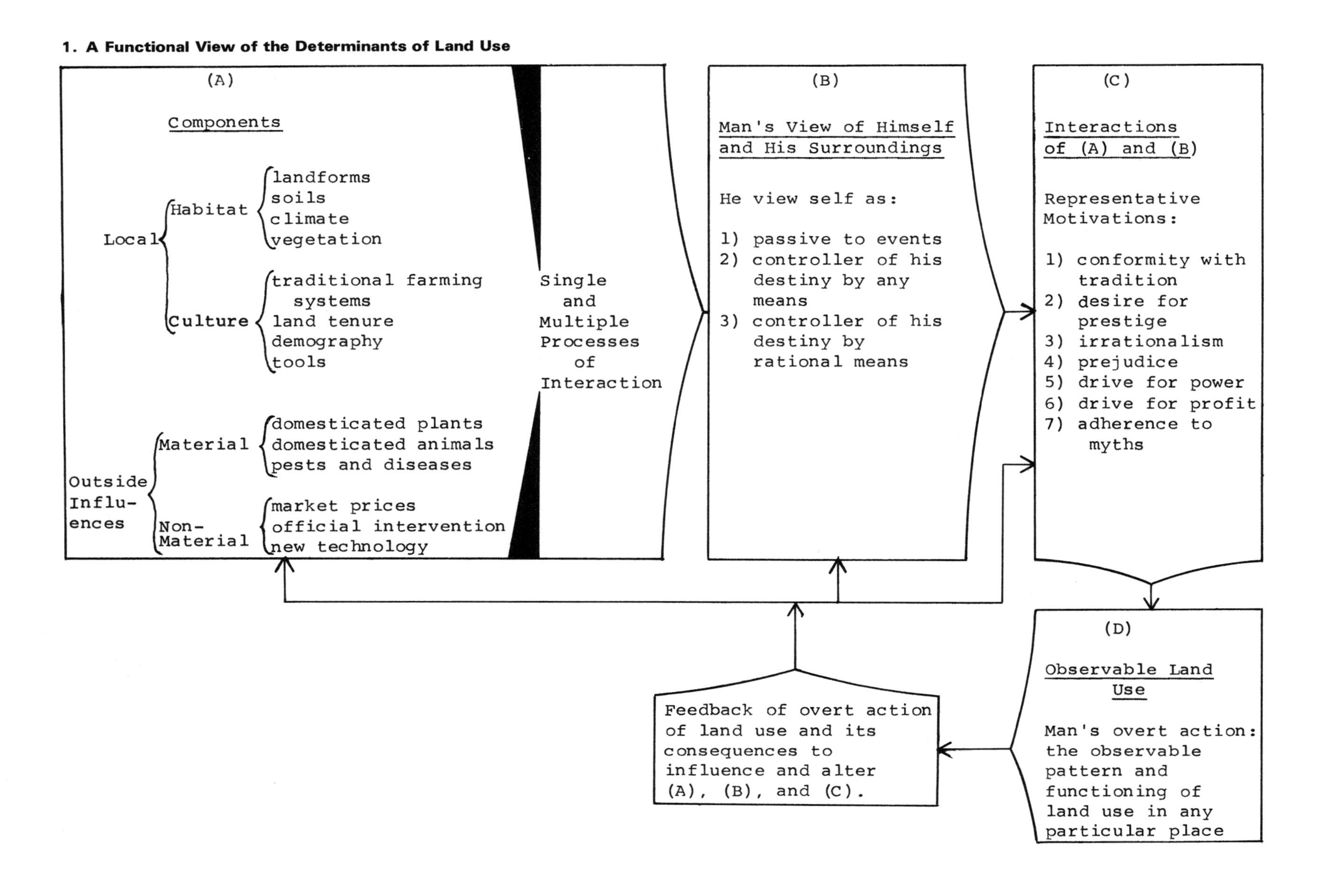

cattle ranching yields the highest return for the available manpower and the low rate of investment *locally considered reasonable* on lands that are not regarded as good for any other activity and which, for that matter, are not very good for cattle.

It is difficult today to imagine the low densities of population that prevailed throughout the Northeast's interior until the twentieth century. Even now there are some municipios (similar to counties), such as Cabaceiras that have an average population density of only five people per square kilometer. In the context of the colonial period this meant that the land per se had value only in proportion to the number of workers available to valorize it. Even now, low productivity per worker and per unit area persists. Only in the sugarcane engenhos (mills) of the zona da mata was productivity relatively high. But, then again, the sugar economy was based upon slaves who had only to be fed and clothed. The chief capital investment was in slaves and machinery rather than in land.

The policies of the Portuguese Crown and of the donotories who received immense tracts of land to develop, and who subsequently subdivided it to others in the form of seismarias (land-grant subdivisions), were expressly to valorize the empty areas, to put people on the land to make it productive, and thereby to generate tax revenues. Today, the undervalorization of both the rural areas and their workers operates against a truly efficient agricultural sector of the economy. One economist, Stefan Robock, who has studied the Northeast thinks that possibly one of the best ways to develop the area is to provide opportunities for work outside of it.[2] This system would make labor scarcer in the Northeast and thus force the entrepreneurial classes to become more efficient in order to remain competitive. In such a process, the worker of the Northeast himself would possibly become more productive and thus be able to secure a higher income and a higher standard of living.

CONCEPT OF LANDSCAPE EVOLUTION—USING NORTHEAST BRAZIL AS A TEST AREA

The idea presented here concerns the nature of the earth's surface as a medium of multiple processes of cultural and physical change, and as an organizing refractor of those processes in time and in space. The concept of landscape evolution holds that the cultural and physical processes that shape any landscape interact continuously, in varying degrees of intensity with each other *and also* with the earth's surface; this surface becomes altered, thereby presenting a continuously changing base upon which subsequent interactions occur.

Easternmost Paraíba and Pernambuco lend themselves well to a schematic, three-dimensional model illustrating the concept of landscape evolution. We will discuss first the functional relationships of the model in a universal context, and then as they apply to Northeast Brazil. (See figure 2.)

In the model, three undulating surfaces—1, 2, and 3—represent, from top to bottom, three successive landscapes of the same area as they have evolved through time. The earliest landscape is at the top; the most recent is at the bottom. Two vertical lines separate the area into three distinct regions from west to east: S (sertão), A (agreste), and M (zona da mata), thereby introducing the element of areal diversity into the model. The hump in the middle section is a schematic rendering of the Borborema massif. In our discussion below, H refers to habitat, and C refers to culture.

We start with landscape S^1 as the given situation. Two sets of processes interact with one another. H^{S1} refers to the total physical properties and processes as they are expressed in the habitat, H—for example in the year 1700. C^{S1} refers to the total cultural properties and processes as they are expressed in that same

[2] Robock, *The Developing Northeast.*

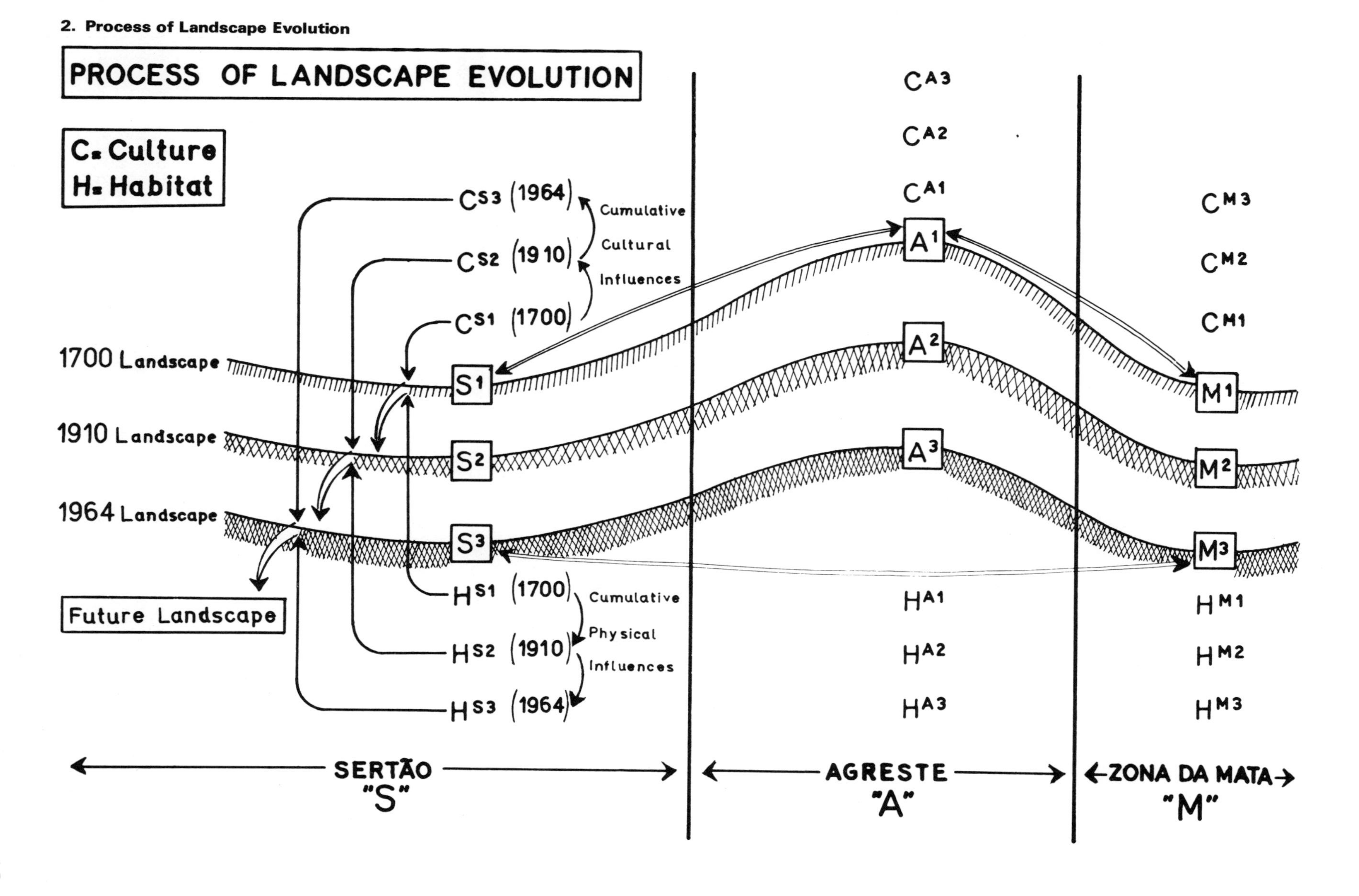
PROCESS OF LANDSCAPE EVOLUTION
C= Culture
H= Habitat
CS3 (1964)
CS2 (1910)
CS1 (1700)
Cumulative
Cultural
Influences
CA3
CA2
CA1
CM3
CM2
CM1
1700 Landscape
1910 Landscape
1964 Landscape
S1
S2
S3
A1
A2
A3
M1
M2
M3
Future Landscape
HS1 (1700)
HS2 (1910)
HS3 (1964)
Cumulative
Physical
Influences
HA1
HA2
HA3
HM1
HM2
HM3
SERTÃO
"S"
AGRESTE
"A"
ZONA DA MATA
"M"

LANDSCAPE EVOLUTION

C^{S3} Rural population densities have risen but are still very low. Greater rationalization of both cattle and crop-raising methods has resulted in less susceptibility to droughts. Sharecropper (morador) tenure system and high concentration of land ownership keep living levels very low. Today, vaqueiros (cowboys) are mostly salaried. Rural exodus continues. Most income from agriculture, not cattle.

C^{S2} Goats, sheep, and cattle continue to decimate the caatinga vegetation. Demand for locomotive fuel in the form of firewood has resulted in accelerated impoverishment of the vegetation cover. Most subsistence crops continue to be humid-land ones like maize and beans which people try to grow in a semiarid region of very uncertain rainfall.

C^{S1} Very sparse population densities associated with very extensive, open-range cattle raising. Herds rarely exceed 1,000 head because periodic droughts every ten years or so reduce herds to 100 to 200 head. Subsistence agriculture only for local needs. One-fourth of the new calves go to the vaqueiro. Cattle products in great demand in the colonial period.

S^1 A vast, dense, arboreal caatinga with cattle fazendas separated by dozens of kilometers. Vegetation and soils'essentially intact.

S^2 Cotton as a cash crop begins to diversify the rural scene, bringing in more workers and a greater need for subsistence crops. Properties are being subdivided by inheritance, but are still measured in leagues.

S^3 The action of man and animals over the years has given the sertao many aspects of a desert, including, in places, bare ground between plants. There is more bare rock exposed today. Overgrazing is evidenced by terracettes and gullying. Any original humus layer has long since been flushed away.

H^{S1} Original vegetation appears to have been a dense, arboreal caatinga with trees up to 20 meters high. Alkali soils in many places. Cloudbursts have not yet had much erosive effect on the essentially intact vegetation and soils.

H^{S2} Cutting of the caatinga for shifting agriculture and cotton makes soils exposed to violent sheet wash. There is greater runoff. Stream beds are drier for longer periods during the dry season.

H^{S3} The economically less useful species of the caatinga prevail today (cactus, etc.). Increased runoff has poured and deposited more silt into stream beds. Sheet wash has left not only exposed bedrock on sloping areas, but also vast areas of quartz pebble-cobble surfaces as the soil fines have been flushed away.

C^{A3} Very high rural population densities for Brazil with many properties having less that 10 hectares (1 hectare is 1.47 acres). Much higher incidence of individual ownership and independence. Mostly intensive subsistence agriculture with some cash crops like agave and mamona. Still practice primitive farming, with fertilizer making inroads in a few places. Rural exodus continues.

C^{A2} Rural population increasing as result of drought refugees, seasonal workers from the sertao, and excess population from the zona da mata. Process of subdivision of properties through inheritance creates smaller and smaller properties. A population spurt is beginning to accelerate.

C^{A1} Very low population density associated with extensive cattle raising. Cotton beginning to enter now. Fairs mark the meeting point of cattle from the sertao and sugar, manioc, and cloth from the zona da mata.

A^1 In 1700 this region was only sporadically exploited for open-range cattle. Land ideal neither for sugar cane nor for cattle in the context of the colonial economy.

A^2 The roca system of shifting agriculture has opened up the original vegetation at an accelerating rate of change. This is the most recent settlement frontier of Northeast Brazil.

A^3 The minifundio par excellence of Brazil today has resulted from subdivision of properties that were not large to begin with. Many properties are at the point of becoming uneconomic and serve only subsistence functions. Local markets create demand for fruits and vegetables. Cattle are scarce. Manioc is the food staple.

H^{A1} Generally undisturbed natural vegetation of mata seca (dry forest) or caatinga. Many tall but twisted woody growths. Soils very few meters deep, but protected and intact. Few floods.

H^{A2} General and selective cutting leaves the xerophytic and unusable species and removes the valuable timber for construction, railroad fuel, etc. Because much of the area is in slope, any crop clearings provoke erosion and removal of thin humus layer.

H^{A3} Only one small area of original vegetation (mata seca) remains; it is kept as an occasional source of timber. Decimated vegetation resulted in greater runoff and collection of water in natural and artificial ponds.

LANDSCAPE EVOLUTION

C^{M3} Consolidation of sugar milling from small engenhos to large factory usinas. Salaried workers live in a money economy and do less home-growing of food. Their life is generally worse today than formerly. Rural exodus. Cities here are absorbing rural exodus from all three zones. Others go on to Rio, Sao Paulo.

C^{M2} Both high rural population densities and cities are growing rapidly. Cane workers receive low salaries but grow their own subsistense crops on backyard plots on company land. Cane will eventually engulf the foot plots. Technology unimproved.

C^{M1} Highest population densities in the Northeast accompany cane growing in the clayey lowlands. Subsistence crops allowed on lower priority slopes and on some bottom land. Slave labor, sugar monoculture for export. Simple technology. Local aristocracy and societal features based wholly on sugar system. Most capital in slaves and machinery. Much deforestation in order to open up new lands for cane planting.

→M^1 Much original forest exists outside the river bottoms. All culture concentrated in the sugarcane valleys.

→M^2 Still little use made of the flat, sandy tabuleiros interfluves except for firewood. Area in cane and in subsistence plots is much greater and more intensively used on the bottom lands and adjacent lower slopes.

→M^3 Cane has pushed all but a trace of subsistence agriculture out of prime bottomland. Rọca cultivation is more intensive on slopes. More use is made of the tabuleiros (firewood, construction, and charcoal materials), and some scientifically grown cane. Also find manioc there. More fruit trees now than before. Tops of hills in cane areas are left as timber and moisture reserves. Lower courses of some "sugar rivers" have been dredged and straightened. Erosion has bared some rocks.

H^{M1} A high proportion of the original forest on the richest clayey bottomlands has been cut. Sandy tabuleiros are relatively untouched. Swamps in valley bottoms limit cane expansion. Little erosion, little flooding, soils intact.

H^{M2} Practically all the original bottomland forest has already been cut. Vestiges remain in very steep or inaccessible places. Erosion evident on overcropped slopes. More flooding due to removal of vegetation in upper reachers of watersheds (agreste).

H^{M3} Few remnants of original forest exist anywhere in the zone. Only second- (and third-, etc.) growth capoeira is seen in varying stages of recuperation. Frequent flooding of silt-laden streams fertilizes the cane bottomlands but also destroys part of the cane crop. On tabuleiros there is a general impoverishment of vegetation both in density and varieties.

area at the same time. Habitat and culture (H and C) interact within the landscape context of S^1 thereby transforming S^1 into S^2, which is the observable landscape at a later date, say 1910.

The cultural state of 1910, C^{S2}, is the recipient of holdover cumulative influences from that of 1700 (C^{S1}), as indicated by the upward-curving arrows. Similarly, the habitat of 1910, H^{S2}, bears many marks of the one existing in 1700 (H^{S1}). Nevertheless, the distinctive culture of 1910, C^{S2}, interacts with the transformed habitat of that same era, H^{S2}, in the context of the 1910 landscape, and eventually produces the new landscape of 1964, S^3.

It must be emphasized that there is a twofold interaction: (1) the processes operating within the natural setting or habitat (vegetation, soils, water régimes, landforms, and, to a lesser extent, climate) interact with the processes operating within the cultural complex (land use, population density, agricultural tenure systems, level of technology, attitudes toward the land, and so on), *and at the same time* (2) each of these sum processes of habitat and culture (H and C) interacts with the existing landscape. The existing landscape is obviously the visible manifestation of both natural and cultural processes, in varying degrees of intensity, as they are frozen at a given moment in a particular place. The landscape at any given time represents the starting base from which contemporary habitat-culture interactions must begin their transformation of that landscape.

In similar fashion the landscape in region A is transformed successively from A^1 to A^2 and finally to A^3, as is the landscape in region M. The mechanics of change mentioned thus far refer only to *intraregional* influences. There must also be allowance for *interregional* influences. The two-way arrow linking landscape A^1 in region A with landscape M^1 in region M is meant to indicate the influence that, for example, a growing market for food supplies in region M in 1700 had upon land use in region A. Other combinations of interregional influence in either direction can be imagined, such as S^1 with A^1 or S^3 with M^3. Not all possible combinations of interregional influences are shown in the model, of course, nor are the details of culture-habitat-landscape interactions for regions A and M—for the practical reason of not crowding the diagram.

The model and the above chart (figure 3) attempt to spell out in abbreviated form how the concept of landscape evolution may be applied to an actual area—in this case, those areas of Paraíba and Pernambuco east of 37°W. longitude. Again, the letters S, A, and M refer respectively to the sertão, agreste, and zona da mata. I have selected the earliest time-section at around 1700 in order to show this part of the Northeast at the high point of characteristic colonial culture, when the sugarcane cycle was still in its heyday and the sertão was already occupied, though very sparsely populated. The second period, taken around 1910, represents a sort of threshold year in terms of area diversification within the agreste and, to a lesser extent, in the other two zones. It is also a date for which there exists extensive source material from interviews with local inhabitants in all three zones. The present situation is supported by air photographs going back over the twenty years from 1944 to 1964, as well as by interviews and personal observation. The choice of exactly where the time cross-sections should be taken is meant to convey some sense of the tremendous rate of acceleration of many processes of landscape alteration since the beginning of this century, and particularly since 1930.

A more satisfactory selection of time periods would be 1500, 1700, 1900, 1944, 1964, and 1984. The advantage of the 1500 date would be the presentation of the precolonial (pre-European) situation as the starting base insofar as it could be reconstructed from colonial documents, the accounts of early travelers, and other means. The year 1944 would be another convenient time section simply because of the photo coverage then.

Chapter Three
THE PHYSICAL HABITAT AND ITS FORMATIVE PROCESSES

The physical environment of Northeast Brazil plays an important, though not dominant role in the development of the area. In Brazil, where there has been a long history of interest in and concern over man-land relationships, and at least an awareness by some people of the rapid rates of environment modification, Northeast Brazil stands out as undoubtedly the section of most abrupt geographical diversity within a small area.

The significance of the physical habitat in the Northeast has usually been seriously misunderstood. The first dominant fact that impresses the traveler is the dryness of the interior. Who in the world expects to discover a true desert in Brazil? There are mountains, valleys, and escarpments, but they are of minor significance compared to the dry interior and the dramatic drought-resistant caatinga vegetation that occupies the area. Probably the most illustrious writer who has described this section of Northeast Brazil, Euclides da Cunha, has fed the notion that *land makes the man.* His descriptions of the sertanejo and his extraordinary adaptations to the harsh environment underline his environmental-deterministic outlook.[1] In other words, a dramatic landscape, sculpted with great diversity and sharp areal differences, is easy to recognize and is also easy to blame for whatever human conditions are found there. This is especially easy if widespread abject poverty just happens to coincide with the most barren and most inhospitable-appearing areas of the region.

An overview of Northeast Brazil, such as one might get from a jet aircraft, is quite simple in basic outline: it is a dry area bordered on the east, south, and west by more-humid zones. The Northeast is a relatively small part of the total national territory but it is an important one because it was the culture hearth of the country and it is where one-fourth of all Brazilians still live, many of whom subsist under extremely difficult conditions.

We have already discussed the mata, agreste, and sertão and it would be well to keep in mind the general orientation of those three zones as we proceed to discuss more detailed aspects of the area. The following general outline is intended to be a rough regional guide but we should be increasingly aware of the transitions between these zones because boundaries are necessarily an abstract compromise that have meaning only insofar as the core regions are clearly understood. We should keep in mind, as we view our representative slice of Northeast Brazil, that the area has not only horizontal gradients (as illustrated by the mata-agreste-sertão variations, progressing inland from the coast) but also vertical gradients of temperature, moisture, vegetation, and even population concentrations (as particularly related to the serras and brejos de altitude and the orographic barriers they comprise), and historical gradients. These time gradients are reflected in the very recent geological history, when eustatic changes in sea level and the sediments deposited in the

[1] Cunha, *Rebellion in the Backlands.*

floodplains or varzeas have a direct relationship to the possibilities for land use. Historical gradients, as more commonly understood, apply to the three main ecological zones insofar as each has had distinctive economic and social experiences. In fact, in some, such as the agreste, the very physical aspect of the area is largely due to the cultural imprint and influence of man.

The habitat base, then, will be presented as the given situation upon which man, with his cultural baggage, has interacted through time. We are interested in the modes of origin of the habitat base, we are interested in its spatial variations, and we are interested in its processes of change. And finally, we shall try to deduce something of the rates of change.

LANDFORMS

Within an area where the highest point of land is only slightly higher than 1,060 meters above sea level, the most dominant landform feature is the broad Borborema plateau with its elaborately dissected margins. This gently undulating surface varies from 100 to 200 kilometers in width from east to west, and is about 250 kilometers from north to south. Its most important function is as an orographic barrier to the prevailing easterly winds, and its relatively low elevation of between 500 and 1000 meters is apparently sufficient to exert a primary determining role in the distribution of different climatic conditions. The Borborema massif is composed of resistant crystalline rocks of igneous and metamorphic origins, but it is not a compact landform unit. On the contrary, it is shaped like an open hand with the fingers pointing toward the northeast. The direction or orientation of these spurs and outliers from the main mountain must exert a primary influence in blocking and redirecting the flow of moist maritime air from the east. Similarly, there are plateau outliers and spurs of still fairly low elevations (less than 800 meters) that point toward the southwest and south. It can be said that the relatively gently rolling undissected core area of the Borborema massif coincides with the highest elevations and that this high-level surface of 600 to 700 meters is surmounted by more resistant serras, or mountain crests, along which lies the border between Pernambuco and Paraíba. (See map 4.)

The geology of easternmost Pernambuco and Paraíba is essentially the same as that of the rest of Northeast Brazil. It is composed of crystalline basement of igneous rocks such as granite, and metamorphic rocks such as gneisses, schists, and quartzites. The age of the crystalline basement is pre-Cambrian—at least 500 million years old. This basement complex has some zones that are more resistant than others. One of these zones is the Borborema massif whose very resistance to the forces of weathering and erosion accounts for its commanding prominence over surrounding areas.

In the Tertiary period, about 50 million years ago, the basement was covered by sedimentary deposits, mainly sandstones with some limestones and shales, and these deposits, with subsequent tectonic uplift of the whole area and with continuing weathering and erosion, were largely stripped away. There are places where the sandstone cap formation still stands above the lower crystalline plains. In the western area, along the border between Piauí and Ceará and the famous Chapada de Araripe, where the standstones are especially notable for their function as a water reservoir, the over-one-hundred resulting perennial streams, sustain agriculture in an area where desert would otherwise prevail. There are other outliers and remnants of the sedimentary cap formation located in eastern Ceará and Rio Grande do Norte, and they are quite easily recognized by their mesalike or table-topped aspect. Within the study area of easternmost Pernambuco and Paraıba, there remains very little of the flat-lying sedimentary cap formation.

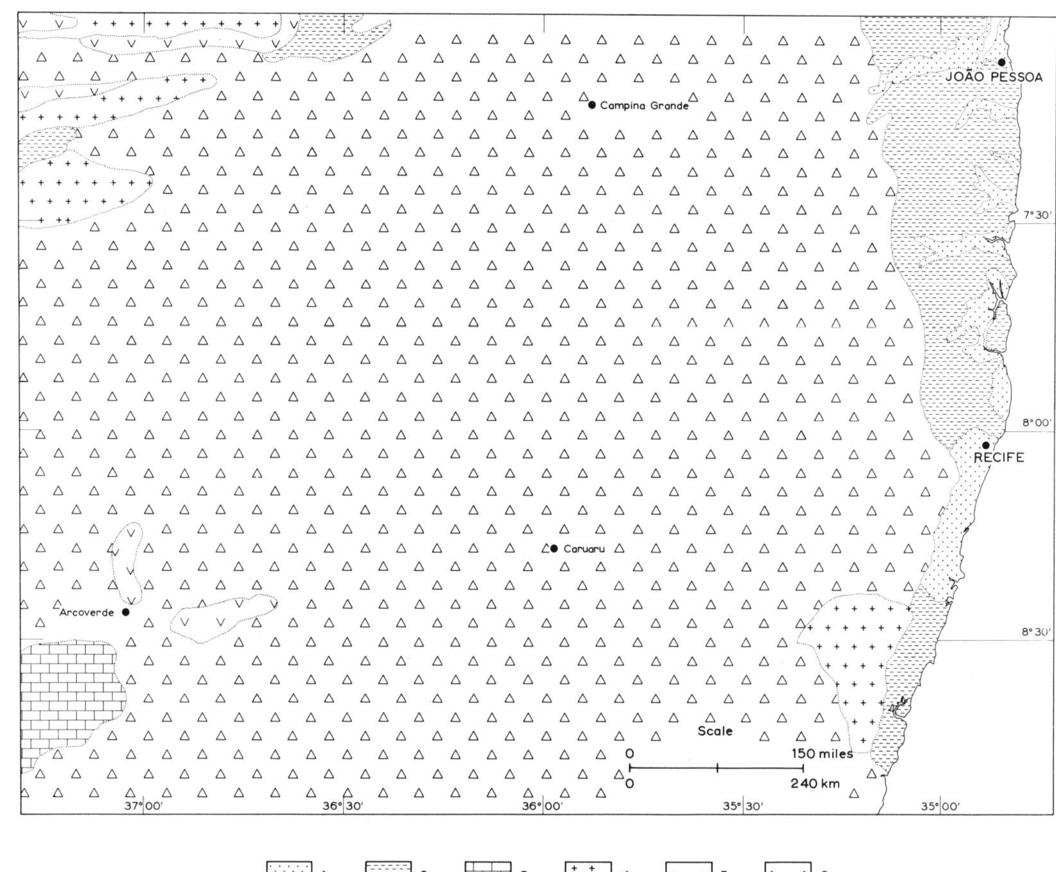

4. Geology

The geological picture of the dry interior of the study area is one of low plains representing zones of weaker crystalline rocks which are punctuated here and there by strongly resistant quartzite nobs and hill clusters or, in some instances such as the Patos plain, a very characteristic inselberg landscape resulting from resistant remnants of crystalline rocks.

To the east of the Borborema massif, one finds an abrupt escarpment leading down to a rather gradual slope toward the Atlantic Ocean. This slope, generally less than 200 meters in elevation, terminates at the Atlantic shore, which is partly protected by extensive reefs, many of which are of sandstone. In fact the very name of Pernambuco's capital city, Recife, means reef.

This narrow coastal plain is of very recent formation, and eustatic changes of sea level have played an important part. The eustatic movements involving a rise in sea level, the latest phase in association with the melting of continental ice sheets at the end of the Pleistocene period, about 10,000 years ago, have formed "ria" inlets whereby the sea occupies or "drowns" former river valleys. As one travels inland from the beach (see figure 4) he passes from the reefs to the quiet lagoons and inlets. In many areas these are also the zones of extensive mangrove vegetation that thrives on the brackish water within the tidal range. One finally encounters the slopes of the very recent Pliocene sediments, the famous Barreiras formation. This formation is 40 to 50 meters above

Spherically weathered granite in the zona da mata at the foothills of the Borborema highlands. Some sections are rotten and disintegrated.

sea level and presents a very broad, gently sloping surface that extends westward. In some places the contact of the Barreiras sediments is made directly with the beaches, especially in Paraıba north of João Pessoa, and there are actual coastal cliffs where the Barreiras formation has been subjected to direct wave action. In other areas there is widespread dissection and erosion of the flat surface. There is less of the Barreiras formation left in Pernambuco than in Paraíba, where the broad areas of the original surface have been preserved and form a wide suspended plain extending westward until it impinges on the abrupt eastern escarpment of the Borborema massif. These broad uninterrupted expanses are known locally as tabuleiros, or table lands. The heavy rainfall of this eastern sector of the zona da mata has provided water for the carving and dissection of the tabuleiro, and the broad valleys have extensive flat floodplains or varzeas where sugarcane dominates. These are the so called rios-do-açucar, or sugar rivers.

In Pernambuco a hilly area rises gradually from east to west and merges with the Borborema escarpment, whereas in Paraíba there is a rather narrow but depressed flat zone west of the tabuleiros. In other words, in Pernambuco there is a more or less gradual rise in elevation from the coast to the Borborema; the Barreiras formation, the tabuleiros, and the crystalline hilly zone form a more or less continuous ascending slope. From east to west in Paraıba one encounters the narrow coastal zone, then the tabuleiros extending westward for 20 to 30 kilometers, and then a sedimentary depression 20 or 30 kilometers wide before one reaches the looming escarpment of the Borborema, just east of Campina Grande. This depression, as we shall see later, forms an unusual orographic pocket where drier conditions prevail than do to the east or west of it. It is a realm of caatinga and cattle raising.

The Borborema has many aspects, but the general orientation is from northeast to southwest. In Pernambuco, the plateau and its eastern slopes form a distinctive area called agreste, which has a relief of more or less parallel ridges and valleys. One exception is the dome-shaped Garanhuns formation that rises to some 850 meters above sea level at a place where the humid zona da mata and the arid sertão approach within 50 kilometers of each other. The primary role of the Borborema massif is as an orographic barrier to the prevailing easterly winds of maritime tropical origins blowing in off the Atlantic Ocean. While the secondary climatic variations depend upon the height and orientation of particular mountain ranges or spurs, the Borborema massif, as a unit, tends to concentrate rainfall on its eastern slopes. Conversely, all areas to the westward side of the summit-divide form the sotavento, or leeward, position that not only receives less rainfall but is also subjected to adiabatically heated descending air. In the context of Northeast Brazil this means extremely desiccating or drying wind that has a pronounced effect upon the vegetation of the area and that gives rise to vast areas of caatinga or tropical thorn scrub.

Two prominent erosion surfaces are evident on the Borborema plateau. The first of these lies between 700 and 800 meters above sea level and is seen in the alignment of the upper levels of ridges and other high step-formations that appear to have the same resistance to erosion and that comprise the remnants of a very old and uplifted peneplain surface.

The second erosion surface is found between 500 and 600 meters elevation. This tends to consist of enclosed basins of roughly the same elevation, such as the Cariris Velhos of Paraíba.

The pattern of river drainage is radial, with the Borborema massif forming the central zone of distribution for much of the Northeast. Rivers flow intermittently to the north, east, and south. The spur of high land west of the Borborema tends to trend in an east-west direction, thereby preventing any stream from flowing directly toward the west.

It is interesting to note that while the climate of Northeast Brazil, within historic times, has attracted much attention and notice because of the droughts, there is a record of climatic variation that can be read among the landforms. The Brazilian geomorphologist Ab'Saber[2] has pointed to widely differentiated climatic cycles in which he cites the disparity between the

[2] Aziz Nacib Ab'Saber, "Relêvo, Estrutura, e Rede Hidrógrafica do Brasil," *Boletim Geografico,* pp. 145–74.

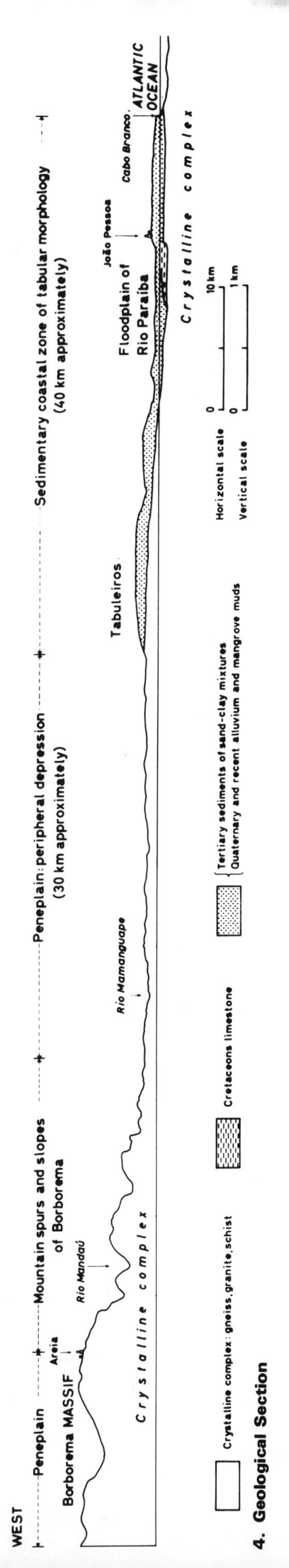

4. Geological Section

amplitude (great width of the valleys) and the very small volumes of water of the rivers that occupy those valleys, which are a product of the present semiarid climate. The broad valleys are clearly a sign of a former humid period, within a context of recent geological history. There was much more fluvial erosion and sculpturing by running water in the past than there is today. And this is noted not only in the semiarid and arid areas but also along the coast. Some writers, such as Georg Marcgrav[3] (one of several scientists brought to Brazil by the Dutch during their occupation from 1624 to 1654), have pointed out that the early navigators who first started up the Capiberibe and other rivers of that coast thought that, because of the size of the river's mouth, they were about to embark upon a trip of several hundred kilometers only to find that, after four or five bends, the size of the river dwindled to that of a small stream. Other evidence from the morphology of the area is found in the presence of small, intermittent streams without the brute erosive force required for superposition of an antecedent stream pattern upon rejuvenated ridges, which would leave water gaps known locally as boqueirões. This fact further reinforces the theory of the former existence of a humid cycle. At the same time it indicates the character of a classic antecedent pattern of drainage, which had been established over a former sedimentary cap formation. As the cap was eroded away, the drainage pattern of large streams was etched indelibly upon the underlying crystalline basement. The former Cretaceous sedimentary cap that covered much of Northeast Brazil dominated the geological past at that time, with only a few outcrops of the basement complex poking through, as in the upper Borborema. The tectonic uplift of the entire land mass resulted in the renewed cutting of valleys by rivers flowing over the sediments, rivers that suddenly cut through higher, more resistant areas in the underlying complex and, thereby, formed the boqueirões, or water gaps.

During the Pleistocene period, other climatic changes occurred. These changes are especially evident in some of the peripheral depressions and also in some valleys. The bajadas and inselbergs found in diverse stages of development are evidence of pediplanation processes, that indicate an evolutionary halt through the interference of a less intense semiaridity. The best example of this semiarid interference is the Sertão Baixo of interior Paraíba, and the sections between the cuestas and ridges of the Pernambucan sertão depression.

Characteristic of this semiarid cycle are the large fossilized bones of Pleistocene fauna found in parts of the sertão depression. The general drying of the climate during part of the Pleistocene caused the extinction of whole species of gigantic animals. The old lakes of the bajadas must have been points of convergence and thus are today bone repositories of those animals who died there. Then, when a more humid phase occurred, the river drainage systems recommenced their work of wearing away and eroding the surface and faintly rejuvenating the pediplain surfaces. Thus, in the Northeast, along with the morphological evidence of a humid paleoclimatic cycle with broad valleys and water gaps, we also see aspects of relief formed in an arid period that was even drier than the one today.

Landforms and mini-climates

One of the most striking results of the great diversity of the terrain within a small area is the chance to observe the apparent influences of very small variations of this terrain upon climate and vegetation. This point is introduced here in order to make the comments on climate

[3] Marcgrav's observations as a naturalist included remarkably accurate descriptions of fauna and flora of Brazil and also, incredibly, daily climatic readings of wind direction and precipitation for 1640, 1641, and 1642.

and vegetation in the next two sections more comprehensible.

The accompanying sections (figure 5) taken in an east-west traverse, one in Paraíbá, one in Pernambuco, show clearly the general profiles from the coast to the crest of the Borborema. What I found in the field was that, for example, around Tracunhaem, the vegetation and soil-moisture conditions on the windward (east) and leeward (west) slopes of a hill as little as 100 meters high were strikingly different. At Tracunhaem I observed mata or dense capoeirão on the windward slope, and caatinga with cactus on the leeward slope. I attribute the presence of caatinga vegetation in that broad zone behind the higher tabuleiros surface to the influence of orographic barriers of perhaps 100 meters in height, perhaps less. Unfortunately, the rainfall data are not sufficiently detailed to present this, but I strongly believe that in that part of Brazil, anyway, the sharp gradients of climate, precipitation, soil moisture, and vegetation can be attributed to these relatively miniscule differences in elevation and particularly to the orientation and exposure of the orographic barriers themselves.

CLIMATE

The phenomenon of drought is dramatic. It is even more dramatic when it is widespread and when human and animal misery accompany it. Much of the history, geography, and social commentary of Northeast Brazil has been written in terms of periodic droughts and of the effects of them. Unquestionably droughts have had an important part in conditioning both people's reactions to their physical habitats and their attitudes toward the relationships of man to the land. The most unfortunate thing is that despite the unquestioned existence of the drought and its terrible aftermath, the fact is that the interpretation of the significance of the droughts has almost always been incorrect, and has certainly been unrecognized by

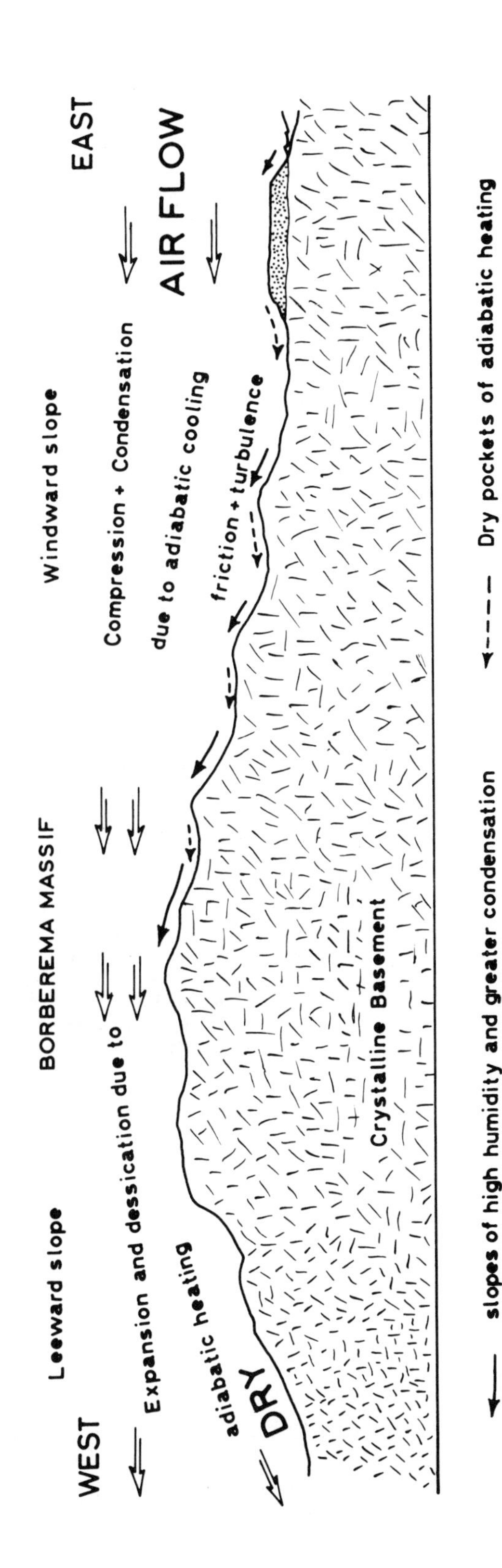

5. Mechanisms of Orographic Rainfall and Drought

most people, including those in a position to know better. In this section we shall examine the climate of Northeast Brazil by introducing the topic of droughts, thereby giving a human dimension to the area's climate. It can be noted that the drought had a different significance in 1932 than it did in 1877, and also that it had a different meaning in 1951 than it did in 1932. In short, the significance of climate, and of drought in particular, has changed with the change of man's culture or, in other words, his attitudes, objectives, and his technical abilities. Through his use of the spineless cactus (palma) for forage during droughts, and the presence of recently constructed reservoirs, man has had unquestionably more control over the drought aftermath than if these and other improvements, such as highways and trucks, had not been developed.

Typical moist agreste landscape in hilly area south of Campina Grande, under wet conditions; spineless palma and cotton plants in foreground, bananas and grass on wet bottomland. Mata seca or dry forest beyond and extending to serra horizon.

We shall follow our discussion of the human dimensions of the droughts (specifically the famous droughts, the Grandes Secas, of 1877 and 1932) with the climatological facts regarding the distribution of wet and dry areas, and then follow that with an explanation of the causes of the drought. The most reasonable explanation to date of the meteorological and atmospheric mechanisms that produce the climatic map patterns has been worked out by Gilbèrto Osorio de Andrade and Rachel Caldas Lins.[4]

The Drought of 1877. The literature of droughts has been written mostly by the wrong people, in the sense that those who were literate and able to record events were generally the ones who were the least touched by them. Euclides da Cunha, in his memorable *Os Sertões (Rebellion in the Backlands),* has given us a vivid account of land and man and the drama of drought in one particular part of the Northeast, the barren wastelands of Northern Bahía near Morro do Chapéu and Canudos where the incredible events of 1896 occurred. Many people who have read da Cunha's *Rebellion in the Backlands* have mistakenly believed that the conditions that existed around Canudos applied to most of the Northeast when actually there is tremendous geographical diversity and the variations are more important to recognize than the generalizations. Da Cunha presents horrible visual images. He portrays the dryness of the air as having such an extreme desiccating quality that the corpses of men after guerilla skirmishes became dehydrated and mummified and did not decompose as they would in a more humid climate. Even one or two years after the death of a person in the sertão, the body would be found with the external skin tissue still essentially intact. Da Cunha also gives us a depressingly vivid picture of the flagellados, the people fleeing the droughts,

[4] In "O Brejo da Serra das Varas," *Boletim do Instituto Joaquim Nabuco de Pesquisas Sociais,* pp. 5–22.

stumbling along the roads and trails with whatever belongings they had the strength to carry, and gradually throwing them away as their strength ebbed. In one image, he confronts us with the picture of an old man lying beside the road, wracked with hunger and disease, and too weakened even to brush away the vampire bat that was sucking blood from his toe.

Probably the most famous and infamous drought was that of 1877–79 in Ceará, during which it is estimated that between 200,000 and 500,000 people died and of which Rodolfo Theofilo has written a chronological month-by-month account, as viewed mainly from the state capital of Fortaleza.[5] He cites the events without benefit of sources or footnotes. He presents a disturbing picture of mismanagement of aid measures; he cites the existence of roving outlaws where the preservation of law and order was scanty at best. There was also considerable exploitation of the flagellados (literally "the beaten ones"), people who had nothing, least of all any bargaining power. Some interesting items are pointed out. For example, during the early stages of the drought there was abundant beef available but this was due, of course, to the fact that people were slaughtering dying cattle with the aim of converting the beef to dried beef, or charque, and of getting the hides before the animals became totally unusable.[6] Some landowners (this is before Abolition, which occurred in 1888) traded a slave for a load of farinha (manioc meal). In Fortaleza, slaves were being sold in southern Brazil because they were a drain on the food resources, and, under the circumstances, in 1877 some 1,775 slaves were shipped out of Fortaleza. By the end of 1877, 42,931 retirantes (refugees) were installed in and near Fortaleza. By December 31, some 83,000 were recorded in and near Fortaleza and the local administrator, Conselheiro Aguiar, stopped sending aid to the interior because he was faced with so many people to feed in the capital.

On December 7, 1877, Aguiar set up a commission of engineers to make studies and to compile a list of public works that might be carried out under the government of Disembargador Estrellita. These were WPA-type projects designed to take the unemployed and the hungry off the streets and to give them enough food to survive, and in the process build some public works. Some of the proposed projects were jails, cemeteries, chapels, streets, and dams.[7] In addition to slaves, other people emigrated in 1877. Some 6,106 people are recorded as having left Fortaleza; 1,496 went to the south and 4,160 went to the north (the Amazon rubber realm). The latter usually ended up in the jungle wildernesses of the upper Amazon Basin as seringueiros (rubber gatherers), never to return. In January 1878 people's hopes were lifted when a few showers fell on the parched land, but the water soon evaporated and the drought continued. However, as a result of these showers, 270 families, totaling 1,343 people, left Fortaleza to take their chances in the interior, expecting more rain to follow, but still more people continued to crowd into the city.[8] Some 30,000 retirantes were put up in emergency shelters such as warehouses and police barracks. Criminals, due to the indifference and incapacity of the government and the laxness of the local police, freely roamed the interior. There were signs that the showers, a hint of an inverno (rainy season), had ceased, and the aliseos, the strong easterly winds, blew once more, destroying any upward convective movements that would have been necessary for

[5] Theofilo, *Historia de Secca do Ceara.*
[6] Ibid., p. 140.
[7] Ibid., p. 148.
[8] Ibid., p. 158.

causing rainfall. Meanwhile, food rations were being distributed to the refugees.

In early February of 1878, enough rain had fallen to put some water in the stream beds and reservoirs. One reservoir, 6 leagues from Aracaú, separated from the sea by a sand dune, was flooded during the floods of 1872–73 and destroyed many farm plots. But there were many fish in the reservoir by 1878, and this proved an attraction to the 1878 refugees. Most of the fish were caught, and as the waters evaporated and receded the retirantes planted vegetables in the characteristic varzea tradition. Some 10,000 retirantes set themselves up by this so-called oasis.

In the thirty-one years since the last great drought, some 6,200 açudes were built, costing an average of 1,000 cruzeiros each. It goes almost without saying that in view of the great disproportion of land distribution in the Northeast, most of the dams were built on the properties of the large fazendeiros.

Aguiar made one mistake by moving the retirantes from the outskirts of Fortaleza to the city center; with the resultant crowding, disease spread. One disease, called de biliosa, was probably an advanced form of hepatitis or liver dysfunction. Patients suffered from fever for thirty to forty days, then died in a delirium. Other diseases were beri-beri, and gastroenteritis, not to mention malnutrition. Some beri-beri sufferers were sent to the refreshingly cool and moist serras for recovery; places such as Sobral's Meruoca, and the Serra da Baturité.[9]

Cases of anthropofagy were reported in the interior, which is not unusual under circumstances where people are dying and there is no food: They eventually revert to eating each other. Less dramatic was the stealing that went on. Fortaleza had 100,000 retirantes in March 1878, and an attempt was made to control prices on government-sold supplies. The population at that time was much smaller than now, of course, but considering the resources at their command, they were extremely hard pressed. People who stole from the state warehouses were called muambas. They stole because "everyone was hungry" or "because everyone steals."[10] Folk songs recounted the numerous feats of the muambas and the tales of the state or federal aid that did or did not arrive.

Yet a number of permanent construction projects were completed, such as the railroad from Baturité, which was begun on June 1 and had reached Pacatuba (33 Kilometers) by September 3, 1878. Further, this drought, in which it is reported that upward of half a million people died (probably an exaggeration), is one where it is noted that there was not a complete absence of rain; there were showers, but the effect of drought is cumulative and far-reaching to the extent that those landless peasants and other people directly dependent upon the land and the cycle of rains normal there simply did not have the means to survive until the next rains. And these people flocked out of the interior to the coastal cities which were not equipped to handle them.

The Drought of 1932. In this account of the great drought of 1932, Orris Barbosa makes his observations with a critical and scathing eye that reflects his disgust and rage at the mismanagement of resources and the serious social and economic ills that contribute to the human misery. He states that the three basic elements of the Northeast's disgrace are (1) the drought, (2) the lazy absentee landowner, and (3) the political chieftain or boss.[11] Each drought is like a forge in which the weak are eliminated and only the hardiest survive.[12] The dull, precarious existence of most sertanejos starts at childhood, and the miserable childhood they

[9] Ibid., p. 167.

[10] Ibid., p. 194.

[11] Barbosa, *Secca de 32,* p. 7.

[12] Ibid., p. 9.

experience leads to early aging. Some march off in search of the sweet verdant lands of the green Serra da Baturité or the moist brejos of eastern Paraıba, or probe southward to the Rio São Francisco or to southern Piauí. With each drought in the late nineteenth century, many retirantes fled to the Amazon, only to vanish and die in the remote corners of the realm of "black gold," or rubber. This was before the collapse of the world rubber market in 1912–13.

The author, Barbosa, was a child during the presidency of Epitácio Pessoa and was still very young when the IFOCS (Federal Inspectory of Works against the Droughts) was established in 1909. IFOCS embarked upon an ambitious reservoir-building program. This was the so-called hydraulic solution that later critics claim was a large failure because of the primary effort expended by the engineer-dominated IFOCS to build anything to hold water. This was the time when the solution to the Northeast's problems was seen to lie in the provision of more water and ever more water.

Northeast Brazil had good land; there were good cotton and sugar market prices after World War I (1914–18). The prices of these commodities were up and the sugar and cotton mills were working long hours. At that time money flowed, and the good life was available in the coastal capitals and even in some of the larger cities of the interior, such as Campina Grande, which processed cotton. But for the great masses of workers who did not participate in this prosperity, the sertão's misery fed the good times in the capitals.

Knowledgeable people noticed that the money spent in Works against the Droughts tended to gather back into the hands of the suppliers of construction materials and machinery salesmen, and into the centers of the market towns to enrich the entrepreneurs and the political chieftains. Federal money flowed alongside the profits of sugar and cotton. The "Golden Period" can be said to have lasted from 1920 to 1923, and in addition to sugar, which affected the states of Pernambuco, Paraíba, and Bahia, and cotton, which benefited mainly Pernambuco, Paraıba, and Rio Grande do Norte, Ceará participated in the prosperity with the carnaúba wax.

While the export cash crops were thriving, owing to high world market prices, the basic staple of diet of most people continued to be farinha de mandioca (manioc meal or flour prepared usually in lard and fried as farofa). It is a truism that "without farinha de mandioca, there is no meal" in Northeast Brazil. And during the 1920–23 period even the production of mandioca was up.

In the Northeast there was a steady awareness of the droughts and the fact that steps should be taken. The memory of the Grande Seca of 1877 was still fresh in the minds of older people. And the Northeast was favored by a number of economic and political factors that facilitated the establishment of a plan against the droughts. Hopes were raised that a lush land, even a possible Garden of Eden, would result from the frenzied building of reservoirs. But what happened, alas, was that the water was impounded behind the dams and it remained there. It was not applied to true irrigation works; its only use for agriculture, except for the occasional showplace experiment station, was for vazante farming in the wet fringe zones of the reservoirs, as the water level lowered by evaporation with each dry season.

Some people mistakenly believed that the mere presence of a few square kilometers of water surface in the Northeast was somehow going to change the climate, and there are still people who believe this today—that the quantity of added moisture through evaporation would somehow get into the atmosphere and then be returned in the form of significantly higher rainfall. This has not been proven, any more than the belief that reforestation measureably influences rainfall. The irony then remained that one could fly in an airplane and see hundreds of reservoirs, large and small, without the reservoirs making much difference in the living level of most people of the area. The "hydraulic solution" had been a failure. Yet the people's faith in the açudes was so strong that they still believed the evaporated water would have sufficient power to give new variations to the laws of nature.

The highway did revolutionize the custom of animal transport, and where the road went, some degree of prosperity tended to become implanted. Places without access remained under a great handicap, as they do today. The increased municipal revenues of the early 1920s were used to install more electric power and it was rare to find any sizable city without its own movie house. This was another of the notable modifiers of customs and a source of the implantation of new dissatisfactions among the people. The new prosperity left a new concept of life in the Northeast and the presence of new roads, telegraphs, movie houses, stores, was a countervailing power to the magical hold upon people's imaginations that such visionaries, prophets, and dominant religious figures as Padre Cicero and Antonio Conselheiro had. Padre Cicero lost some of his prestige in the face of machines and electricity, in the opinion of Barbosa.

In 1923, during the Bernardes government, public works were stopped, and unemployment and labor disorders occurred. Skilled workers sought jobs in the permanently wealthy capitals of the coast, and were hired at rock-bottom wages. Life was more tolerable in the well-watered brejos and mata zones of the east. This was also the year that the infamous bandit leader Virgulino Lampeão of Alagoas began to rampage. Then there was a catastrophic inverno (rainy season) with too much rain which washed out a lot of cultivated land with their crops.

Some of the dam projects continued. Even foreign (American) engineers were brought in, and while many were proficient dam builders, there was a serious lack of engineering geology competence, so that the dams were well built but they were constructed with inadequate knowledge of the suitability of the site. Several dams were later discovered to be incapable of holding water because of the porosity of the country rock or the existence of joints or other escape channels for the water which was to have been impounded.[13]

Then, in further catastrophe, a plague killed several million coffee plants in two years. Cotton was piled up in the warehouses, awaiting possible higher prices, and yet higher prices were not quoted because the world demand was for a better quality of cotton. Sugar was also falling in price. There was no United States market for it. And the rebellious Carlos Prestes revolutionist column began its long trek toward the Northeast. It was a period of general unrest and, as is common in Brazil, the blame was placed upon the government in general and not on the fall of world market prices. The Great Western Railway raised its rates by 30 percent and so did trucks. People were battered by political hates. There was a spirit of revolution. The town of Princesa in interior Paraíba revolted. There was a good deal of anti-American and anti-British feeling.

As far as what happened on the land, it is clear that drought is the faithful ally of the large landowner. This is because during the crisis of a drought period, the wealthy landowner forecloses on the small landowner. This has to do with the production indices. One hectare of land, which is worth 150 cruzeiros after an abundant rainy season and is usable for grazing after crop harvesting, is worth only 30 cruzeiros during a drought. Cotton lands vary in price between 600 and 40 cruzeiros

[13] Hilgard O'Reilly Sternberg, personal communication to author, 1959.

per hectare. Is it any wonder that land tends to become concentrated and reconcentrated in the hands of a few while the small-scale farmer not only flees the drought but also flees having lost everything?

The healthy zones for subsistence were the Serra da Baturité, a traditional oasis of higher agricultural production; the agreste zone of the Borborema where beans, maize, mandioca, and potatoes could be grown; and also along the margins of the perennial rivers and the fringes of the açudes.

People began to anticipate a drought around 1926. A critical day is always the day of Santa Luzia, December 13; if rain does not fall by that day it probably won't come later.[14] Along the eastern coast the critical rains are called the chuvas de cajú. In terms of their impact, the droughts tend to drive out the landless salaried workers first, those who have the least security and control over their lives. Next follow the small renters, followed by the small landowners. The large landowner, the fazendeiro of substance, usually has the resources to buy food, and usually he owns a house in the capital city and can move there to wait out the drought. Regarding resistance to disease, Barbosa notes —and it is probably true—that the sertanejo or the worker of the sertão probably lives better than the more sickly man of the mata zone. The physical habitat of the mata is more humid and hotter. It is a physical milieu within which even people with access to the best medical care are constantly afflicted with problems of intestinal parasites, fungus, boils, and other diseases that are inherently much more a part of the ambiente than they are in the drier sertão The sertão is a far healthier setting. The workers in the sugarcane areas of the zona da mata frequently go barefoot and are therefore more subject to parasites that enter the body through the soles of the feet. The sertanejo usually wears some kind of footgear, either boots or alpargata (a kind of slipper-sandal).

In the context of that day and age, the landowner tended to distrust and fear the agronomist and engineer. These técnicos were generally people of a higher level of education and represented authority because they were usually employed by the government. And because the government (federal or state) had always been a symbol of outside interference, and there had never been any association of anything good with it—it only took things away, such as money for taxes—landowners feared and resisted outside help.

The average farmer tended to want little from his land. His was not an intensive mode of production; it was a mode of extensive techniques applied to extensive areas of land. In that period, farm wages ranged from 1 to 3 cruzeiros for a ten-hour-long work day, with a half hour off for lunch (farinha, beans, and charque). In the cash-crop areas of sugarcane, cotton, coffee, and carnauba wax production, the wages ranged from 2.5 to 4 cruzeiros a day, and women and children were paid 1 to 2 cruzeiros a day to plant and weed the sugarcane and to weed and harvest the cereals.

In the caatinga and sertão, the pastoral economy dictated lower salaries. For a ten-hour day, the foremen or bosses earned 12 to 15 cruzeiros a day and enjoyed strong influence because they kept their jobs during the droughts and were afterward responsible for rebuilding the decimated cattle herds and generally restoring the land. Elpídio de Almeida[15] recalls that during his long memory, and throughout his research on the Paraíban interior, he never encountered mention of any cattle herds having over 1000 head. Most of them were 500 to 600 head. The droughts that came on an average of every ten

[14] Manuel Correia de Andrade, *A Terra e o Homen no Nordeste,* p. 37.

[15] Almeida, personal communication to author, April 1964.

to twelve years destroyed the herds until only a remnant of ten to twenty head remained, and that constituted the seed of a new herd. Thus, the fazendeiros of the sertão were periodically recommencing their herds, and the key vaqueros were essential to building up the herds after the droughts.

Some notion of what other salaries were can be gathered from the fact that a master carpenter earned 10 cruzeiros a day, a mason 12, a sheet metal worker 10, a mechanic 15, and a chauffeur 8. Factories paid very low wages because of the abundant labor supply, and unions were undreamed of. It was a buyer's or employer's market.

The drought of 1932 was a Grande Seca like those of 1877 and 1915. The rains had been diminishing since 1926, and that was a bad sign. When the seca arrived, there was widespread panic. In some of the interior towns the flagellados attacked and looted stores for the scarce and expensive food supplies. When they trudged into the coastal capitals, they were established in camps outside the cities, as during the seca of 1877. In 1931, a new plan for relieving the effects of the droughts was approved and the IFOCS acted again to relieve unemployment. Refugee camps were set up in Ceará where the worst effects of the drought were felt. They were located at Fortaleza (camps of Piramba and Octávio Bomfim), in Patu, Quixeramobim, Crato, Carius, and Ipu. These camps were hastily erected in the year between April 1932 and April 1933, and some 800,000 people were housed. These camps diverted many flagellados from the already crowded cities. The new plan of IFOCS called also for public works. Some 8,000 refugees were shipped to Pará and given land. One such refugee colony was the Colónia David Caldas in Piauí state. Most of the labor contracted by IFOCS, however, was put to work on the dams.

In IFOCS, the priority programs included (1) the construction of federal dams, federally financed, which would ultimately feed a national network of irrigation canals; (2) state or municipal dams, federally financed; (3) private dams, where the federal government paid the contractors; (4) road systems, to help connect producing areas with markets; (5) the division of irrigation-improved lands among small landowners; (6) the establishment of cooperatives of credit, production, and consumption. Needless to emphasize, some of those programs were less successful than others. It may be observed that the private açude was not a preponderant factor in the social and economic transformation of the Northeast. It simply tended to ease, protect, and strengthen the position of the landowner who remained on top of the social-economic-political hierarchical heap. There was incidentally, and as mentioned before, a certain amount of fish farming carried on in the açudes, and this helped somewhat to ease the protein deficiency for some families.

The author Barbosa spent a week, from September 10 through 17, 1933, touring with President Getulio Vargas to visit the Northeast, and drove from João Pessoa to the brejo of Areia in two and one-half hours. In his description of Campina Grande, he explains how its prosperity is due to the rise of cotton; he describes the famous regional feira (market) and states that Campina Grande lies between "the brejo and the sertão." He uses *brejo* as the equivalent of *agreste*. In other words it is a "hinge" city, a fact to which we shall return later. He notes that during certain dry periods of the year, a can of water (probably 5 liters) costs more than 1 cruzeiro, equivalent to two to four hours labor in those days. He notes that in Soledad, only 60 kilometers west of Campina Grande and in the heart of the sertão, there was no rainfall recorded for eight years. (This may possibly be because no observations were made.)

These foregoing accounts of the droughts of 1877 and 1932 convey something of the flavor of those times. The drought of 1932 occurred against a background of a much more integrated national life so that it was possible for goods and people to be moved from disaster areas to relief areas.

Distribution of climates in the northeast

Northeast Brazil is, with some exceptions, an extremely dry area. For centuries the recurrent droughts have attracted considerable attention because of their profound effects, both direct and indirect, upon the land and the people. In this section I will attempt to show (1) *where* the dry and humid areas of northeast Brazil are, and (2) *how* the Thornthwaite system of climatic classification qualitatively and quantitatively demonstrates the fact of average dryness over most of the area.[16]

The technique of interpolating, and in a few cases extrapolating, temperature values for specific localities, from isotherms drawn on the basis of elevation *and* the records of 33 temperature stations, has been used to obtain estimated temperature values to complement the measured rainfall data for a total of 140 stations. This procedure is justified for Northeast Brazil since the characteristic high-latitude effects of differential heating and cooling on equatorward- and poleward-facing slopes are minimized in equatorial latitudes, owing to the obliquity of the sun's rays. Also, because the maximum relief of the Northeast seldom exceeds 1,000 meters, the differences in temperature from place to place, in any one month, over the whole area, are relatively small. Under the limitations of such a method, however, only an approximation of average existing conditions in the Northeast is herewith proposed.

Altitude and, more important, surface configuration are critical in determining temperature distribution and orographic concentrations of rainfall. As shown on map 5, the 200-meter contour roughly parallels the coast 80 kilometers inland, with the exceptions of rather broad embayments in western and eastern Ceará, and narrower embayments along the east coasts of Alagoas, Sergipe, and Bahia. The 500-meter contour encircles a large part of eastern Pernambuco and Paraíba, as well as western Bahia and the intersection of the Piauí, Ceará, and Pernambuco borders. Small areas near Morro do Chapeo, Garanhuns, Tacaratú, and Triunfo rise above 1,000 meters.

With respect to general air mass characteristics, frontal activity takes place mainly in winter when cold polar air seeps northward along the coast, lifting and cooling the surrounding warmer air, thereby causing precipitation in the zone of contact along the east coast. In summer the Northeast may or may not receive rain, depending upon the strength and size of the monsoonal indraft of maritime tropical air that moves southward from the Atlantic toward the Chaco "low." Because Northeast Brazil is not in the direct path of these rain-bearing warm winds, and because of the shifting position of the easternmost edge of that moist indraft, the area is subject to great variability of rainfall.

Temperature distribution in Northeast Brazil consists of a more or less uniform reduction of temperature with elevation, with the lowest temperatures coinciding approximately with the highest elevations. Areas of highest rainfall, moreover, although concentrated for the most part along the east coast, also correspond generally with the more highly elevated inland areas. In summary, therefore, one observes the expected correlation not only between low temperature and high elevation, but also between high rainfall and high elevation.

Thornthwaite defines potential evapotranspiration, or water need, as the amount of water that would transpire and evaporate if it were available. Because potential evapotranspiration is computed as a direct function of tempera-

[16] Kempton E. Webb, "The Climates of Northeast Brazil According to the Thornthwaite Climatic Classification."

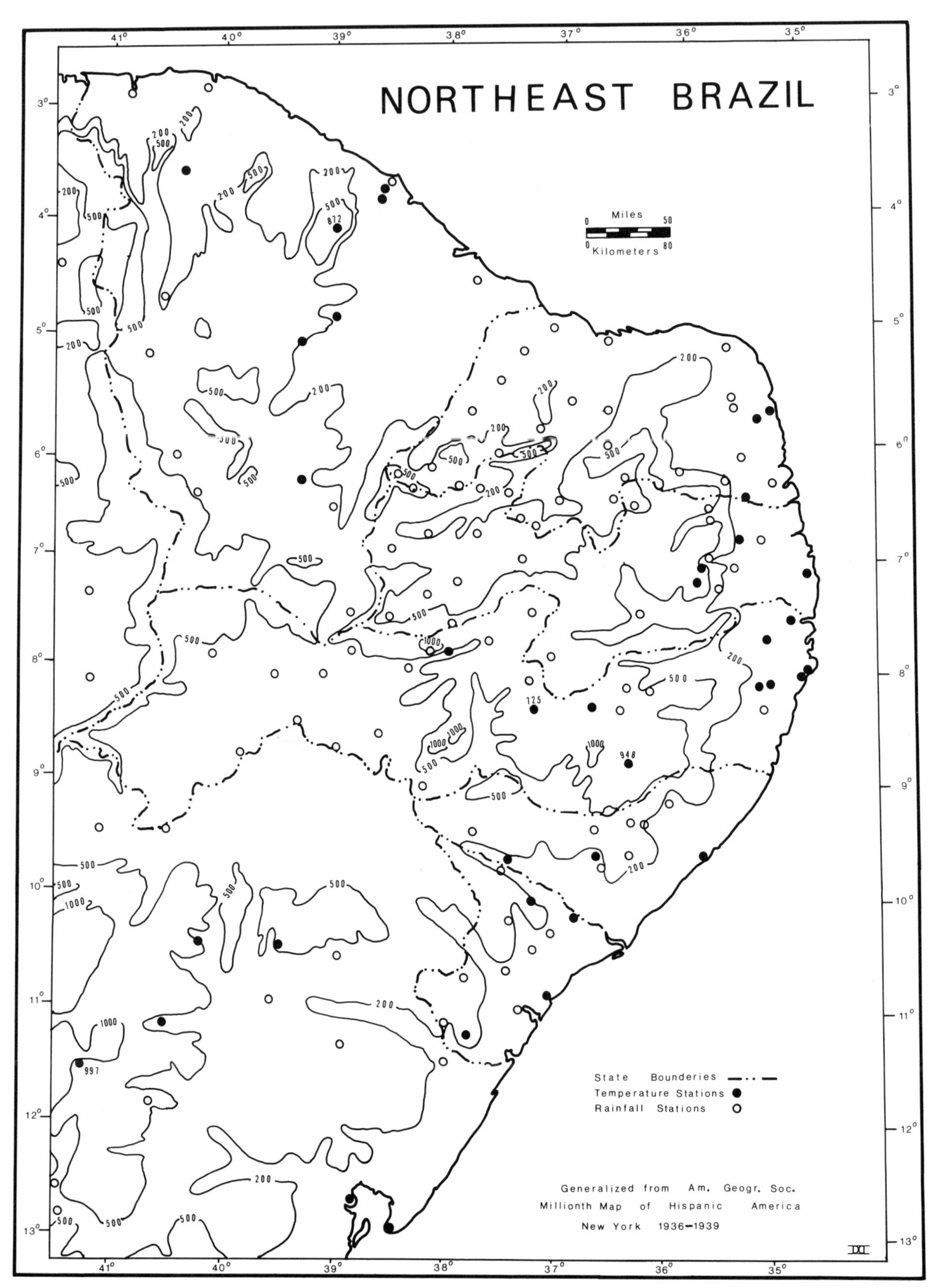

5. Generalized Elevation above Sea Level

ture, with minor corrections for length of day and month, the pattern of isarithms of potential evapotranspiration must be expected to resemble that of isotherms, for a given area. The relationship between elevation and temperature, and therefore between elevation and potential evapotranspiration, becomes apparent when one observes Guaramianga, with an elevation of 870 meters and a low potential evapotranspiration of 94 centimeters of water, *or* the Chapada de Araripe area, with an elevation of generally more than 500 meters and a potential evapotranspiration of generally less than 114 centimeters of water. Conversely, high potential evapotranspiration values are associated with low-altitude stations: for example, Recife, with 60 meters of elevation, has a high potential evapotranspiration of 165 centimeters. Aracati, 30 meters above sea level, has the highest computed potential evapotranspiration of the whole area—181.1 centimeters. Because of its position close to the equator, Northeast Brazil has values of potential evapotranspiration that far exceed the lower limit of Thornthwaite's present megathermal category. Additional intervals of potential evapotranspiration need to be included in the system.

The graphs shown in figure 6 demonstrate the relationship between potential evapotranspiration, rainfall, water deficit, soil moisture recharge, water surplus, and soil water utilization. Thornthwaite has found that approximately 10 centimeters of rainfall may be stored in the soil at the end of the rainy season and may be used later at the beginning of the dry season. The first 10 centimeters of rainfall surplus at the beginning of the rainy season is recharged to the soil and is therefore not available for runoff.

The following stations are selected for their representation of a variety of conditions in the Northeast, and not because they necessarily depict average conditions. Average conditions are shown in map 6.

Jaboatão, elevation 50 meters, is located near the area of highest winter rainfall on the east coast of the Northeast, and has pronounced dry and wet seasons. Rainfall drops below water need in September, the 10 centimeters of stored soil water being used by mid-November. A deficit, equivalent to 11.4 centimeters, lasts until January, when rainfall exceeds water need and subsequently puts the 10 centimeters back into the soil. A large water surplus exists between March and September, in which 99.1 centimeters passes off as runoff, not all of which need be surface runoff.

At Aracatí, elevation 30 meters, potential evapotranspiration is uniformly high throughout the year, ranging from 14 centimeters in June to 17 centimeters in December. The high total annual potential evapotranspiration of 181.1 centimeters largely counterbalances the heavy rainfall. Rainfall, however, has a sharp maximum between February and May, when there is 25 centimeters of runoff. Extremely dry conditions for the rest of the year result in a deficit of 91.8 centimeters between July and February. Aracatí is more or less typical of the area of large summer deficit in northern Ceará.

In contrast to Aracatí, Morro do Chapeo, elevation 997 meters, has a low total annual potential evapotranspiration of 85.6 centimeters. The total rainfall of 74.6 centimeters is considerably less than that of Aracatí, yet, owing to its low potential evapotranspiration, Morro do Chapeo has a higher effective moisture. Like Guaramianga, it is typical of the places of higher elevation, higher effective moisture, and lesser variability of rainfall.

Cabaceiras, the driest station in Northeast Brazil, lies 390 meters above sea level and has a total annual moisture deficit of 80 centimeters. Almost no rain falls between September and December; moreover, very little falls during the remainder of the year.

Of all the lines drawn on a series of Thornthwaite climatic maps, the most important is the zero-value isarithm of moisture index,

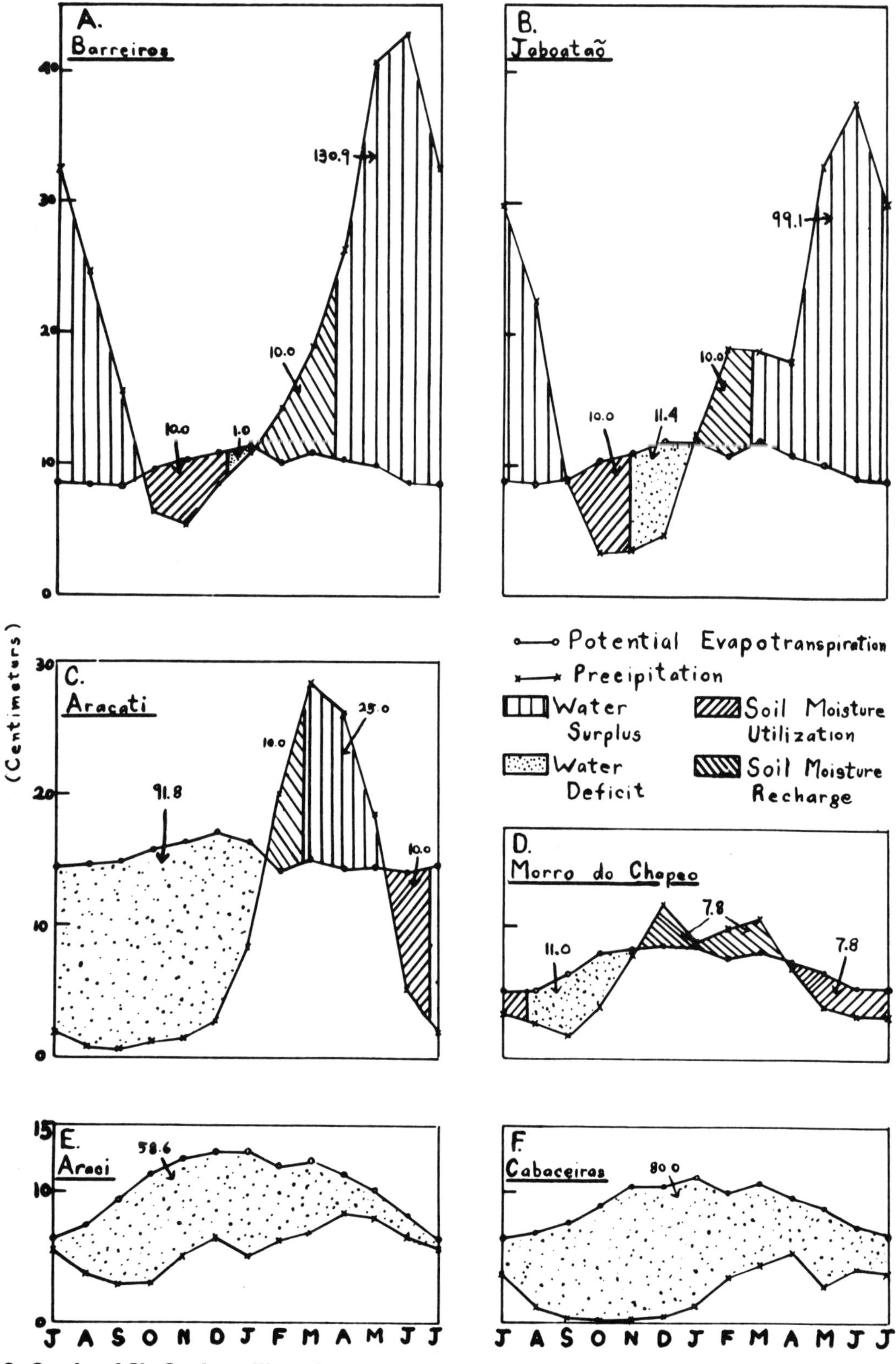

6. Graphs of Six Stations: Water Surplus and Deficit

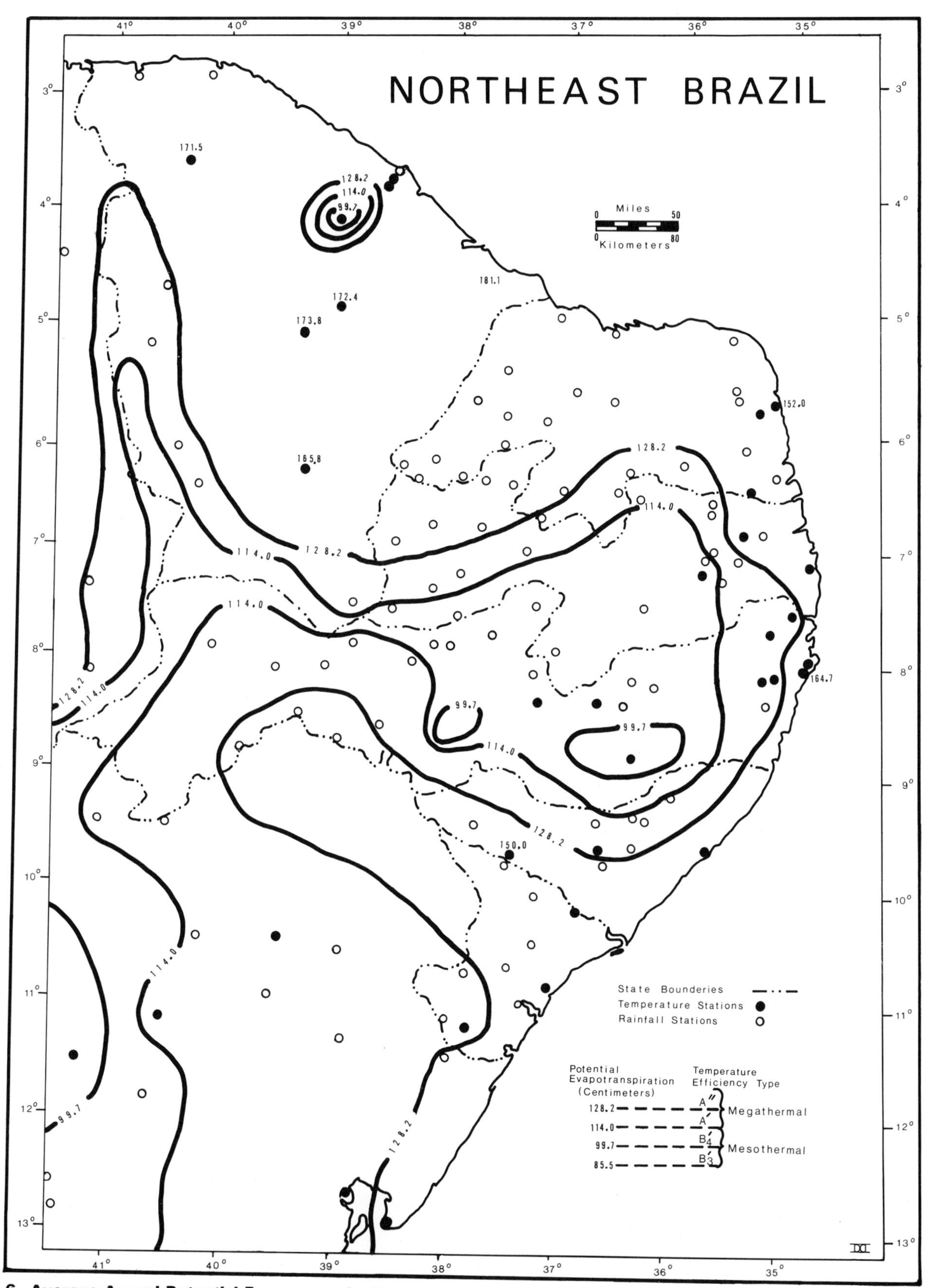

6. Average Annual Potential Evapotranspiration

which separates the moist from the dry climates on the map of moisture regions (map 7). The indices of moisture from which the isarithms are drawn define a relationship between total water surplus, total water deficit, and total potential evapotranspiration.

The zero line separates the rainy coast from the generally dry interior of Northeast Brazil. The following dry areas have moisture indices of less than −20: the interior of Ceará, most of Rio Grande do Norte and Paraíba, and northern Bahia and eastern Piauí. Cabeceiras has the lowest moisture index of all stations in the Northeast: −44.5.

Positive moisture indices, indicating moist climates, are found in Piauí, Paraíba and Pernambuco, Bahia, Guaramianga in Ceará, and all along the east coast.

In general, negative moisture-index values are found in the low places of Ceará and Bahia, and in central Rio Grande do Norte and Paraíba. High moisture indices are found along the east coast of Pernambuco; other moist places are associated with relatively highly elevated locations. The distribution of stations, by percent and with respect to the moisture index, is as follows: E (arid) stations: 4 percent; D (semiarid) stations: 51 percent; C (subhumid) stations: 40 percent and B (humid) stations: only 5 percent. Thus, 91 percent of the stations are either semiarid or subhumid.

To indicate differences from season to season, Thornthwaite classifies climates according to seasonal variation of effective moisture. The moist areas with little or no deficit of effective moisture are concentrated along the east coast of Pernambuco and at scattered inland areas of higher elevation, such as Guaramianga, Triunfo, and Andaraí. On the other hand, the dry areas, having little or no surplus of effective moisture, occupy the greater part of the interior of Northeast Brazil.

Thornthwaite's last element of classification is the summer concentration of thermal efficiency, which is derived by summing the potential evapotranspiration of each station for the three summer months and then expressing this sum as a percentage of the total annual potential evapotranspiration of each respective station. All stations of the Northeast have a summer concentration of thermal efficiency of between 25.2 percent and 31.1 percent, which, in contrast to situations in higher latitudes, indicates little except that there is only slight seasonal variation of potential evapotranspiration. It should be emphasized, moreover, that, for equatorial areas, a distinction of seasonality couched in terms of winter and summer is meaningless compared to a distinction expressed in terms of wet and dry seasons.

By way of summary, it has been noted that the primary factors accountable for the main areal differences in moisture regions of Northeast Brazil are elevation, surface, configuration, and location with reference to the zone of dependable summer rains in central Brazil and the zone of dependable winter rains on the east coast of Brazil. The main factors that account for low effective moisture are low latitude and low elevation, insofar as they produce extremely high values of potential evapotransportation.

The contribution of the Thornthwaite classification toward an understanding of the climate of Northeast Brazil consists mainly in the delimitation of moisture regions that can be quantitatively compared to other moisture regions. Application of the Thornthwaite classification in a low-latitude area, such as the Northeast, emphasizes the importance of potential evapotranspiration and its influence in modifying the effects of rainfall. With one exception, the interior of Northeast Brazil has little or no surplus of effective moisture. In contrast, the entire coast has a moderate winter surplus, with small areas of little or no deficit scattered along the east coast and at higher elevations farther inland.

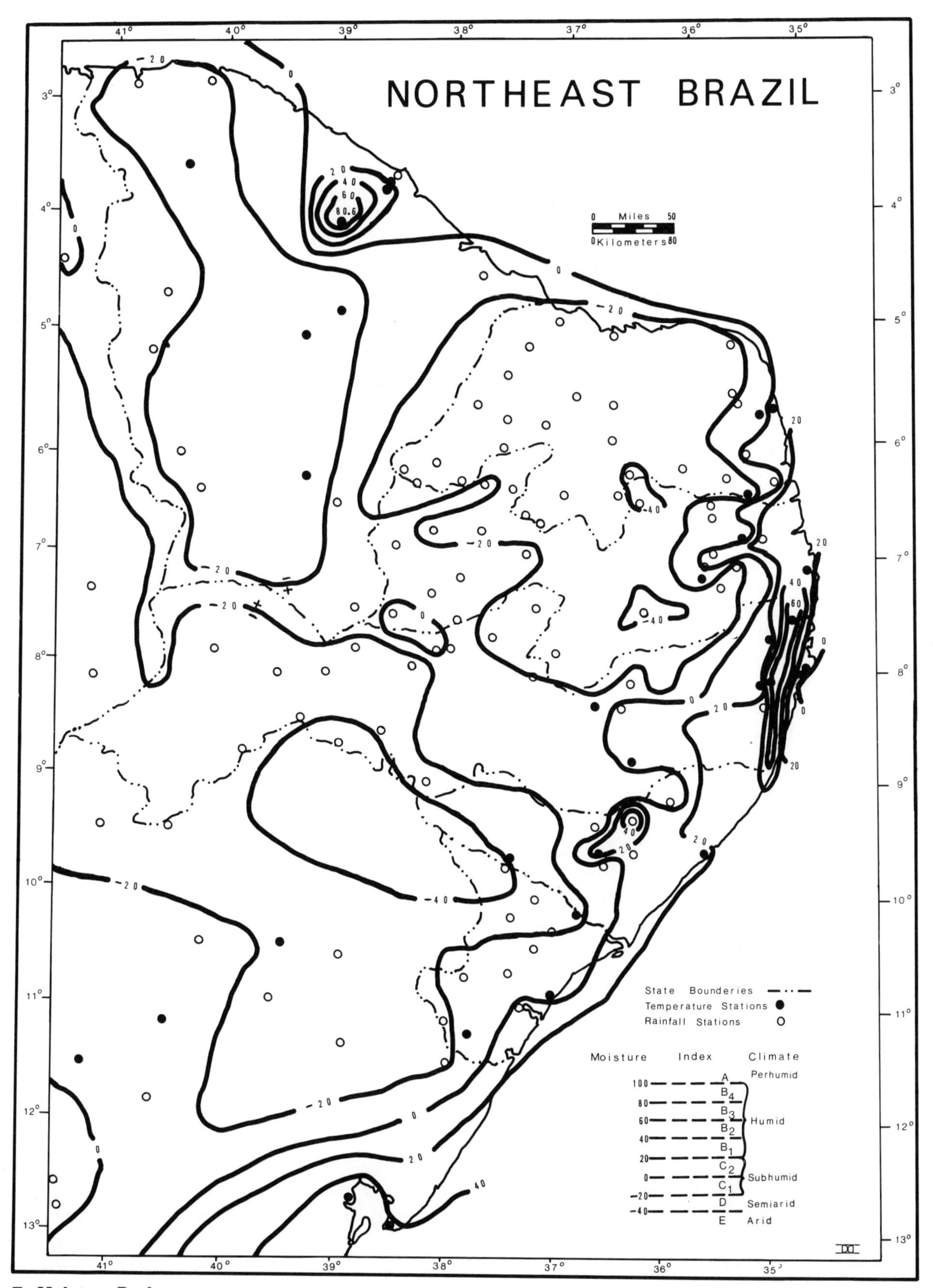

7. Moisture Regions

As a final point, it is suggested that, for an area the size of Northeast Brazil, and for the degree of generalization implied in the application of the Thornthwaite system of climatic classification, the resulting maps yield the type of detailed information that might be useful in regional planning operations conceived on a similar scale.

Explanation of the droughts

There has been a long history of attempts by climatologists and geographers to explain why and how the droughts occur. We have already seen the impact of the droughts upon the lives and economy of the area during the Grandes Secas of 1877 and 1932; we have also seen the results of climatological investigations that have indicated generally where the dry areas are. We now have to explain the mechanisms and processes whereby the droughts occur. The first fact to recognize, and it is easy to miss, is that the key distinguishing characteristic of the Northeast's climate is not the low rainfall per se, but rather the high degree of rainfall variability. The fact that the droughts are unpredictable, that there may be ten or twelve rainy years and suddenly a profound and long-lasting drought, makes life and livelihood precarious.

The regional atmospheric circulation and the rainfall régimes. The precipitation-causing influences of foreign air masses can be better appreciated when they are considered in relation to the more or less permanent atmospheric conditions with which they interact (or interfere).

The most persistent climatic influence throughout the year in Northeast Brazil is the vast subtropical high pressure over the South Atlantic which provides the prevailing easterly winds that continually flow against the coast of the Northeast. This is clear air with fairly low relative humidity—the skies are blue with few cumulus clouds—and it dominates the entire coast from the coast of South Africa to the bulge of Northeast Brazil. This is the same stable air mass that provides the brilliant, transparent nights in the sertão. Many poems and songs have been inspired by the "luar do meu sertão."

The prevailing southeasterly winds flow out from the center of high atmospheric pressure over the South Atlantic between the latitudes of 35°S and 40°S. This is a semipermanent high-pressure cell from which the winds flow out in a counterclockwise direction, owing to Coriolis Force, the apparent horizontal deflective force that acts upon all moving bodies on a rotating earth. In the southern hemisphere the anticyclonic wind motion is counterclockwise; in the northern hemisphere it is clockwise. In south Africa, the eastern edge of this subtropical high-pressure cell lies over—and largely causes—the Kalahari Desert. It is from this eastern flank that the easterly winds proceed in a northerly, then westerly trajectory curving around to finally impinge upon the coast of Northeast Brazil. Throughout their prolonged trip over the ocean, these winds absorb enormous quantities of moisture, since the warm ocean surface is a particularly effective evaporating surface. At the same time, the air is heated and therefore its capacity to hold water vapor is increased so that the relative humidity (the ratio of the amount of water in the air to the amount of water the air is capable of holding) remains at a fairly low level. It is this clear and stable air that arrives at the coast of Northeast Brazil and dominates the region throughout the year, and that accounts for the low precipitation. When rain falls, it is because the atmospheric stability has been interrupted owing to vertical air movements caused by connection with or the invasion of cold antarctic air from the south.

The coast is generally low in elevation, but, even so, the low elevations are sometimes sufficient to trigger conditional atmospheric instability. Moderate rainfall that moistens only the coastal fringe east of the Borborema does

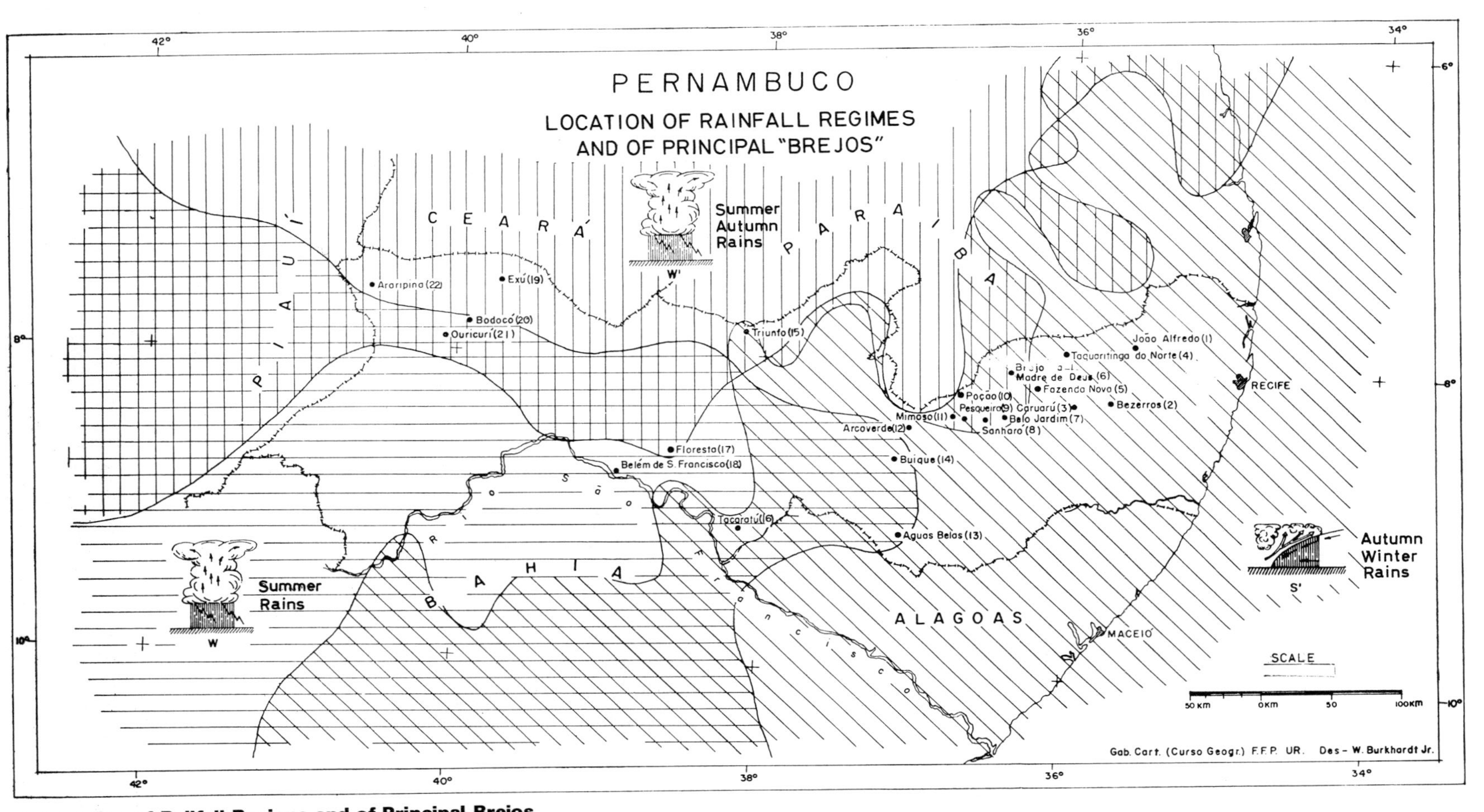

8. Location of Railfall Regions and of Principal Brejos

occur. These simple orographic rains would be the only ones if it were not for competition and contact with other air masses.

Competition for at least temporary dominance of the Northeast comes from three distinctive air masses, each of which is active and makes its influence felt in a particular season. Paradoxically, it appears at first glance that in a region where there are three different rainfall régimes in succession that cover nine months of the year, there are also conditions that are capable of defining one or more characteristic areas of semiaridity in South America. In fact, it appears that the interior of Northeast Brazil comprises the extreme limit of penetration of each of these three air masses which converge, however weakly, upon it. Restated, the Northeast's interior *can* be reached by any or all of these three air masses, but there is absolutely no assurance that it will, in fact, be their destination. The specific consideration of each air mass and of the mechanics of the annual convergence accounts for the niggardly and irregular rainfall in the different areas.

There are, successively, summer rains, summer-autumn rains, and autumn-winter rains. Other areas, of course, come under the almost exclusive influence of each of these air masses, but within the study area of Pernambuco and Paraíba each of these rainfall maxima corresponds with a large area that is delimited on map 8. Some small areas can come under the influence of two air masses. Fewer are privileged to be visited by all three in rare years. In the Köppen climatic classification the notation suffixes of w, w', and s' are combined with A and BSh to designate most of the Northeast's climates; tropical (Aw, Aw', and As'), and semiarid (BShw, BShw', and BShs').

The A climates have annual rainfall that exceeds the amount of evaporation. These would be positive moisture indices in Thornthwaite's system. The combined notations shown above indicate a well-defined rainy season in relation to a lengthy dry season. If the yearly amount of evaporation exceeds rainfall, BSh climate results, which is the climate of semiaridity in low latitudes, connoting not only warm but also dry conditions. In summary, in the Northeast the climates are warm and humid and also warm and dry.

Summer rains

These chuvas de verão (summer rains) register maxima in February (or even in March when they crowd in on the summer-autumn rains) and are controlled by the yearly expansion of the equatorial continental air; this is warm, humid, convective air whose source-region lies in the upper Amazon and Rio Negro basins. The expansion-invasion of this warm humid air occurs in summer, covering most of Brazil; it expands southward, and the eastern edge of it expands eastward to reach Northeast Brazil. It accounts for the Aw climates of Piauí and Maranhão. Although greatly altered, it is still manifested in the form of BShw climate in western Pernambuco, and therefore it produces reduced yearly rainfall even when it is added to the summer-autumn and autumn-winter rains, because all these influences are met there in the extreme limit of their effective reach. The years in which the penetration of the common equatorial air mass is weak are the dry years in the areas of summer rains, and particularly in the areas of BShw. In other words, the summer rains have their origins in the deep interior of the continent, and the semimonsoonal indraft of moist tropical air is felt in the Northeast to the extent that it has sufficient size and strength to penetrate that far. In some years, the indraft simply does not penetrate that far and the people of Ceará anxiously look westward toward the Serra da Ibiapaba for the first dark clouds.

Summer-autumn rains

These rains have a less precise origin. It is said that they come from a stable, moist air mass, but the presence of this mass is determined by the annual latitudinal migration of the ITCZ (Intertropical Convergence Zone). The ITCZ shifts southward during the southern hemisphere summer. Rains associated with the ITCZ begin in summer, but the heaviest rains fall in March and April. The Köppen designation w' means "summer rains delayed into autumn." The strength of the migration of the ITCZ varies from year to year. Sometimes this particular regime can be felt in the eastern coast south of Natal, in Pernambuco and in Alagoas. When this occurs, autumn rains are added, along that coast, to those of the S' (winter) rains.

Along the coast of northern Brazil, which is the prime domain of the ITCZ migration, this moist unstable air is introduced into Northeast Brazil and penetrates southward up the valleys of the Parnaíba, Jaguaribe, and Piranhas rivers. The moist air masses actually overflow the great drainage divides because they are convective air (with vertical movements) and their trajectories are not controlled by lines of relief, as is common with advective air. Continental equatorial air covers Maranhão and all of the Pernambucan sertão. It covers all of Ceará and practically all of Rio Grande do Norte, and the western half of Paraíba. Even these, as happened with the expansion of equatorial continental mass, the farther removed it is from the source region, the more reduced are the rainfall totals, and the more irregular is the annual rainfall distribution.

Whether from west to east or along the northern coast or the interior, the summer-autumn rains define extremely sharp transitions between the tropical humid and the tropical semiarid areas. Fortaleza remains Aw' although Macaú, to the east, and Quixadá, to the south, are already classified as BShw'.

Autumn-winter rains

The third regime is that of the Atlantic polar front of remote antarctic origins, which dominates the middle latitudes of the South Atlantic. Being a zone of strong discontinuities, characteristic of all midlatitude zones, the polar front discharges bursts of antarctic air northward, which advance toward southernmost Brazil. In the face of the imposing escarpments of the southern Planalto, the cold-air masses can move either (1) northward along the valleys of the Paraná-Paraguay river systems into the upper Amazon valley bringing the famous friagems, or cold snaps, to that area, or (2) northeastward along the Brazilian coast until they reach, and include, coastal Northeast Brazil. The Northeast is more or less the end of the range of these antarctic discharges. These are wedges of cold air that penetrate northward and, by being denser and heavier, insert themselves under the warmer Kalaharan air, forcing it to rise and causing atmospheric instability that usually produces frontal precipitation. The precipitation from these frontal passages is said, in the local weather lore, to "refresh" the prevailing easterly winds.

The autumn-winter is the time when the energy of these polar outbursts is most evident along the Northeast coast. During the spring they are reduced to a minimum. The summer is anticipated by the arrival of the chuvas de caju, or "winter rains anticipated in autumn." For this reason they are rains whose maxima are registered in June although they had begun in the autumn. Of the rest, the greater frequency with which the cold discharges reach the Northeast coast does not necessarily coincide with the greatest energy with which the ITCZ emits them. For whatever reason, the rainfall totals of the Pernambucan zona da mata, year after year, and the irregularity of the rainfall distribution, are a function of the regional energy frequency. The surpluses and deficits of these rains, their early arrivals and delays, the brevity or length of their duration, are constant preoccupations of the farmers of Northeast Brazil.

In summary, a yearly competition occurs between the weakened leading edges of three air masses of distinct and distant origin. The effects of atmospheric instability from this triple advance, perhaps only less random or less unpredictable except for the regular passages of the antarctic cold fronts, burdens the Northeast with a very severe physical handicap. This competition gives the Northeast a most irregular distribution of rainfall. It is, moreover, a progressive reduction, because of three separate trajectories, of the rainfall totals. The ultimate result, in that "no man's land" where the three air masses expire, is the barren, spiny caatinga of the semiarid sertões.

Map 8[17] shows that part of Pernambuco and its neighboring states that form the battleground for the three competing air masses. To sum up this influence, one can say that whether or not any weather station receives rain depends upon its position relative to these three air masses. Some places are influenced by essentially one mass; others may benefit from frequent annual exposure to two of the air masses; and some places, like Triunfo, are located near the convergence locus of all three air masses. Whether or not a place gets rain depends upon not only the altitude, the elevation that would largely determine the temperature conditions there, and the degree to which the orographic mechanism might be triggered, but also the directional orientation of the site—that is, whether the moisture-bearing winds impinge upon the slope at right angles, giving optimum rainfall conditions, or whether the winds blow parallel to the slope, where there would be no significant vertical air movement, and consequently no rain-making situation. (See figure 7.)

This explanation, which is largely the work of Gilberto Osório de Andrade and Rachel Caldas Lins, is the one that best accounts, so far, for the great variety of rainfall regimes and the geographical diversity of the patterns of the regimes. There is no other way to account for such sharp gradients of moisture. Later on we shall examine the complex situation of the brejos and serras that are the ecological surprises in interior Northeast Brazil. These are the areas that are generally hidden from main roads and yet that have an overwhelming role in local and regional life and livelihood that is generally underrated.

The Grandes Secas (great droughts) occur when vast areas of several states are not reached by any of these three air masses. These areas might miss a rainy season one year, two years, or even three years in a row. The great gamble of the local inhabitants is that there is no way in the world to be able to forecast the drought, which may abruptly follow a dozen or fifteen years of abundant rainfall.

The year during which I did most of my fieldwork in the Northeast (September 1963–June 1964) turned out to be one of the rainiest on record. My photos of the caatinga showed it a verdant green and my photos of vaqueiros frequently had backgrounds of ominous black clouds heralding an imminent downpour. It was an opportunity to see the calamity of excessive rains where crops are washed away, but it was not the time to observe the gray-blue, barren-leaved caatinga in all its parched glory as I had seen in 1957 in Ceará.

In conclusion of this section of climatic patterns and processes in Northeast Brazil, it might be interesting to describe what it is like to live there. In the coastal cities from Alagoas through Pernambuco, Paraíba, and Rio Grande do Norte, the wind blows constantly from the east. The wind is warm, relentless, and damp. Its very humidity prevents it from being refreshing. One gets the impression that he is standing in front of a fan inside a Turkish bath. The winds blow from the southeast most of the time, although in the drier months from September to February the coastal winds blow with greatest frequency from the east and northeast, and during the rainiest season from March to August, south and southeast winds predominate. This pattern applies especially to the Pernambucan and Paraíban coast.

[17] From Gilberto Osorio de Andrade and Rachel Caldas Lins, "Circulacão Atmosferica Regional e Regima de Chuvas," unpublished manuscript, 1963.

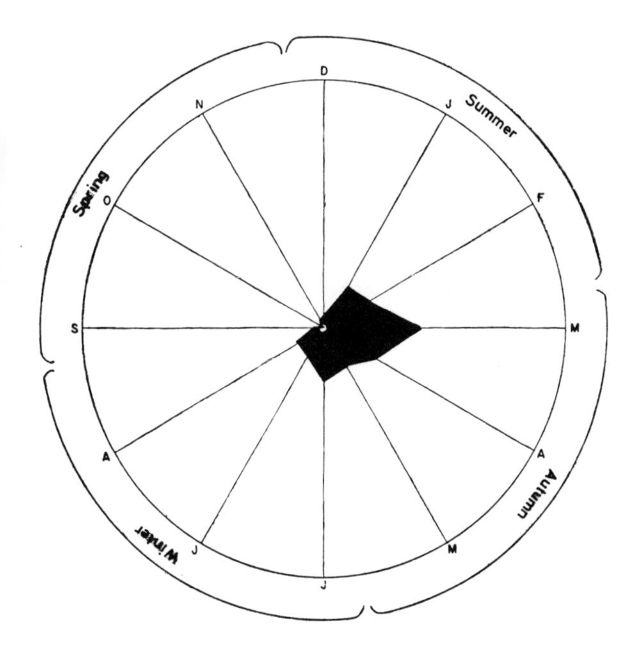

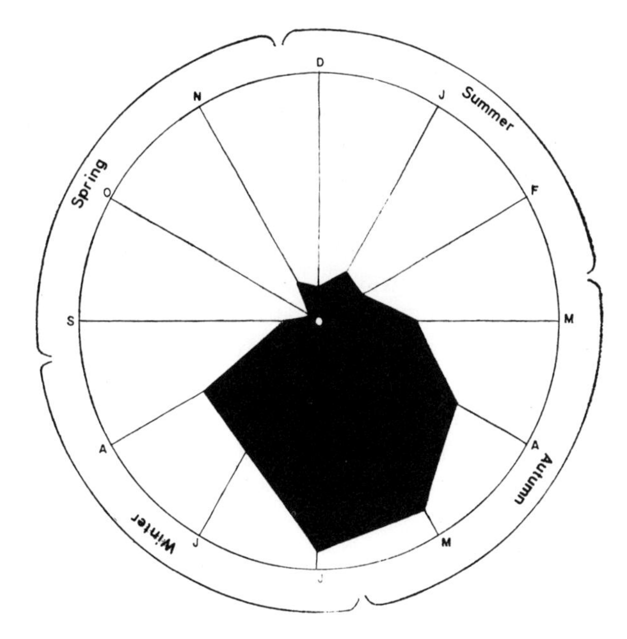

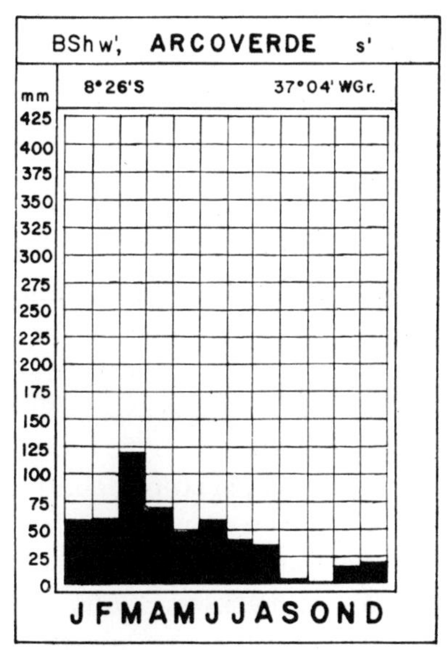

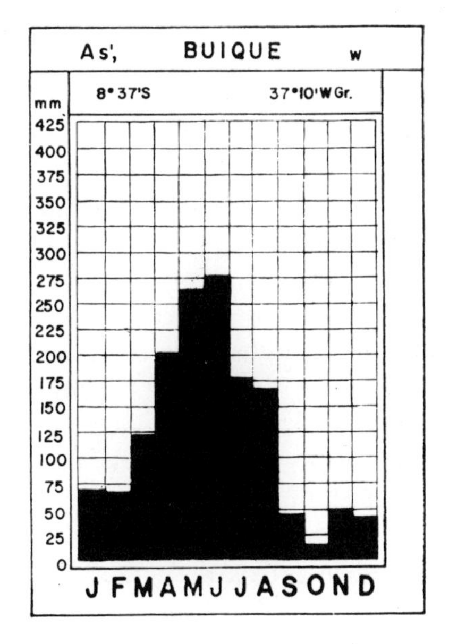

7. Rainfall Distribution

The dominant role of orographic barriers of even as little as 100 meters relief cannot be overestimated. As one travels into the interior, one notices differences in both vegetation cover and relative humidity on the windward and leeward sides of such a barrier. A striking example exists near Remigio (Paraíba) where, approaching from the west, one is traveling in extremely dry air that is being heated adiabatically, and then, within a distance of 2 to 3 kilometers, passes from air so desiccating that one's lips are chapped, one's nasal passages dried, and the air itself is brilliant and crisp, to air that is warm and humid, practically saturated, and full of all the discomfort one associates with walking fully clothed into a hot shower room. Along the coast, because of the high relative humidity, the temperature almost never falls to a level that could be considered chilly. The wind is not cooling or refreshing; it stirs the air around but it does not evaporate perspiration. It is a climate where one perspires freely just by sitting still in the shade. It is common for people to take three, four, or more showers a day.

Upon reaching the agreste, however, one is subjected to much lower relative humidity and, as he ascends the Borborema massif, also to lower temperatures. This means that in the sertão itself and most of the agreste, the climate is comfortable and pleasant. The sertão is the most comfortable because of the dry air, brilliant sunshine, and, at night, a definite chill. The low humidity and absence of cloud cover permits rapid rates of radiation from the earth's surface and gives the sertanejo nights a brilliant clarity that is unforgettable. Sertanejo songs and poems rhapsodize about "O luar do meu sertão" (the moonlight of my sertão). The stars are naturally observable in an area where many of the smaller towns of less than 5,000 people still lack electricity. The reader is asked to stop and consider whether he has ever been in a town of 5,000 people where there is not one single electric light. The blackness of the night is broken only by the light from dim candles and weak lanterns. On a cloudy night or a night of a new moon, the blackness is complete. One has to feel his way along the sidewalls, touching walls and doorways and hoping he does not stumble into a pothole. The prudent fieldworker in the Northeast carries a flashlight at night.

VEGETATION: TYPES AND PATTERNS

Vegetation is a mirror of a combined effect of rock types, climate, soils, and human actions and interference. In Northeast Brazil it is the human actions that have been most responsible for producing the aspects of vegetation that are seen today. For example, the very designation zona da mata (forest zone) is now a purely historic designation for the simple reason that there are no longer large areas of semi-deciduous tropical evergreen forest in that part of Brazil. There used to be, but man has substituted sugarcane, other crops, and scrubby second- and third-growth capoeira vegetation for the mata. Let us observe how the vegetation pattern reflects the rainfall and general climatic conditions.

Within the Northeast the highest average temperatures of Brazil are found. In the zona da mata the more prevalent cloud cover and sea breezes keep the highest temperatures to around 24°C. In the lower elevations within the sertão, temperatures are around 26°C. The highest temperature ever recorded in Brazil occurred in the Northeast because of the higher rates of insolation compared to those of the Amazon. On the serras and higher areas of the planaltos, temperatures decline with elevation at an average rate of 3.3°F per 1,000 feet. The average yearly temperatures there are around 22°C, as at Garanhuns and at comparable elevations such as Esperança in the Paraíban agreste. The yearly range in between average maximum and average minimum temperatures is only around 5°C owing to the low latitude of Northeast Brazil.

This pattern of sustained high temperatures, without much annual variation, contrasts with the pattern of great variation in rainfall distribution. Along the Atlantic coast there is a zone of rainfall of between 1,000 and 2,000 millimeters (40 to 80 inches), and the zona da mata can be thought of as having that amount of rainfall. The interior sertão receives as little as 500 millimeters (and there is as little as 250 millimeters in Cabaceiras, Pernambuco). In fact, one climatic classification, by Pimentel Gomes,[18] considers the matas to be those areas

[18] Gomes, "Agua no Nordeste," *Revista Brasileira de Geografia*, pp. 23–60.

with over 1,000 millimeters per year (the highest rainfall he cites in Mamanguape (2,280 millimeters per year). His second category is the caatingas, with 600 to 1,000 millimeters per year, and the cotton areas, which he calls mocolandia, with 400 to 600 millimeters per year, and which is found in the Cariris Velhos of the study area and the Curimataú of Rio Grande do Norte.

In the study area of eastern Pernambuco and Paraíba the lines of equal rainfall, or isohyets, parallel each other, and decrease in value toward the interior until they reach the value of 1,000 millimeters, which is a response to the orographic barrier that the Borborema massif presents. The exception to this parallelism of isohyets to the coastline comes as a response of the moving air to special relief situations, such as are found in the lower agreste area of Paraíba, essentially a leeward adiabatic heating phenomenon, and the brejos of altitude.

The climate of the Borborema is 2° C to 3° C cooler, sometimes more, and has a rainfall of 650 to 1,000 millimeters per year. This is the so-called agreste region, and in Pernambuco and Paraíba the zone of immediate-volume rainfall is enhanced by islands of higher humidity known as brejos. The original vegetation type in this agreste region is called agreste by some people. It was probably originally a type of mata seca with many species of the zona da mata, but with a more barren aspect and sparser distribution. It is a kind of intermediary stage between the mata of the coast and the caatinga, or tropical thorn scrub forest, typical of warm semiarid climate.

West of the 650-millimeter isohyet lie the vast reaches of the sertão. In Northeast Brazil there are three pockets, as shown on the previous map of moisture indices, located in central Paraíba, Ceará and northern Bahia. One, the Cariris Velhos of Paraíba, is in our study area. The vegetation cover associated with the semiarid climate is an association of xerophytic (drought-resistant) plants—the caatinga Caatinga is an indigenous Tupi expression (from caa [forest] and tinga [white, clear, or open]) and it represents the results of forest adaptation to a dry climate and bare soil. It is an extremely heterogeneous association of plants and trees and one of great interest and beauty. The interior of both Pernambuco and Paraiba have enormous areas of caatinga.

As we review the vegetation characteristics of this part of Brazil, we must constantly remember that the vegetation we observe and photograph in the field today is vastly different from that which Europeans saw when they first came to this part of the new world in the early 1500s. Dense covers of capoeirão (the second- and third-growth vegetation) which appear as virgin and primeval forests are really areas that simply have not been cut for the past sixty or seventy years. And even in places where one is assured by the oldest resident that there has never been a cutting down of the mata seca, as behind Sao José da Mata, just west of Campina Grande, there is at the same time an admission that certain desirable trees had been cut down for construction purposes. So, by definition, that "uncleared area," although not clean-cleared, as in preparation for a field of beans and maize, had been subject to selective cutting over the years.

José Guimarães Duque has drawn a map (map 9) of natural regions which is essentially a vegetation map.[19] However, for guidance and perspective on the topic of vegetation, one must go back to Philipp von Luetzelburg, the indefatigable German botanist who worked for IFOCS and traveled extensively in Northeast Brazil for ten years between 1911 and 1921. His monumental three-volume *Estudo Botânico do*

[19] José Guimarães Duque. See map 9 for his map of "natural regions." IBGE, Conselho Nacional de Geografia, "Tentative de Classificaçao das Regioes Naturais do Nordeste," 1963.

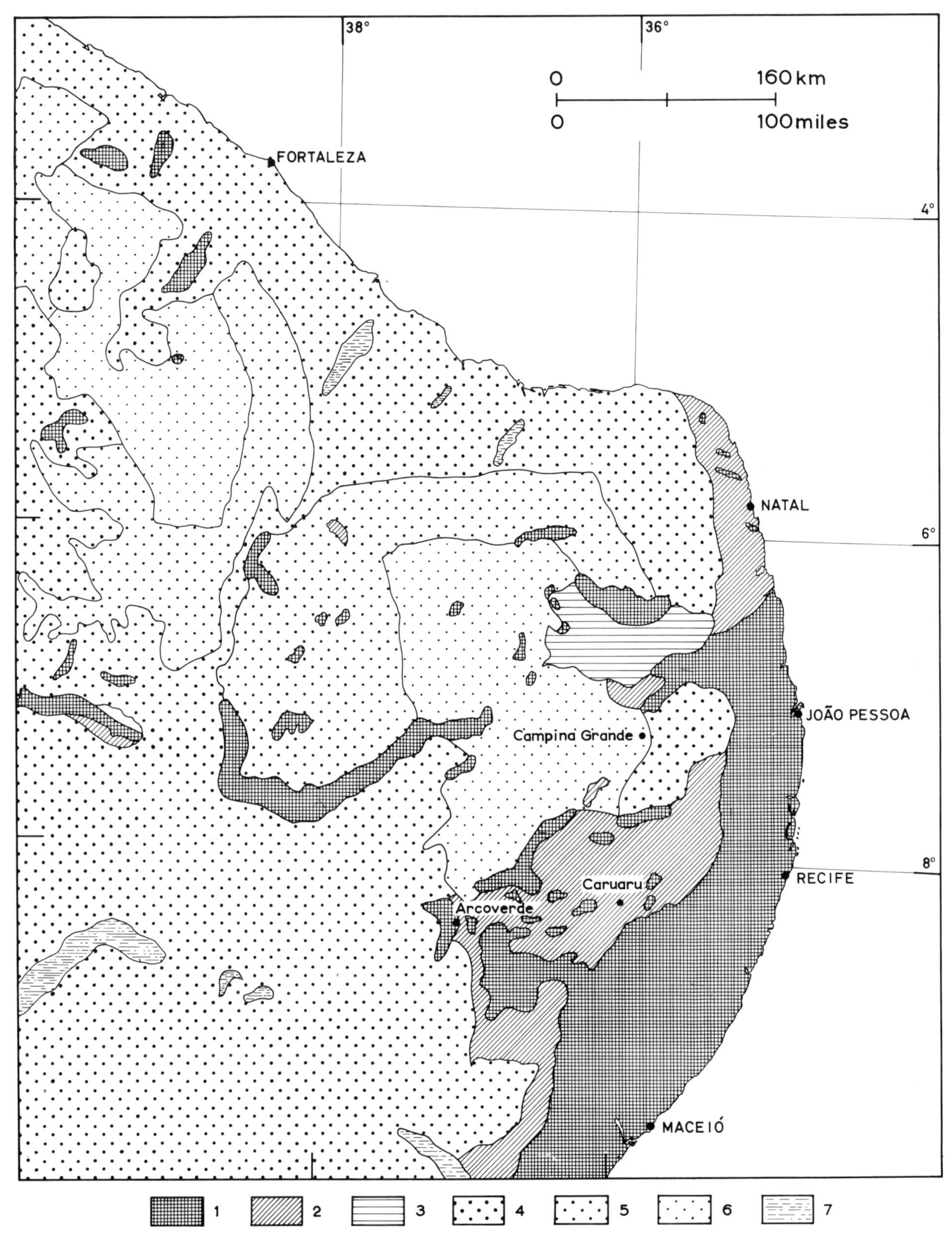

9. Natural Regions of the Northeast
1. Mata or humid highlands (serra); 2. Agreste; 3. Curimatau; 4. Caatinga; 5. Sertao; 6. Serido; 7. Irrigation basins

Nordeste is a classic of first-class scientific field observation, research, and analysis of a difficult area in a difficult period. His first volume is an account of his travels to Piauí, Bahia, and Sergipe and includes many excellent photographs, although without much analysis. Volume 2, which we shall refer to frequently, is his work in Pernambuco and Paraíba from May 1919 to February 1922. The trips were made by car, horse, donkey, and on foot. The numerous photographs he took make it possible for one to compare the vegetation of that period with that of today, since most of the trails and roads he followed are now transitable by car or jeep, and I was able to follow many of the same routes in 1963–64. Volume 3 is a general discussion of vegetation types in the Northeast. It is less regionally oriented.

The vegetation along the Pernambuco coast was formerly composed of an extensive dense and high mata that was hygrophilous and megathermal—that is, it required much rainfall and supported high temperatures and high relative humidity. This mata extended inland up the Rio Paraíba valley to the Borborema slopes. "Of those matas today," Luetzelberg writes, around 1920, "we find only small vestiges in the deepest hollows of the valleys or on the rugged slopes of the serras. The rest of the area, which was formerly occupied by forests, is presently occupied by sugar cane, maize, beans, and so on. To the west of that zone of matas extends caatingas, interrupted to the north and west by the Serra de Santa Luzia, and the farther one proceeds from the coast the more mixture there is between the elements of mata and of the caatinga." In table 2, cited by Magnanini, we see a comparison of the areas of each vegetation category, mata and caatinga, as estimated by Gonzaga de Campos and Luetzelberg for each Northeastern state.[20] The disparities are a reflection

Sheep can survive in the harsh environment of the sertao. Caatinga vegetation.

of the incomplete information available and of the problems of category definition. After presenting a description of the major vegetation types, we shall describe what has happened to each of these types in terms of their destruction and decimation, and read some of the estimations of other writers as to the degree of this decimation.

Mata means high trees, a warm humid climate, and a soil rich in mosses and well-developed epiphytes (hanging vines, air plants, and other parasitic plants). This dense, arbored vegetation depends mostly upon light and humidity. The light comes only from above, the zenith, and the trees compete and struggle upward to reach it. In the true mata there is very little open land, and the sunlight rarely penetrates to the forest floor. The continuously working bacteria that keep the soil fertile is one of the strong advantages of the mata.

The *caatinga* has all the qualities of the xerophilous forests of the semiarid region (such as agreste, campos cerrados, serido, and carriscos in the sense of sertão). Trees and bushes average about 3 meters in height. Light comes from

[20] Alceu Magnanini, "Aspectos Fitogeograficos do Brasil," *Revista Brasileira de Geografia,* pp. 98–99.

all directions; moisture is deficient; there is no humus to speak of. Whatever thin layer of humus exists in the driest sertão suffers from lack of the bacteria that would decompose organic substances and form nitrogen. It is well known among fieldworkers in Brazil that the word *mata* is practically synonymous with fertile farmland and *caatinga* with poor farmland. Therefore, the caatinga is rich in leguminous families that manufacture their own nitrogen from their root nodules. The lack of humus limits the amount of herbaceous verdant flora.

The plants themselves have interesting morphologies. Many have spines to protect them from the territorial encroachment of other plants (if the plants grow too close they are punctured by the defending spines) and from animals. There is little parasitism of the type that produces epiphytes in the zona da mata, since there is no need to climb the trees to seek the sunlight. It is all around; in fact the brightness of the daylight in the sertão is almost overwhelming. Even with extra-dark sunglasses one is continuously squinting to avoid the glare —especially from the ground, which is light and comprises a reflecting surface of very high albedo.

Waxy leaves on the sertão plants cut down the transpiration of water, and the leaves themselves are narrow in order to minimize the evaporative surface.

A further breakdown of the major vegetation types may be useful as a reference:

1. *True matas* have tall trunks of a gray-whitish color and seek sunlight from above. The true remnants of original vegetation are found now only in the protected remote nooks and crannies where man and his axe cannot get at them. The use of timber for fences that encircle many square kilometers has contributed to the destruction of the matas, as has the burning to clear land for crops. What results is an inferior capoeira that moves in because of the complete chemical-bacteriological alteration of the soil.

2. *Capoeira* refers to the vegetation that comes into an area after the original or virgin vegetation has been cut down. It is the second or third or thirtieth growth. What happens when an area of virgin mata is first cleared? First of all, the direct sun's rays kill the fertile-soil-forming bacteria and the new seeds cannot become as readily established as before clearing. The shrubs and bushes and trees become smaller. The vegetation acquires a more xerophytic appearance. The secondary growth will never revert to true mata although it takes a trained eye to distinguish between a true mata and an old, tall, dense capoeirão.[21]

Anaerobic bacteria cease working because of the strong light and drying soil. The deficient action of humus kills the shallow horizontal roots, and the leaves of the lower growths are toasted by intense sunlight. The drought-resistant, or xerophylous, plants then invade the cleared area. They (xerophilous bombaceas, bignomiaceas, and melostomaceas) crowd out other new shoots and only the hardiest shoots of the original mata survive. Subsequent deforestation and repeated clearings by the traditional slash-and-burn system of roça agriculture makes the lower bushy growths denser, and the aspects of xerophytism increase. Xerophitous grasses invade, as do purely xerophytic cactus plants. The carrasco vegetation represents, in Luetzelberg's opinion, the ultimate decadence of capoeira. As might be expected in the semi-arid interior of Northeast Brazil, the areas of capoeira tend to follow the river valleys and humid serras, since the watered places are the sought-after and cultivated areas.

3. *Capão* refers to the scanty remnants of true mata that have been invaded by herbaceous and xerophytic plants.

4. *Palmares* or palm trees often occur in stands or graves of one type. The carnaúba palm

[21] *Capoeirão* is the superlative form of capoeira, meaning a very tall, dense, second-growth vegetation.

is valued for the wax of its leaves, and it festoons the lower sertão surface of Ceará state. The humbler buriti palm is prized for its large fronds or branches that make a practical roofing material.

5. *Agrestes* are not physiological matas; they lack the exclusively vertical sunlight and rainfall of the matas. There is little epiphytism in the agrestes because of the low relative humidity in the atmosphere. Parasitic plants do not climb upward because there is abundant sunlight on the ground. Grasses are not succulent but, rather, are dry and siliceous (high in silica) and do not retain moisture. Trees are widely scattered since they require considerable growing space in view of the low moisture available for all plants. The tree trunks are fairly tall and straight, averaging around 10 meters in height. The soils are rocky, sandy with much hard pan formation, and generally hard to farm.

6. *Vazantes* belong to the agrestes and refer to the low spots that are flooded temporarily. The soil stores water that subsistence crops can then use. Palm trees are common in the varzeas but other trees are rare because the vazantes lack the humus of the true mata. Farmers plant sugarcane, squash, tobacco, maize, and beans in the floodplain zones but these crops are always lost during the large floods. Such floods and crop destructions occurred on a wide scale in 1964. Too much rain can be as bad as drought.

7. *Veredas* is a vegetation mixture of agreste and caatinga in the sandy alluvial soils of valleys. The sertanejo regards the veredas as good pastureland. They are generally criss-crossed with myriad cattle trails in the vicinities of reservoirs, wells, or water holes, especially in Bahia and Piauı. Once the veredas are cut back and burned over they lose their woody growths (trees) and the space is given over to hard and tough grasses and widely spaced raquitic shrubs and bushes that are useless for agriculture. Sound observers such as Luetzelberg believe these to be good prospective areas for reforestation efforts.

Caatinga vegetation and sheet erosion in the sertao. Deteriorating forage base for cattle.

8. *Tabuleiros* have already been discussed as low-plateau landforms. The sandy soils provide them with such excessive drainage of rainwater that an edaphic semiaridity prevails, as in the Pernambuco-Paraíba border where the vegetation strongly resembles the campo cerrado of central Brazil.

9. *Campos cerados* are the characteristic savanna vegetation of grasses with scattered trees that cover most of the state of Goias, Mato Grosso, and a large area of Minas Gerais. In central Brazil the long intense dry season causes this adaptation; in Northeast Brazil specific soil drainage conditions, as found on some tabuleiros, produce the same stunted vegetation (short, twisted trees less than 2 meters in height and a sparse cover of grasses and other bushes less than half a meter high).

10. *Caatinga* is an association of spiny and woody plants that get along with little water, can survive many months without any water, thrive on sunshine, and grow anywhere. The original caatinga can be thought of as a dense, xerophytic mata composed of shrubs and trees with small, shriveled, thorny leaves; it is rich in spiny plants like the cactaceas, which are

armed with all the protective morphologic and metabolic means to prevent too much loss of water by transpiration.

The sertanejo divides the caatinga into three main types according to its height, density, and suitability as pasture: (1) *Caatinga baixa* (low caatinga) is dense, with no openings through which man or animal might move easily. It dominates the chapadas (plateaus) of Piauí state. (2) *Caatinga alta* (high caatinga) has an approximate ratio of two bushes to every tree. It is found in the flat areas (bajadas) between the mountain serras. The soils there are less hard, dry, and stony than usual. Common trees are the aroeira, barauna, angico, mimosa, pereiro, marizeiro, joazeiro, and carnauba. (3) *Caatinga verdadeira* (true caatinga) is usually called sertão by inhabitants of the dry areas of Paraíba and Ceará. It is composed of legitimate xerophytes. The soil is covered with a discontinuous carpet of bromelias, and tall cactaceas. Another distinction made by some people is that of (4) *caatinga legitima,* which is the areas where Cereus Jamacarú grows (popularly known as cardeiro) together with mandacaru. Both are used as cattle fodder during droughts, and after their spines are burned off. The popular understanding of *sertão* is those areas where the cereus squamosus ("facheiro" in popular usage) grows, which is of little or no use. Those areas are hard to travel or subsist in. Some 800,000 of the 1,232,000 square kilometers that comprise Northeast Brazil are covered with caatinga, according to Leutzelberg.

The composition of the caatinga and its various parts varies with soil quality, river systems, surface configuration, and the activities of the caatinga's inhabitants, animal and human. The caatinga does not admit outside elements from more humid settings. They simply cannot survive the harsh competition from the hardier caatinga species.

Many characteristic features and aspects always accompany the plants in a caatinga grouping. Xerophytism is the chief factor. The plants are deciduous in order to conserve the water that is in them. The lack of humidity means that fallen leaves cannot be turned into humus. There are nitrogenous plants with tuberous roots that have their nitrogen-fixing bacteria *(Knoellchenbacterien).* These bacteria cease activity during the long dry season, then resume with the first rains. The leaves of the caatinga plants bend to avoid the direct rays of the sun, and are small in order to cut water transpiration loss. Roots and tree trunks (such as the amusing barriguda ("belly" tree) have bulbous sections with open intercellular spaces for water storage.

The leaves of many caatinga species are protected by fine hairs that secrete gums and resins. There are thick, and economically profitable coverings of wax on the genus *Cereus* (carnaúba palm). The woody growths or trees have hard resistant wood, and they grow slowly. They tend to have irregular twisted and contorted trunks with thick rough barks; they have flat crowns or semicircular crowns of great circumference. The branches are highly ramified from the ground surface upward. In other words, there are many branches, giving a "brambly" aspect that is very characteristic of the caatinga. Both the trunks and the branches of trees are grotesquely twisted. The dry soil under them means no mosses, algae, or fungi. Only a very few miserable epiphytic plants survive there. Table 1, adapted from Luetzelberg, presents the tree arboreal aspects of xerophytic vegetation.

The high cactaceas are all capable of growing to the majestic heights of 10 meters. They include the *Cereus Candelabros, Cereus Jamacarũ* (popularly known as mandacaru de boi), and *Cereus Squamosus* (facheiro). Where the mandacaru succeeds in invading the agreste, which is a perfectly natural occurrence in view of the relentless "desertification" of the entire Northeast, it can reach a height of 12 meters

Table 1. Arboreal aspects of xerophytic vegetation

	Agrestes	Carrascos	Caatinga
Trunks	High (av. 10 meters), thick (50 cm). More trees than shrubs and bushes.	Low (av. 4 meters), thin (10 cm). Dense, only one-third of growth is trees.	Low (av. 4 meters), thick (20 cm); one-twentieth of vegetation is trees
Crowns	Rounded or oval	Oval	Umbrella-shaped
Leaves	Large, whole, digitated, leathery	Large, hard, leathery, whole or digitated	Small, pinnates or multi-pinnata, delicate and soft
Ground vegetation	Grasses and low palms	Tufted scrub	Opuntias, low cactaceas, bromeliaceas carpet
Cactaceas	Rare. Jamacaru occurs in isolation.	Only low and scattered cactus, rarely the large columnar Cereus.	Frequently 30% of total flora. Has columnar Cereus as well as low cactaceas.
Bark	Smooth or rough types found	Rough or crusty	Smooth or rough

if it can manage to survive the rains and floods that are its natural enemies. The facheiro occupies and typifies the driest places.

The cactaceas have very little use, but the sertanejo can use them as forage by cutting them down, piling them up, and then burning off the readily combustible spines. Constituted of over 93 percent water, these cactaceas are a welcome forage to cattle during droughts.

Desertification of the northeast

There is one central fact upon which all writers agree—that of widespread and repeated deforestation over the centuries. Luetzelberg believes the former vegetation was so dense that it tended to keep people out. "Without doubt, the extraordinarily dense and luxuriant forests along the coast and on the serras of the interior were the greatest obstacle to the first penetration."[22]

Alberto Loefgren, another botanist, writes at the same time as Luetzelburg (around 1920);

> The incessant devastation of the forests and the frequent burning of the caatingas, and perhaps, to a certain extent, the overgrazing by goats, have transformed those lands into a vast zone of caapueras [old orthography for capoeiras, meaning secondary growth vegetation] in which tall trees are already extremely rare.
>
> In the mountains and uplands of the interior, whose lower surfaces are more hilly, as in the serras of Uruburetama, Maranguape, Baturité, and Machado, the primitive [original] vegetation must have been virgin forest. Today [that is, around 1920] capoeira is the common vegetation and, in the more protected places is found capoeirão [high, dense capoeira], still with its magnificent maçarandubas, ipês, louros, pao d'arcos, jatobas, and other trees of great size; but we could not find any truly virgin forests despite the fact that all of the vegetation in those places was originally tropical rainforest.[23]

Fieldwork in 1963–64 turned up numerous examples of the "devastaçao das matas." On May 6, 1964, I visited the town of Mata Virgem, which lies perched some 646 meters above

[22] Luetzelburg, 1:3.

[23] Loefgren, *Notas Botanicas*, p. 12.

sea level on the Serra do Oratório, which forms part of the Pernambuco-Paraíba boundary. I was interested in finding out whether there still remained any "virgin mata," for which Mata Virgem was named.[24] The town is a settlement of the municipio of Umbuzeiro and was elevated to the category of a vila by Decreto-law no. 1164 of November 15, 1938. The last trees had been cut down since 1944, and some of the first trees were preserved and evident in the construction beams of the two dozen or so houses and structures of the hamlet. The name Mata Virgem is therefore a toponomic relict reflecting the earlier vegetation. The town is now stagnant. A noontime interview with five residents, conducted in the town bar—which lacked any refrigeration—revealed that, in response to my question of how many vehicles pass through Mata Virgem per day on an average, only about four or five pass through it per *week*. It seems that Mata Virgem was, during the last half of the century, an important feira to which people brought goods from as far away as Suribim. The serra slopes were not that much of an obstacle to pack trains in that era, and the land of the serra around Mata Virgem was producing abundant crops in the years following the first forest clearing. Today it is a stagnant eddy away from the main roads where the action is.

Another example from the agreste of Pernambuco near Bom Conselho will illustrate the recency and completeness of the land-clearing process. José Cirláco de Godoy bought some land in Bom Destino, some 18 kilometers north of Bom Conselho. Godoy, who was over seventy years old but active in 1964, told what it was like: "When I arrived here in 1908 it was all forest and the maçaranduba trees were of this size [he stretched his arms out fully as if to embrace a tree whose trunk might have a diameter of 120 centimeters, or about 4 feet] and this height [implying tall trees]. We had thick forest close to the house. At that time there were only three houses between Bom Destino and Bom Conselho [a distance of 18 kilometers]. Now there are over 200 houses between here and there." It is indeed difficult for one seeing that thoroughly humanized and domesticated agreste area today to imagine it being a vast closed forest as recently as 1908. Yet this and many other similar examples underline the fact that the agreste was really the last frontier zone to be effectively settled in the Northeast. It is the transition or "hinge" area in terms of physical characteristics, of historical gradients, and of land-use patterns. Its somewhat tenuous character gives it a susceptible quality that is most evident in its low tolerance to human interference in the ecological setting.

How does the vegetation change with increased human intervention—through cutting and burning by man, and by the overgrazing by cattle, goats, and sheep? Luetzelberg pointed out how the aspect of basic vegetation types changed when more moisture was available. Referring to the regional context of the sandy Serra de Araripe (southern Ceará), he states that when that soil of the Serra is more moist, the arboreal aspect becomes more exuberant: the caatinga becomes carrasco, and the carrasco becomes agreste. Referring to the regional context of Goiás state, he says that greater moisture would cause the grasslands (campinas) to become savanna (campo cerrado), which in turn would become a cerradão (denser campo cerrado), which would become an arboreal carrasco, and finally an agreste.

The strong implication of the foregoing discussion is that there is a sequence of vegetation types through time within the same area in addition to the sequence of vegetation through space from the humid east to the arid interior of the study area. Luetzelberg's accompanying diagram attempts to show the sequence for the two extreme regions. Within the zona da mata, with increasing cultural interference, the origi-

[24] Field notes, May 6, 1964.

nal first-class mata would become mata seca (dry forest) or capoeirão. Further pressure (depending upon the local edaphic and orographic variables) would reduce that vegetation to a caatingão (my own term for a dense caatinga) and finally caatinga.

In the sertão, the original vegetation was probably a mata seca. The succession of progressively poorer and sparser vegetation types is, in order, capoeirão, capoeira, caatingão and caatinga, and possibly cerrado.

The progression to poorer vegetation forms is similar in the wet and dry zones. Only the starting point is significantly different. In over 13,000 kilometers of field travel in Northeast Brazil during 1963–64, I encountered very few areas where the vegetation cover was denser, higher, or otherwise more luxuriant than it had formerly been. Local inhabitants remembered clearly the kinds and sizes of different trees that populated their local vegetation. What varies is the rate of deforestation and the rate of attrition on the vegetative cover.

The improvement and elaboration of a highway network has enabled trucks to reach deeper into the sertão to bring out charcoal for the burgeoning cooking hearths of the coastal cities of Recife, João Pessoa, and so forth. Thus we see an accelerated rate of destruction of the caatinga at this time.

The least-touched areas are the remotest areas, usually large fazendas where there is no necessity or incentive to cut over. The largest trees found in the caatinga were about 20 to 25 centimeters (8 to 10 inches) in diameter and 8 to 10 meters tall (25 to 30 feet). The only example I could find of an undisturbed piece of mata seca, or what I regard to be the original vegetation of the agreste, was just 12 kilometers west of Campina Grande at São José da Mata, another indicative toponomic example. The patch of mata seca was about 300 meters wide by 400 meters long, extending back behind the houses of the hamlet. Zacarias Salvino de Oliveira is the acknowledged first inhabitant of the settlement; he arrived there in 1934 and built the first house. He said that that section of mata was never cut. No one remembers any roças (farm plots) existing where the mata now exists.[25] That piece of mata seca contains several species of trees used for construction (juca, cedro, pau d'arcos, umburana, barauna, and carvai) as well as the barriguda, sucupira, pau leite, aroeira, vassourinha, caatingueira, bacheira, sepauba, cumaru (bark used for medicine), jabotiabeira, umbuzeira, angico, and a few maçaranduba trees.

A rare vestige of dry forest (mata seca), original vegetation in the agreste zone at Sao Jose da Mata, just 13 kilometers west of Campina Grande, Paraiba.

The hunger for the useful species of the forest, whether of the humid mata of the coast or of the drier zones of the agreste and sertão, has existed for a long time. "From the end of the last century up till now," writes Major João de Mello Moraes in 1948, "the expansion of the sugar mills has been accompanied by an enormous absorption of firewood and of railroad ties by the railroads, cotton textile manufacturing plants and cement plants, brick and ceramic kilns, and thermoelectric plants which supply power to towns and industries."[26]

Some attempts have been made to calculate just how much devastation has occurred. Through long experience of fieldwork in different parts of Brazil, and of extensive travel on

[25] Personal interview, April 13, 1964.

[26] Moraes, *Aspectos da Regiào Litoranea do Nordeste,* p. 6.

TABLE 2. Estimated extent of vegetation types: A.D. 1500 and 1958–59

		Area of state	Area of primitive forests		Area of primitive caatingas		Area of primitive campos	
Epoch A.D.	Name of state	(in 1,000 square kilometers)	(in 1,000 square kilometers)	Percent of state	(in 1,000 square kilometers)	Percent of state	(in 1,000 square kilometers)	Percent of state
1500	Paraíba	57	15	26.13	39	68.42	3.00	5.27
1958–59	Paraíba	57 still intact	3	5.26	17	29.82	0.57	1.00
1500	Pernambuco	98	20	20.40	73	74.50	5.0	5.10
1958–59	Pernambuco	98 still intact:	5	5.10	39	39.70	0.98	1.00

	Cultivated land, pastures	
	in 1,000 square kilometers	Percent of state
1500	Paraíba: none	none
1958–59	Paraíba: 37	64.92
1500	Pernambuco: none	none
1958–59	Pernambuco: 54	55.10

land and by air, Alceu Magnanini has combined his personal observations with the insights gleaned from travelers' accounts over the centuries in order to estimate the degree of alteration in Brazil's vegetation. In table 2, Magnanini points up the massive reduction in the areas of the states of Paraiba and Pernambuco covered by mata, caatinga, and campos (grasslands). The actual numbers presented are less significant than the relative orders of magnitude of the deforestation. The author notes that probably more areas of mata were declared than ever actually existed because (1) many people included caatinga as mata (considering the local tallest vegetation in the sertão as their "forest"), and (2) many people confuse mata (true forest) with mato (natural vegetation that invades cleared areas—and that can even mean the weeds in one's garden).

Curiously, the map of Brazil showing the supposed vegetation at the epoch of discovery, around 1500 AD. (map 10), is so highly generalized that it shows a band of forest 100 to 150 kilometers wide along the coast of Northeast Brazil and a strip of forest following the serras of only the present state boundaries. The rest of the Northeast is shown as simple caatinga.

The map is my crude attempt to particularize the pattern of vegetation as I judge it to have been around 1500 A.D. The technique used has been one of extrapolation of observed processes of desertification projected back in time, using the windward serras slope and brejos as the relatively wetter places and the interior lowlands and leeward slopes as the drier ones. The crest lines have been emphasized to draw attention to the angle of incidence of the prevailing southeasterly winds against the variously trending orographic barriers.

SOILS

Resource inventory studies are greatly hindered in Northeast Brazil by the lack of detailed soils maps. While much of the geology has been mapped, using mostly air photographs with rare field checking, soils involve much more on-the-scene fieldwork and direct observation. The following comments constitute, then, only a general introduction to the subject, while other references to soils and their significance will be found in a later chapter on the major geographical regions of Northeast Brazil in the zona da mata, sertão, and agreste.

The soil cover of the Northeast is really no more static or permanent than the vegetation cover. The same deletereous effects on vegetation act in concert upon soils, and leave their marks. While to a limited extent the vegetation can be rejuvenated and restored, soils suffer a more permanent damage if they are abused too greatly over too long a period. Let us look at soils in each of the three main ecological zones of Northeast Brazil.

1. In the *zona da mata* the depth of the soil exceeds twenty meters with little evidence of erosion. Processes of chemical weathering and erosion predominate over processes of mechanical weathering and erosion in this humid, well-watered setting. In the areas where man has interfered least with his axes and plows, the streams carry little sediment. The A horizon, or uppermost soil layer, measures about 10 centimeters in depth, and is composed of rotting leaves, stems, and the trunks of fallen trees plus the earthworms, microfauna, and bacteria needed for the formation and maintenance of this humus layer.

2. In the *agreste*, where the rainfall is lower, generally less than 1,000 millimeters per year, there is a pronounced dry season. The soils are not as deep as the mata soils, and they are generally a lighter color. Agreste soils usually range from less than half a meter up to five meters in depth with most soils near the lower figure. The commonly encountered half-meter of soil usually covers a bedrock that is heavily jointed and is being weathered into rounded and angular blocks. One reason for this is that the gen-

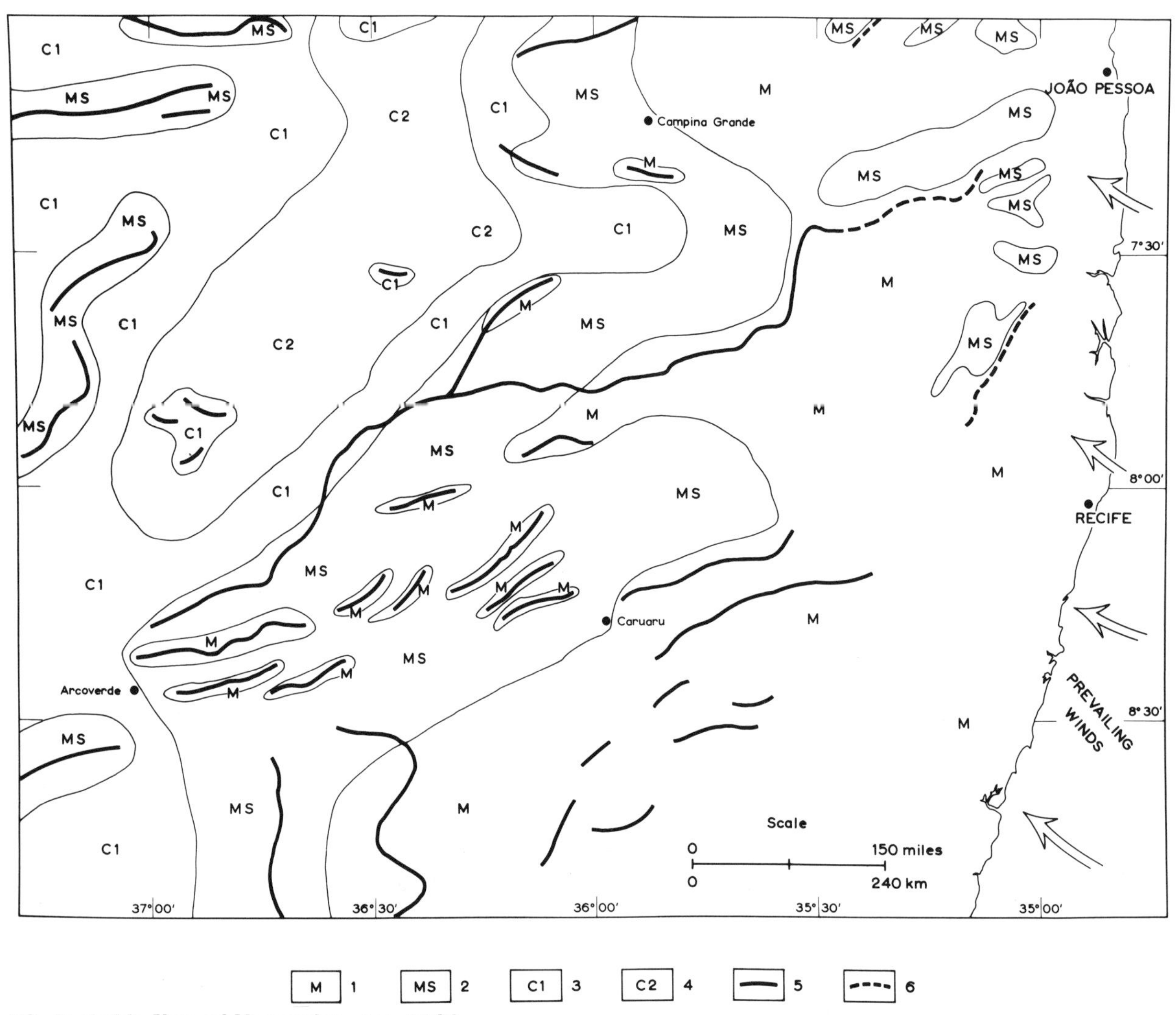

10. Probable Natural Vegetation, A.D. 1500
1. Mata—tall, dense, evergreen, tropical forest with epiphytes; 2. Mata seca—shorter, less-dense forest, with fewer epiphytes; 3. Caatingao—tall, dense, tropical, thorn-scrub forest (dense caatinga); 4. Caatinga—tropical, thorn-scrub forest; 5. Crest lines more than 200 meters above sea level; 6. Crest lines less than 200 meters above sea level

eral lack of humus obstructs the formation of organic acids that play a decisive role in the chemical breakdown of otherwise very resistant silica (SiO_2).

These soils of the agreste are sandier than those of the mata, and they have an insignificant humus layer. One effect of the sparse protective vegetation soil cover is that the first showers after the end of the rainy season tend to wash away much fine, weathered rock material and thus further expose the underlying bedrock.

As a transition region, the agreste is and has been especially sensitive to climatic oscillations. For this reason one can find indelible remnants of former climates, both wetter and drier, in the landscape.

3. *Caatinga* soils are thinner and lighter than those of the agreste. In some areas there is no soil at all, and the "bare bones of Mother Earth" are exposed to the harsh sertão elements. High

rates of potential evapotranspiration (as high as 1,810 millimeters of water in Aracatí, Rio Grande do Norte) combined with low rainfall (generally less than 600 millimeters per year) means that upward percolation of water in the soils, by capillary action, is more common than is downward movement of rain water. This is the manner in which alkali salts are brought to the surface of the ground and contribute to the high albedo of the sertão or caatinga landscapes. The uppermost millimeters of the caatinga-covered soil are highly susceptible to the sheet wash and sheet erosion that occur suddenly with the torrential downpours characteristics of the dry interior.

During my fieldwork, I observed an essentially impermeable soil (A horizon) near the driest pocket in Brazil (São João do Cariri, Paraíba) during a downpour. The rain does not sink into the parched earth, but stands, only to be evaporated within a half-hour, or to run off, carrying with it a layer of topsoil to the nearest rivulet and stream.

At least one soil scientist offered the opinion that the major obstacle of soils of Northeast Brazil is the physical characteristics, not the fertility. Thousands of square kilometers of otherwise arable land, assuming the availability of water, would be unusable because of the vast numbers of rocks and cobbles that make it impossible or at least uneconomic to try to plow the areas. In these and in other areas of the sertão, the plow frequently uncovers a B horizon which is even more infertile than the original surface, or A horizon. These statements of course contradict the prevailing notion that all that the sertão needs is the magical application of irrigation waters to convert it into—if not a veritable Garden of Eden—at least the bread-basket of Brazil. Such are some of the sobering considerations one should keep in mind when viewing the resource potential of Northeast Brazil.

Soils in the Northeast can be classified not only according to regional characteristics, but also according to generic characteristics. Agronomist José Guimarães Duque lists five principal types of soils commonly observed within those broad basins of Northeast Brazil that conceivably might be irrigated.[27]

1. *Alluvium* is the azonal soil formed in the lowlands, riverbeds, and stream beds by the fluvial transport of clays and sands over the years. These soils are flat, dark colored, deep, of normal drainage, and fertile due to the mixture of a variety of largely unweathered materials. They are first-priority soils for irrigation. They are the best soils, physically and chemically, of the entire dry zone.

2. *Massapé* soil originates with the deposition of fine sediments in low, flooded fields or lake beds that dry up during summer; it is a morass of clayey mud in the winter rainy season, and is covered by sun-baked mud cracks in summer. The massapé has poor physical qualities, such as low permeability, but it does boast a fairly high content of minerals that enhance its fertility: calcium, phosphorous, magnesium, and potassium. Because of its impermeability, the massapé requires immediate drainage to prevent the accumulation of salts. The salty massapé is an older soil that has been submitted to many summers of evaporation and precipitation of salt due to the summer sun. The massapé of the tabuleiro owes its name to the peculiar decomposition of clayey schists on a gently rolling surface configuration; it is better drained than the true massapé of the low areas.

3. *Salão* soil is probably a former alluvium that has become salty and, under the action of climate, has dried out, become hard and cemented. It is grey, flat, impermeable, is alkaline (pH around 9.0), and is very clayey. Despite its unsuitable physical qualities for irrigation, it has considerable fertility because of the presence of calcium, sodium, potassium, phosphorus, magnesium, and manganese. This soil

[27] Duque, *Solo e Agua no Polígono das Secas*, pp. 137–39.

is usually used for growing cotton, carnaúba, or simply for unimproved pasture.

4. *Tabuleiro* is a reddish soil found on flat or undulating surfaces, containing rounded pebbles of all sizes, and alternating or mixed sandstone and clayey schists. Because of the high proportion of sand, the tabuleiro has the highest permeability of all the soils and is used for cotton and pastures.

5. *Varzea* soils are carried down and deposited in lakes and low areas where the flooding of winter and drying of summer begins to develop a salão type of soil. The varzea has normal chemical fertility, but it is hardened and lacks permeability and natural drainage. Unless proper precautions are taken, it becomes overly salty if irrigated. Areiusco soil occurs in only a few areas, such as the Baixo Açu and the basin of the São Gonçalo rivers. It overlays other lower soils and is poor in nutritive elements, except for calcium. It drains readily, lacks any organic material, and dries rapidly, thus making it of little use for farming.

Chapter Four
THE SPREAD OF SETTLEMENT AND LAND USE

The toeholds of early coastal settlement by the Portuguese in Northeast Brazil were where the states of Pernambuco and Bahia are now. Those colonial outposts served as the "culture hearths" or centers of diffusion for the settlement of the entire area of Northeast Brazil. The hardy explorers and adventurers struck out from zones around present-day Recife and Salvador to reach and eventually settle along the dry coast of Ceará and in the Middle North (present states of Piauí and Maranhão). Because of the common cultural roots over all of the Northeast, there is similarity of cultural and economic traits observable today, despite the obvious regional physical differences. One can almost even speak of a peculiarly Northeastern cultural complex in that the Northeast has held on tightly to its Luzo-Brazilian roots, which have not been adulterated by sizable foreign immigration as have those of southern Brazil.

Economic continuity through the centuries has been provided by an agricultural basis of settlement along the humid coast, and a pastoral basis of settlement in the drier interior. This two-way basic division of land use persists today. As the twentieth century has progressed, Northeast Brazil has become increasingly differentiated. The relatively homogenous character of sertão life, as contrasted to life in the zona da mata, has been altered both by innovations and by outside influences of an economic and political nature, and the result is that subregions are appearing and that the intermeshing of the cultural elements with the natural habitat has become more complex.

The coastal zone was the primary locus of Portuguese colonization in Northeast Brazil. It was there that settlement was begun; there had been earlier abortive attempts by the French and Dutch, but permanent success was achieved by the Portuguese. The Portuguese were, for many years, able to develop the resources there only through a close tie with the mother country, upon which the Brazilian colony depended demographically, economically, and politically. The entire venture of exploration and settlement was a complex undertaking that varied between the colonial outposts, which were merely commercial operations in the classic mercantilistic sense, and the permanent settlement within the rudimentary context of the Brazilian economy. Both the agricultural and the extractive activities persisted side by side. Agriculture satisfied the subsistence needs of the colonists, and the extractive industries satisfied the demands of the mother country. The balance between extractive and agricultural activities was only interrupted when the normal colonization process became based on sugarcane (plantation) production. This changing of emphasis and outlook accounted for some of the irregularities and surprises that one observes in the settlement process along the Northeast coast during the sixteenth century.

Zona da mata

The coast of Northeast Brazil was an early and frequent target for various expenditionary forces representing Portugal and other European powers as well. What attracted them was brazilwood (pau brasil), which was abundant in coastal forests. The existence of this dye wood, which brought high prices on the European markets, created an excitement in Portugal which was translated into an energetic drive to obtain and sell this exotic raw material. The desirability of the pau brasil attracted foreign competition and eventually forced Portugal to stimulate the settlement of Brazil in a more or less sustained and systematic manner in order to assure its rule and control there. The hereditary captaincies-general provided the administrative means for securing the area for Portuguese control, and also for doing so with a minimum of investment by the Portuguese Crown.

The colonization or settlement of the coast was a joint venture involving private as well as public capital; private individuals, under strict controls of the Crown, took it upon themselves to develop the land, to provide the tools and means necessary for its development, and to guarantee the settlement of the area. It early became apparent that the brazilwood, by its very nature an impermanent form of exploitation, was not the economic activity that would fix man firmly on the Brazilian land. The intensive cultivation of sugarcane appeared to be an ideal solution to the problem because sugar was being eagerly bought in Europe, and in Brazil there were most favorable natural conditions for sugarcane cultivation. And it is something less of a historical accident that the Portuguese had been known as cultivators of cane, based on their experiences in their Atlantic island territories.

As Pernambuco and Bahia began producing cane, their prosperity made them centers of attraction and population growth even before the sixteenth century ended. They were boom areas, the urban centers of expanding agricultural frontiers. The sedentary nature of cane production created the conditions for fixing man on the land and provided a concentration of people that was being added to constantly by new Portuguese immigrants, by the miscegenation of Portuguese with the indigenous Indians, and mostly by the forced immigration of Africans and of Indians from other areas of Brazil who were brought, as slaves, to work in the cane fields.

It was from the town of Igaraçú and Olinda, and later from Salvador (Bahia), that the first colonists struck out, stimulated by the grants of sesmarias, to occupy the coastal fringe, and built engenhos (sugar mills). To the extent that sugarcane became defined as a source of steady income, the ownership of land in the sugar area also became desirable. The fertile areas of the zona da mata proved a tremendous economic boom to sugar growers and produced larger fortunes than the brazilwood exploitation had or, for that matter, than the mineral deposits that various prospecting parties had sought and often promoted, without benefit of facts.

Gradually, the areas of forest were cut down and sugarcane spread and began to dominate the coastal areas—first in Pernambuco, and soon afterwards in Alagoas and Bahia in the Reconcavo. Olinda (Pernambuco) and Salvador (Bahia) began to compete for the defense of lands threatened by foreigners. This political vying of the two cities, together with the creation of the general government in 1549 and of the royal captaincies, revealed the growing economic importance of Brazil, and was another element of extraordinary importance that explains why the coast of Northeast Brazil was settled so rapidly.

Areas to the north of the lower course of the Rio São Francisco were generally explored and settled by Pernambucans, while Baianos (people from Bahia) concentrated their explorations south of the Rio São Francisco. Sugarcane cultivation began along the floodplain of the lower Rio Capiberibe, which flows through present-day Recife, and on the fringes of the Bahia dos Todos os Santos, near Salvador. And from there the cane spread to neighboring zones. That sea of green cane inundated the floodplain along the coast, which facilitated the access of sugar to European markets. The building of the engenhos was determined largely by the distribution of rivers along the coast; communications were mostly by water, and very few roads linked settlements. Most lines of communication ran from the interior toward the coast, and bulk items almost always moved by water.

As long as overland communication was poor or nonexistant, proximity to navigable water continued to be a prime requisite for any kind of permanent settlement or economic venture. The fertile alluvial soils were conducive to cane cultivation, and the proximity of these rivers also helped solve problems of food production and transportation, and of energy (water wheels) to drive the engenhos and to transport the sugar to the ports from which it would be sent to Europe. The rios Berberibe, Una, Ipojuca, those of the Reconcavo, the Mundaú, the two rios Paraíbas, and the Potenji became true axes of agrarian settlement. They were important not only for their economic value but also for the defense of the coast. Occasionally French contrabandistas would anchor in the mouths of these rivers, attempting to conduct an illicit brazilwood trade. To stop the French and other foreigners from being able to do such things, thus also exploiting the upper reaches of these rivers, the Portuguese government resolved to occupy and settle the mouths of most of the rivers itself.

The combined currents of economic expansion and settlement of the area, and the danger and recurrence of foreign attacks, caused an accelleration of the colonization process. Under the influence of the hereditary captaincies and of the governor-general, a number of villages and cities were established. At the end of the sixteenth century the Northeast coast was rather effectively occupied between the Bahia dos Todos os Santos and the mouth of the Rio Potenji. The outstanding communities along this strip were the villages of Igaraçú (1536), Olinda (1537), and Conceição (1527), which is on the small island of Itamaracá. Other cities founded as direct results of the colonizing impetus furnished by the government were Salvador (1549), Filipéia de Nossa Senhora das Neves (present-day João Pessoa [1585]), São Cristovão do Rio de Sergipe (1590), and Natal (1599). These towns were the product of a colonizing process in which the fighting of Indians as well as of French raiders proceeded alongside the economic expansion of the sugarcane enterprise.

The urban communities occupied maritime positions and had an incipient colonial form but they were still extremely dependent upon the mother country and upon European markets, from which came most necessities of life and where lay their hopes for economic exchange and independence. At the same time, this line of cities formed a defense perimeter at a time when the territory was viewed covetously by other countries.

French, Dutch, and English entrepreneurs raided and sacked the coastal communities. These attacks were frequent in Pernambuco and the Bahian Reconcavo because the greatest prosperity and therefore the most loot was to be found there.

The invasions by the Dutch and subsequent battles against rebellious Indians and runaway black slaves slowed down the expansion of settlement toward the interior of Northeast Brazil. Once the troops were organized to remove or destroy these hostile elements, and after the victory, there was a generous distribution of land. Various sertanejos became established in the areas of the matas and agrestes, beginning a kind of second economic front that was alternately agricultural and pastoral. Naturally, this second front was maintained by close cultural and economic ties with groups and commercial activities in the coastal cities.

Sertão

The growing development and expansion of sugarcane cultivation, occupying most effectively and lucratively the lands close to the coast, dominated the entire economy of the area and relegated the relatively lowly and mundane activity of livestock raising to the less desirable, lower priority dry zones of the interior. Even the Ordenações Reais (Royal Orders) underlined the priority of sugarcane cultivation, ruling that the grazing of beef cattle could only be done if it did not interfere with cane production. Yet cattle raising, which in the early colonial period occupied a secondary place, came to have its own life and became the outstanding vehicle for the valorization of the sertão lands whose physical character did not allow sugarcane to be grown. Boiadas, or cattle herds, were driven from the corrals of Bahia, Sergipe, and Pernambuco to advance upon the sertão. It had become evident that the raising of cattle was economically legitimate because of the great demand for work animals, as well as for meat and leather products in the zona da mata. The only problem in the sixteenth century was that there was no suitable place to raise animals. With the opening up of the sertão, ample room was provided. As a matter of fact, the sertão is not really very good for cattle *or* for sugarcane, but cattle can survive there and sugarcane cannot.

This was the beginning of the westward movement of livestock raisers in the direction of the Rio São Francisco. The big push was characterized by the elimination of obstacles to penetration, such as the former Indian raids and the niggardly nature of the physical habitat where the procurement of drinking water was a serious problem, and where recurrent droughts wiped out whole herds. The expansion, however, into the sertão was made at great sacrifice because the conditions of the expansion differed widely from those of the humid coast. The zona da mata not only had a different climate but it was also tied directly into the Metropole, or mother country. Nevertheless, due to this interior penetration, the administrative and political apportionment of the Northeast in the seventeenth century became a real fact. The captaincies-general, which had been given out during the sixteenth century, had been mostly gestures, which did not have the least reflection on the landscape or on the maps. They involved lands whose rights were given to individuals but there had not yet been any interaction of man with the land; no use had been found for the sertão until essentially the seventeenth century. Then, through the combined efforts of farmers and ranchers, the captaincies of Pernambuco, Paraíba, Bahia, Rio Grande do Norte, Ceará, and Maranhão began to show the imprint of man upon the landscape. These many colonizing currents led to the creation of new towns: Itabaiana (1665), Jaguaribe and Cachoeira (1693), São Francisco do Conde (1693), and Santo Amaro das Brotas (1697).

These towns and other settlements, which reflected an increasing march toward the interior (Vargas' "Marcha para o Oeste")[1] characterized the early eighteenth century, in which the raising of cattle became fully recognized as a primary function of Northeast Brazil. Many towns were founded along the trails of penetration and, subsequently, along the roads that linked the pastoral centers with the consuming regions on the coast. A radial pattern of roads became elaborated. The roads trended toward the interior at right angles to the coast.

Obviously, the settlement that accompanied the livestock-raising activities differed greatly from that of the coast. In the beginning, the fazendas were established as enormous sesmarias and were not designed to create a concentrated settlement. These enormous properties were scattered throughout the sertão. Their central axis of communication was usually the cattle trails, which ran parallel to or close to streams. Later, when cattle raising acquired a greater viability and had even become com-

[1] Vargas' "Marcha para o Oeste" refers to former president of Brazil Getulio Vargas and his Horace Greeley-like exhortation to his countrymen to "march westward."

mercialized, the isolation decreased. Concentrations of people appeared at the meeting places of the salinas (salt licks) of the pousas (rest areas), of the travessias (fording places and passes), and of the cattle fairs. Such was the origin of Feira de Santana and of Joãzeiro. But the expansion of cattle raising brought a new problem whose seriousness could not be anticipated during the settlement of the zona da mata—namely, fierce Indian resistance.

The Indians of the coast were assimilated by miscegenation, they were converted to Christianity, or they were killed off or destroyed by the white colonizer and his diseases. Numerous Indian reserves, representing the Tupi, Ge, and Cariri tribes, existed hidden in the sertão where the Indians had retreated. Cattle raising produced something of a shock when the successive grants of land (sesmarias) and the natural increase of cattle came to require larger and larger areas. A long pioneer frontal zone was implanted between the rios São Francisco and Parnaíba, and this zone eventually enclosed all Indians of the Northeast.

The cattle encountered generally favorable natural conditions: saline soils and the resulting salt licks, as well as acceptable indigenous sertão plants as forage. As the favorable prospects for cattle raising became more evident; the desire for land increased, and a broad pioneer front formed.

Cattle raising became a thriving activity. In the greater Northeast, cattle raising had as its centers of dispersal Bahia and Pernambuco, and the thrusts toward the sertão were divided into two main channels which eventually met in Ceará (1) one channel was the sertões de fora (outer sertões), clearly of pernambucan cultural origins, which passed over the Borborema massif, the Cariris Velhos (west of the Borborema), Cariris Novos (around Crato, Ceará), and the Serra de Ibiapaba (frontier of Ceará with Piauí), and finally reached Piauí and Maranhão; (2) the second channel was the sertões de dentro (inner sertões), which represented the Bahian expansion that passed through the sertão of Jacobina, flanking the Espinhaço mountains, and reached the Rio São Francisco. Having crossed that river, this channel of cattle raisers reached the right bank tributaries of the Rio Parnaíba, the rios Gurgueia and Canindé, and eventually attained southeastern Maranhão through Piauí. Both streams of cattle raisers were linked to the powerful landowning dynasty of Garcia d'Avila, who dominated much of the land between Piauí and Paraíba in which the towns of Oeiras and Souza mark their origins.

The great power of the fazendeiros and their representatives provoked a general revolt because these wielders of power did not respect the lands reserved for the christianized Indians. Known by such various names as the Guerra dos Barbaros (War of the Barbarians), Guerra do Açu, and the Confederação dos Cariris, these clashes spilled much blood in the Northeast and ended by wiping out almost all of the Indian rebels. The Indian survivors were enslaved or placed in settlements run by missionary priests. This victory eliminated the last obstacle to Portguese colonization of the interior.

The eighteenth century witnessed a gradual evolution of the land settlement in the Northeast that had been supported by these two economically significant colonizing currents. Naturally the interior continued to develop, but much more slowly than the prosperous coast, and although hostile Indians were no longer a problem, the severe habitat was.

In general, the eighteenth century manifested the main lineaments of settlement. The development of cattle raising provided the means whereby different areas within the Northeast became linked for the first time and, in that way, the Northeast avoided the stultifying isolation that Maranhao had suffered when it was first settled. The Portuguese Crown created the captaincy of Piauí, and Ceará and Paraíba became separate political units in 1761 and 1799, respectively. In 1722 Piauí was annexed to Maranhão, which greatly retarded its development until the early nineteenth century, when it became an autonomous state.

New towns were founded that attested to the initial vigor and promise of development in the sertão: Oeiras (1712), which later became Piauí's capital of Teresina, Fortaleza (1726), Icó (1736), Aracatí (1747), and Souré (1755).[2]

The settlement of the interior of Paraíba is representative of the process that enveloped most of the interior of Northeast Brazil. For this reason, and because there is generally less known of the settlement processes in the sertão, compared to that of the sugar zone which has become widely publicized in many languages, let us review how the interior, and particularly the Paraíban sertão, was occupied.

Until around 1650, the captaincy-general of Paraíba—that is, the area of it that was known—was restricted to a narrow coastal zone, amounting essentially to the floodplain of the Rio Paraíba.

All of the sertão, from the Borborema highlands to the area of the Rio Piranhas, remained untrod by the Portuguese colonizers and was inhabited exclusively by Indians who were organized into tribes, each with its own radius of influence. The penetration of the Paraíban sertões, except for a few minor incursions, began in the latter half of the seventeenth century, and came by three main paths: (1) up the valley of the Rio Paraíba, (2) along the Rio Pianco from its headwaters or the water-divide with the Rio Pajeú, a tributary of the Rio São Francisco, and (3) along the trail for settlement of the western part of the capitancy-general, linking the zone of the Rio São Francisco with the Piranhas River basin.

At this time, the margins of the Rio São Francisco were already occupied from its mouth, inland, by cattle raisers. Fleeing the Dutch invasion, these cattlemen moved inland with their herds, settling both banks of the valley. Following the expulsion of the Dutch in 1654, the movement to intensify the settlement of the interior quickened. Within a short time the pioneers reached the northernmost shores of the Rio São Francisco. They crossed it and penetrated its tributaries in a northerly direction, arriving as far as the flat land of Piauí and Maranhão. This zone, as mentioned previously, was called the sertões de dentro.

The raising of cattle, "that merchandise which is self-transporting," was the main stimulus in opening up the Northeast's interior. Other motivations also stimulated the sertanejos, such as the capture of Indians to enslave, the hunting for gold and precious stones, and the ease with which land could be obtained. "It cost only paper and ink for the request of a sesmaria." The Portuguese Crown favored and encouraged exploration and the migration of people to the inland fastnesses.

As for the captaincy of Paraiba, whose interior sertão still remained essentially unknown, the natural routes inland were along the rivers, since by following a river there is no way to get lost. In the west, the colonizers moving to the north crossed the tributaries of the Rio Pajeu and descended into the Pianco valley, ending up in the Piranhas region. Tramping inland by way of the Borborema, leaving the Rio Moxotó, they reached the headwaters of the Rio Paraíba and were in the vicinity of the Cariris Velhos (the domain of the Cariri Indians until they were displaced westward to the "New Cariri" zone of southern Ceará). Ascending the Rio Paraíba valley, from east to west, the colonizers soon arrived at the Borborema highlands. The link between the two zones, the center and the west, was made around 1670 by Antonio de Oliveira Ledo, who was following the Rio Taperoa. Arriving at the end of his journey, in the extreme west of the captaincy, he came upon an area cleared

[2] Brazil, Conselho Nacional de Geografia, *Grandes Regiões*, p. 166.

and occupied by sertanistas from Bahia, an occupation not known of in the capital.

The central part, that of the Borborema, began to be explored and settled in 1663, according to the date of the first sesmaria awarded. What was granted in February 1665 by the Count of Obidos, the governor-general whose seat was in Bahia, has special significance and is worth recording, as it is representative of the sesmarias that were awarded in Paraíba and other captaincies of the Northeast:

> Antonio de Oliveira Ledo, Custodio de Oliveira Ledo, Constantino de Oliveira Ledo, Luis Albernaz, Francisco de Oliveira, Maria Barbosa Barradas, and the officers Sebastião Barbosa de Almeida, all residents of this State, [note that] in the Captaincy General of Paraíba, in the area of a place which the Count of Atouguia conceded to Governor Andre Vidal de Negreiros, exist unused lands which were never given to anyone nor cultivated by anyone; and whereas the said supplicants are residents and own much livestock, cattle as well as horses, and other beasts, and other animals with which they could occupy all the useful land of the area, and which the area cannot accommodate; and whereas the supplicants have themselves discovered and settled with cattle of two years of age this area without any complaints from anyone, and have otherwise served Your Majesty, whom God protects, for twenty years in this place, taking on considerable expenses in improving the area thereby rendering service and riches to Your Majesty by settling the broad empty sertão which is otherwise inhabited by savage Indians. The supplicants humbly request Your Majesty to grant, in the name of Jesus Christ, sesmarias 30 leagues of land to the above-mentioned petitioners, which would begin to extend along the Rio Paraíba above the place where terminate the lands given to Governor Andre Vidal de Negreiros, and 12 leagues of breadth, with the understanding that they would extend 2 leagues to the south, and 10 leagues to the north.[3]

The names of three members of the Oliveira Ledo family appeared for the first time, requesting lands for the settlement of the Paraiban sertões. The first two, Antonio and Custodio, were brothers; the third, Constantino, was Custodio's son. They were all Portuguese. As the petitioners declared, they had discovered these unoccupied lands and had grazed cattle there for two years. This leads to the conclusion that some people had arrived in the Borborema area at least by 1663.

Of this group of "petitioner-colonizers" who requested 30 leagues of land along the Rio Paraíba in 1665, there is reason to believe that only one ever really exploited the concession. That was the first signatory, Antonio de Oliveira Ledo, who married Isabel Pereira de Almeida and raised a family there. Ascending the valley of the Rio Paraíba, he discovered a group of Indians of the Cariri family beside the river at a place where the Serra Carnoio rises, forming a boqueirão, or water gap. He proceeded to pacify and domesticate the Indians and settle the area in order to secure the zone for livestock herds. For this reason, he traveled to Pernambuco to find a missionary priest who would convert and "catequize" the Indians. He returned with the French Capuchino priest, Teodósio de Lucé. This initial phase of the colonization of the Cariris Velhos occurred in 1670, according to the account of another priest, the Franciscan Brother Martin de Nantes, who spent eight months as assistant to Father Teodósio. That initial nucleus of colonization or settlement has become the present city of Boqueirão (also known as Carnoio).[4]

The cattle fazenda of the interior. The fazenda de gado, or cattle ranch, was to the vast interior sertão of Northeast Brazil what the casa grande, senzala, and engenho complex were to the zona da mata of coastal Northeast Brazil.

[3] Elpídio de Almeida, *História de Campina Grande*, p. 17.

[4] Ibid., p. 15, citing *Documentos Históricos*, 12:62.

Each of these defined the economic and social routines of life and livelihood in each zone, and they had a profound impact upon the evolution of Brazilian society. Let us listen to an authoritative voice of a Nordestino, that of Luis da Camara Cascudo, the outstanding historian of Rio Grande do Norte, as he relates in vivid language something of the fazenda de gado and its importance in the Northeast.

The fazenda de gado fixed the population of the interior of Northeast Brazil. The grazing of livestock on the open range, free and unfettered on the endless plains and tabuleiros, gave men a sense of freedom. Cattle raising had a conspicuous absence of a direct control system which was clearly manifested by the straw bosses, the masters, and administration of the sugarcane economy of the coast. For the vaqueiro this freedom of action was an invitation to his initiative and a challenge to his lively imagination and personal inventiveness.

The old cattle fazendas, in the mid-nineteenth century, were no longer 3 leagues depth by 1 league stream frontage but rather 1 league in depth by half a league of stream frontage. The house of taipa [daub and wattle], covered with tiles, was unpretentious and was not separated from the front thatched shade roof which protected the gathering and conversation area which also served as a place to rest and to cool the saddles. There in the shade was a long narrow smoothly worn hardwood bench, made of peroba, aroeira, or jacaranda, which beckoned one to sit down and calmly discuss the chores and details of the daily routine.

The house itself was a very simple and unrefined dwelling, and very uncomfortable by modern standards. For those who regard the seat of the fazenda with the eyes of city dwellers, and who do not appreciate the unique rustic traditions of that sertão setting, the simple homely comforts and accommodations of fazenda life will elude them. A doorway opened from the front porch into the front room, or living room.

In the front room was a table, wall pegs to support leather animal trappings, wooden chairs, another long bench, a soft leather chair for special visitors, ceremonies, and protocol. A corridor led back to the kitchen-dining room, as in the old Portuguese farmhouses, thus taking advantage of the cozy fire during the damper, cooler nights at the end of autumn and during winter [meaning the rainy season]. Because there were no cold spells beginning in November, the kitchen gained added space and became the living room, or family room, for the members of the family, domestic helpers, relatives, and close friends. Off the corridor were the small windowless bedrooms with their hammocks or beds. On the poorer fazendas were crude cots which had straw or reed mattress and were covered with a thinner layer of bedding. The first steel bedsprings, which really encouraged sleep, were not readily accepted by the old traditional senhoras who were accustomed to the harsh "franciscan" contours of the straw mattress. The children slept in the small bedrooms, and the parents in the large bedroom. That master bedroom was also part storage room. It was the repository for cheeses, shelves for storage of vegetables and containers, leather sacks of manioc flour, trunks for clothes, and butter jars. There was also hidden in some corner a money box.

Most houses had only two doors, a front door and a rear door leading out of the kitchen. Utensils for the dining table included knives, and spoons, but few forks. The food was cut with knives and eaten with the hands, as was done at the table of the King, Dom João II of Portugal. The spoon, an enormous one, was sufficient to hold everything: soup, farofa of manioc, and a piece of meat, and what the spoon could not manage, one's fingers could.

Behind the main house was the fenced area for goats and sheep, who were entrusted to the watchful eye of the lady of the house. To one side of the front of the house was a corral of interwoven sticks and branches, with a gate leading to the dairy cattle. Drinking water came from a well or a flowing spring. Baths were taken on Saturdays if one wished.

Very little milk was drunk, either raw or boiled; milk was always taken with something else; milk with jerimum, with potato, with farinha. There was no bread, and the sertanejo still does not take to bread. In the popular old folk tales and stories, there is no mention of bread. People liked bolachas [crackers] which became popular around the 1860s and spread to all corners of the sertão.

Rapadura; unrefined brown sugar which stores and travels well in this bricklike form.

Little white sugar was used. It was used to sweeten medicine syrup, for the tea given to the newborn baby, and to cut the bitterness of bitter elixirs. The common sweetening was rapadura and light brown sugar. The crude hard rapadura was like sugar candy and it was the heart's desire of every child licking and sucking and chewing its delicious dark sweetness.

Fresh-water fish from the rivers were rarely eaten. Vegetables were used only as condiments and as a garnish to liven up the platters of cooked food. My cousin Polibio refused a lettuce salad offered to him in Natal, saying "that's only lizard food."

I never saw coffee drunk with milk in it. People drank much black coffee sweetened with the flavorful rapadura.

Men got up at the crack of dawn to tend the heifers who were lowing and famished. People went to bed by 9 P.M., and generally lived by the solar clock. The hours of daylight organized one's personal regime. Before going to bed, the children washed their feet and generally hung around listening to the talk of the adults. When a storyteller got warmed up, the youngsters would be entranced, mouths agape, with the storyteller as much as the story.

Coffee was at dawn, lunch at 9 A.M., dinner at 3 or 4 P.M., supper at 6 P.M. When Venus, the evening star, was high, it meant the "sandman" was bringing sleep. A glass lamp was in the front room and small common lamps served elsewhere. No whale sperm oil was used in the lamps. Rather, candles made from the wax of the indigenous carnauba palm tree. At times, the low murmer of voices out on the front stoop would fade away in the darkness, leaving only the glow from cigarettes rolled from cornstalk paper and tobacco from the brejo, and the savory smoke drifting off from puffing pipes. You could hear the sporadic bleating of the goats out back, or a peremptory snort from the pigs, but the atmosphere in the early evening was one of complete tranquility.

The goats were regarded with both appreciation and suspicion. Children were fed goat's milk because it was believed to be richer and stronger than cow's milk. The risk was that the child might acquire the cantankerous temperament or maliciousness of the she-goat. Some people believed that the she-goat became invisible for an hour each day when she visited Hell. True or not, the sertanejo had a high regard for the goat because it could survive the droughts and also find food for itself where no other living being could. The goat which furnished milk to the children came to be thought of as the comadre [literally "co-mother"] of the man of the house. Henry Koster noted this during his 1810 trip by horseback from Recife to Fortaleza.[5] The goats and sheep were reputed to predict the rains by their antics and behavior.

The children's games were deeply rooted in the milieu; they played fazendeiro and cowboy—repeating on a child's scale what they saw going

[6] Henry Koster, *Travels in Brazil.*

on around them. They "worked the range," galloping around on wooden "horses," rounding up cattle represented by bones. They had rodeos [vaquejadas] with spectacular "dogie wrestling"; they made dams with broken pieces of pottery; they gathered water and made it run through the "irrigation" channels dug with their fingers. They were enchanted, seduced, and made jealous by water. A full river was a fascination.

Already in the twentieth century, cotton had modified the landscape by replacing the trees along the riverbanks with the endless cultivated fields. You can see the barbed-wire enclosure and the fence, giving the sertanejo another novelty to consider. In contrast to the old days when the vaqueiro knew the limits of his work territory by almost nonexistant divides, such as travessões which the caatinga covered, and places where a landmark tree of pau d'arco grew, now there was a closed border of sharp and hostile barbed wire. And the gates and mata-burros [rail cattle fence-gate] multiplied. In the former days one could gallop for league after league in an illusion of common land, unfettered by individual ownership. The barbed wire presented for the first time to the vaqueiro the dominant impression of alien individual possession and the image of limits.

The pastoral cycle or phase, with a strong dominant influence in most of interior Brazil, still leaves a mark in many municipios in their names: Capim [grass], Curralinho [little corral] in Pará; Pastos Bons [good pastures]in Maranhão; Campo Maior [large field] in Piauí; Currais Novos [new corrals] in Rio Grande do Norte; Bezerros [heifers] in Pernambuco; etc., etc. Moreover, in each state exist hundreds of place names faithful to the cattle culture. There are mountain ranges, hills, stream crossings, wells, mountain passes, whose simple naming is a cultural, geographical, and historical fact of life and a testament to that cattle culture.

We are the children of a great cycle of vaqueiros. The work of ranching guaranteed the success of Rio Grande do Norte and of interiors of Paraíba and Pernambuco, and assured their survival. Thousands of place names attest to this: Rio do Gado Bravo [wild cattle river], Boi Morto [dead cow], Curral Velho [old corral], Lagoa dos Cavalos [horse lake], Queimadas [burnings], Boa Agua [good water], Agua Ruim [bad water], Casa das Cabras [house of goats], Carro Quebrado [broken wagon], etc., evoke this entire history. And as man entered the sertão, he found it to be difficult, harsh, and filled with all sorts of wonders for which he bestowed names on the land: Serra das Almas [mountain of souls], Passagem do Tapuio [crossing of the savage], Passagem da Onça [leopard crossing], Gameleira dos Macacos [monkey tree], Serra da Apertada Hora [range of the late hour], Lagoa do Sapo [frog lake], Baixo do Cangaço [bandit hollow], Rio do Vento [windy river], etc.

Other names spoke of enchantment, hope, and dreams of the future: Fazenda Nova [new ranch], Salva Vida [safe life], Boa Esperança [good hope], Paraiso [paradise]. Names of other places are like photographs: Remanso [tranquility], Descanso [rest], Bom Lugar [good spot], Alivio [relief], Aleluia [happiness], etc.[6]

Agreste

One of the principal conclusions of this study is that the agreste did not really exist as a physical or cultural landscape much before the nineteenth century. The so-called agreste is essentially a man-made association of features that add up to a very real and distinctive landscape today. The agreste, with its diversity of production, as well as of property sizes, was a response to the rise of cities and the greater specialization of functions within Northeast Brazil. In traditional Northeast Brazil there were really only two activities: sugarcane raising in the zona da mata, and cattle raising in the interior. And until the nineteenth century the interior embraced both the sertão and agreste, as defined in this study. The traditional colonial regions of sertão and mata could not handle or satisfy the demands of the nineteenth and twentieth centuries. Hence the agreste was invented.

Another way of viewing what happened in the Northeast was that there was a shift from earlier valorization of the sugarcane-growing areas to a valorization of cities, of industrial processes,

[6] Cascudo, *Tradições Populares da Pecuaria Nordestina,* pp. 11–19.

and of overland transportation and true cities outside of the sugar area, and that never really existed until the nineteenth and twentieth centuries.

John Galloway, in his unpublished doctoral thesis, has done an excellent job of reconstructing life and livelihood in nineteenth- and early twentieth-century Pernambuco, and he writes of two regions: the coast and the interior.[7] He could do this to the extent that there really were only two regions at that time. If one analyzes the details of population change in his so-called interior zone, he will find that the agreste, as I have suggested, represents the third, final chapter in the chronological settlement of Northeast Brazil. First came the zona da mata, second the sertão, and third the agreste—speaking of essentially effective settlement as contrasted to early explorations or even sesmaria grants that may or may not have been exploited. The fact that Galloway writes of two regions supports exactly this study's conclusions. A historical geographer could write of two zones until the nineteenth century because there were in fact only two zones, which illustrates beautifully the evolutionary character of landscapes in response to changing cultural contexts. The options of land, capital, labor, and market in each period led to the creation or invention of this new region—the agreste, so that in any evaluation of Northeast Brazil we must ask what the writer's perspective is, from what historical period is he writing, and, therefore, from which geographical context is he writing, because the geography of each period is quite different.

This late opening up of the agreste is underlined by the late-eighteenth-century appearance of the towns of Pombal (1772) and of Campina Grande (1790), which were important points in the expansion of cattle raising in interior Paraíba. The highlands of the Borborema, between the coast and the dry interior, played a decisive role in the location of these population nuclei. The deployment of these towns along with that of other similarly sited communities—in a semicircular sweep from Rio Grande do Norte until the boundaries of present-day Alagoas—permitted the passage of cattle drives (boiados) if they were conducted through certain mountain passes and along certain water courses. Campina Grande grew up from one of the hamlets formed along the margin of these routes of penetration. It was a meeting place of the cattle fairs, and its growth is due especially to combined conditions of an amenable climate, a favorable site for a city, and a position as a magnet of population attraction.

As the population grew, unevenly to be sure, in all three zones, the impact of droughts had increasing effects in the dislocation of refugees. The droughts, which caused a continuous exodus, benefited the agreste and mata, and the cool moist serras.

The general panorama of Northeastern settlement, beginning in the second half of the nineteenth century, is a monotonous repetition of land-ownership disputes and feuds and the general stagnation of the sertão in contrast with the relative prosperity of the agreste and the mata zone. It is worth mentioning that only on the coast and the agreste was a continuing trend toward the birth of new urban centers maintained, compared to the still isolated and undervalorized areas of the sertão, which retained an extensive type of economy and land use as well as a rarefied, dispersed form of settlement. While the sugarcane industry was transformed from the old engenhos to the modern usinas—and created new centers such as Catende, Escada, União dos Palmares, Murici, Riachuela, and Laranjeira—the agreste took on new life, regional economic diversity, and specialization from the development of cotton and, later on in the twentieth century agave (sisal) in addition to the earlier cattle raising and specialization in dairy cattle.

It takes considerable intellectual effort to imagine that the diverse and almost completely humanized landscape of the agreste that we see

[7] John H. Galloway, "Pernambuco 1770–1920."

today was once considered fit only for cattle. Elpidio de Almeida said that in the environs of Campina Grande and the agreste in general there was at first only cattle, and that after around 1700 cotton and other crops became more common. And so it was that stock raising was instrumental in opening up the agreste, as it had been in opening up the sertão. The agreste has the distinction of being that intermediate zone that participates in, and has aspects of, both the humid zona da mata and the dry sertão. As the wave of human settlement spread westward from the sugar zone, it became apparent that the Borborema area was not well suited to sugarcane growing; and, as a matter of interest, neither was it ideal for cattle raising.

The town of Campina Grande was a way station that started out as a weekly market or fair of cattle, cotton, and cheese from the sertão, and at which the sertanejo could buy rapadura and farinha de mandioca grown in that area and to the east. Later, manufactured goods such as cotton cloth was sold there.[8]

The people who settled in the agreste came from both flanks. Those who came from the sertão in the west were usually fleeing the droughts. We must remember that to the sertanejo the agreste must have looked like a Garden of Eden, a place where rains could be depended upon and the crops could be harvested every year. On the other hand, to the person coming westward from the zona da mata, the niggardly physical habitat, where the rains and amounts of soil humus were not nearly as abundant as along the coast. Most of the people who eventually settled in Campina Grande came from Pernambuco because there were simply not enough opportunities for one to own land in that sugar zone that had been settled and owned for centuries. Good land was not available unless one moved westward—and dryward—into the agreste. In 1864 Campina Grande had only 4,000 inhabitants. Only cattle trails connected it to the rest of the country. In 1907 the railroad arrived, and then began the real growth of the city. Cotton was exported directly from there; foreign buyers of cotton located there.

The dominance of cattle raising thus changed to a dominance of agriculture and, most important, of diversified agriculture, ranging from cotton to subsistence crops (mandioca, white Irish potatoes, rice, beans, maize, and so on) and coffee, before the coffee plague of the 1920s. After the 1940s, agave became the new boom crop, but it was backed up by the other crops as well, thus maintaining a diversified land-use economic base.

The early cattle raisers who settled the agreste built fazendas and located the first permanent human settlements that were the nuclei of future villages and towns. Most of the present towns and cities started out as the seats of fazendas. Naturally, their founders chose the areas of best pastures and abundant water.

In the early colonial period the agriculture practiced in the agreste was almost exclusively of a subsistence character, alongside livestock raising. It was not until the late nineteenth and early twentieth centuries that an accelerating rate of settlement occurred in the agreste. (It is worth noting that one reflection of growing population in Brazil is the rate of the dismemberment of municipios that have attained a sufficient population for new municipios to spin off from the older ones.) It is interesting that the agreste possessed conditions favorable to agriculture although cattle raising was the initial means of opening up the area. Then, by switching from mainly grazing activities to mainly agricultural activities, the agreste showed itself as contrasting strongly with the dispersed and rarefied settlement patterns of the

[8] Almeida, personal interview. Interviews with this amateur historian and ex-mayor provided valuable insights into the development of the agreste. Much of the information in the remainder of this section comes from him.

sertão. What distinguishes the agreste from its neighboring zones is that it is an area of polyculture where not only sugarcane can be grown, although not with the same efficiency as in the zona da mata, but also cotton, maize, beans, potato, fruits, agave, pineapple, and so on. The area functions as a passageway through which the channeling of goods from the sertão (charque, hides, cheese, and the like) proceeded toward the coastal markets and made possible the growth of a great number of cities along the routes of communication that served the area.

In summary, it can be said that the agreste exhibits the greatest versatility of any zone of Northeast Brazil. Its physical character will tolerate and support a much wider range of economic productive activities than either the zona da mata or the sertão. A second factor in its favor is that it is located between the other two areas, and is a natural exchange point, or zone, for the products from the adjacent zones. Third, the agreste, by this curious historical accident, happened to gather to itself a wide range of activities that could respond to the economic opportunities of each decade, beginning with cattle and going on to cotton and, more recently, agave and manufacturing, generally. Moreover, the area has been able to participate in the economic booms in each period. Because of its great diversification, even though it is small and despite the serious problems of the minifundio there, which will be discussed in detail later, I believe that the agreste today is *socially* the healthiest region of all Northeast Brazil. If one writes, as does Luiz Camara de Cascudo, that the sertanejo has an air of freedom and independence about him, he is right, but so has the person of the agreste, and with greater justification because he has more options and choices of available work. As one travels from the sugar area toward the agreste, he is impressed by the aspect and attitude of people. The worker of the sugar area, when addressed, frequently holds his hat in his hand and casts his eyes downward, whereas the man in the agreste will leave his hat on and look you directly in the eye. There is an air of independence and a viewing of people more as equals in the agreste than in the zona da mata, also. It is in the agreste that I feel that the answers to many of the Northeast's problems can be found. Solutions have already been found there, but they are not widely known.

Campina Grande; fast-growing urban center of interior Northeast Brazil. A population of one million is projected by 1985, from a population of only 120,000 in 1963. Subdivision on outskirts.

The city of Campina Grande is one of the most impressive in all Northeast Brazil. Its operating norms, its "rules of the game," are different. It is the only place in the world I know of where you can arrive with a broken-down automobile at 6 P.M. one afternoon and have a complete engine overhaul so that you can drive away at 8 A.M. the following morning. Yet, oddly, it is easier to send a cable or telegram from Campina Grande to London or New York than it is to Recife. Its international communications are much better than its local ones. The numerous banks there make it possible to transact business all over Brazil; there are branches of Campina Grande–based banks in southern Brazil. The city has a civic pride and community spirit that is unusual. It has been blessed with enlightened progressive municipal governments. Elpídio de Almeida was prefeito (mayor) for two terms (1947–51) and (1955–59) and brought about innovations such as the construction of a new Mercado Municipal, much like a supermarket adapted to Northeast Brazil, and of municipal laundering facilities, also built in a Northeast mode. If a prediction had to be made, I would venture that the population of Campina Grande will reach 1,000,000 by the year 1990, which is certainly a quantum leap from 120,000 in 1964 but is entirely possible.

One small anecdote of no great significance but of some interest relates to the occasion when my Brazilian-made Jeep station wagon (a Rural) was stolen from in front of my hotel. Having no idea of where to look for the car or what to do, I asked the members of the hotel staff for advice. Their suggestion was to telephone the local radio station immediately and give a description of the car and the number of its license plate. (It was a blue and white car, and almost all Rurals were blue and white; it was probably the commonest car on the road except for the Brazilian-made Volkswagen). We heard the announcer instantly broadcast the news of a stolen car, and within twenty minutes three phone calls were received from observant citizens who noticed a strange car being driven in a strange manner in their three different barrios of the city. The car was recovered, out of gas and undamaged, on the outskirts of town the next morning, but it was due to the observant and cooperative populace that we knew where to look for it.

LAND USE

Patterns of land use in Northeast Brazil have a pronounced historical as well as geographic and economic dimension. While the famous cycles of economic boom and bust swept like waves across the other regions of Brazil, they tended to leave eddies and backwaters in Northeast Brazil that remain today as relict landscapes.

One writer, Affonso Varazea, noted that within Northeast Brazil the normal succession of more perfected and productive forms of economic exploitation did not replace the older rudimentary forms.[9] Rather, older inefficient modes of land use were replaced by newer but also inefficient modes of land use, thus displacing the former to remoter zones. Generally, the less developed the area and its transportation system and infrastructure, the greater protection the inefficient producer will have from efficient and lower priced competition.

The uniqueness of Northeast Brazil, in comparison with other parts of the country, lies in the fact that the economic cycles that came and went in the rest of the country remained and became an integral part of the regional, Northeastern agrarian structure. Throughout the centuries, the traditional dominant activities of livestock raising and sugarcane cultivation have been maintained in traditional forms typical of Northeast Brazil.

When one compares the quality of land use in Brazil, he finds that there is the lowest degree of land-use intensity in the Northeast. There is also a great variety in the number of products cultivated, which derives not only from a complexity of physical settings providing the options and choices open to the farmer, but also from a number of social, historical, and economic factors. Let us look at some of the general land-use characteristics in Northeast Brazil and then outline briefly the dominant characteristics of each form of land use.

General characteristics of land use

The patterns of land use in Northeast Brazil are characterized *mainly* by their stability and lack of change throughout four hundred years. It is the part of the country where the different forms of land use of the colonial period are best preserved. Besides the traditional agrarian activities—the large sugarcane plantation, ex-

[9] In *Geografia do Acucar no Leste do Brasil,* p. 195.

tensive cattle raising, small subsistence and commercial farming—that characterize the humid Northeast, the drier sertão and agreste have two quite different agricultural landscapes. One is the vegetal extraction represented by the caroa, babaçú, and carnauba (since the coconut is grown mostly on plantations today) and the presence of new crops that are adapted to the physical conditions of the Northeast and are changing the traditional landscape. We can cite here the planting of tomatoes (Pesqueira, Pernambuco), agave, and palma (spineless cactus).

The agrarian organization of this region clearly reflects the type of settlement—that is, the way colonizers penetrated the interior, and the way they perceived the sharp differences between the humid coast and the semiarid sertão, as well as the verdant serras, which were true oases, favored by higher rainfall.

Extensive cattle raising resolved the problem of how to occupy the dry sertão where the semiarid climate was incapable of supporting subsistence crops without the aid of irrigation, which was irrelevant in that context, and still is today. In the humid zone, from the earliest days of the colonial period, more favorable climatic conditions permitted the development of sugarcane. But even today, in most of the sertão the raising of cattle on large properties occupies most of the area.

When agriculture began to pass through an industrial phase during the nineteenth century, the installation of modern sugar usinas replaced many of the old traditional engenhos. To guarantee their supply of raw material, the usineiros were obliged to buy up more and more land, thereby becoming the owners of truly enormous tracts. The latifundios were responsible for the indirect use of land. The frequent absenteeism of ranch owners and of the senhores de engenhos determined and influenced directly the different forms of land tenure and work systems used in the exploitation of land and man.

Contrasting with the latifundios, small properties were commonly found on the serras, the pés de serra (moist piedmont areas), or even in the wet bottomlands where greater concentrations of moisture permitted a diversification of farming. Subsistence polyculture characterized those areas.

The other quite different—and recent—element in the traditional agrarian landscape are the new crops which are industrialized and bring higher profits compared to alternative crops. Agave, mamona, and banana are some examples of these new crops. The forage palma is not commercialized but is consumed by cattle on the fazenda.

The practice of land rotation (or slash-and-burn, or roça) is the prevalent system in the Northeast for subsistence-crop cultivation, and modern conservation practices are not part of the daily routine of most farmers. This lack of a system of land rotation is partly responsible for the continual migration of people from place to place, and for the low living standards that are aggravated by the droughts. We can see, then, how the land tenure system as a work régime is not conducive to rooting or fixing the farmer on the land. The very primitive and rudimentary farming methods and tools are other obstacles that keep down the productivity per unit area and per hour of work of the farmer.

Let us now outline briefly the major characteristics of each of these five forms of land use.

Sugarcane plantations. Sugarcane, which the Portuguese brought to the New World in the early colonial period, found ideal growing conditions in the zona da mata. This zone extended along the coast from Bahia to Rio Grande do Norte.

The sugarcane landscape of Northeast Brazil is a bright green sea of cane extending over vast areas, flowing over the slopes of rolling hills that are topped with forest reserves in varying stages of recuperation (capoeira). The main buildings were the casa grande (big house, or owner-family residence), the senzala (slave quarters), the chapel, and the engenhos bangues (the actual place where the cane was squeezed and the juice boiled down to sugar).

Because in the remoter areas, especially the brejos, the rudimentary engenho is still milling the way it was in the old days, it may be of interest to describe it. The seats of the older sugar properties were called engenhos; these were small, crudely installed, home-industry operations that produced sugar much in the way North Americans imagine Vermonters made maple sugar and syrup. The usual location beside a river reflected the need for water in the industrial refinement process. One can quickly spot an engenho by its tall, rectilinear chimney. Beyond the engenho, on slightly higher land, is the big house and sometimes the slave quarters, shade and fruit trees, and a chapel. Completing the scene were the houses of the other workers, warehouses, and stables.

In the environs, the cane fields were alternated with capoeira and dense capoeirões indicating a system of land rotation as the means of preserving the soil's fertility. The cane fields of the engenhos are small and not contiguous, manifesting a less intense use of the property. One geographer[10] has defined the bangue's function in the agrarian structure by stating: "Economically and socially, the engenho bangue, or simply the bangue represents a typically rural activity much more than the usina. For centuries the bangue provided the locus for an indigenous distinctive social structure in the zona da mata: that of rural patriarchy," which has been so abundantly described by Gilberto Freyre and others.

Replacing the engenho on the most productive lands, but continuing the agrarian tradition, were the usinas, or modern sugar mills, which were installed in the form of a large monocultural property supported by modern industrial processes that used machines, capital, economies of scale, and so on, for the first time in the Northeast.

Modern sugarcane management involves the spreading of bagasse (shredded pressed cane) on sandy soils of Alagoas.

The usina landscape reveals the innovations at first glance: the endless cane fields, the use of selected cane strains, the application of chemical fertilizers, irrigation, and mechanization. All these improvements were intended to raise the productivity of sugarcane.

The usina was the center of a large agroindustrial system. The large buildings and the giant chimneys are the signs of busy activity. Narrow-gauge railways cover the property with a network of tracks over which the raw material is brought to the plant. Sugar storage was done by type and quality of the sugar. The tall distillery reflected the use of a byproduct, residual syrup, for the making of alcohol. Aluminum-colored cylindrical tanks stored the alcohol, as also did the tank trucks, and railroad truck cars transported the alcohol. Administrative buildings, the houses of the workers and employees, the school, and the church or chapel were elements that were closely tied to the prime industrial activity.

Despite these impressive developments of the usina, the basic fact remained that sugarcane and its sugarcane culture continued to dominate the zona da mata as much in the twentieth as in the sixteenth and seventeenth centuries.

[10] Mario Lacerda de Melo, "Aspectos da Geografia do Açucar no Brasil," *Revista Brasileira de Geografia*, p. 157.

Ranching. Extensive cattle raising is the characteristic mark of sertão land use. It was due to cattle and the fact that they could survive the sertão that the vast interior of the Northeast became populated. Following the cowpaths of the early years came the men who built the ranches and corrals, from which later grew towns and cities.

The aridity of the Northeast's climate, the shallow stony soils and the sparse and spiny vegetation, offered few opportunities for human occupation. The raising of cattle appeared to offer a viable solution for the economic utilization of the caatinga where each fazenda had many leagues of land, only loosely defined or bounded, and few workers.

The cattle were left in a half-wild state to multiply on the open range. Animals from different fazendas mixed freely and were differentiated only by their brands. Nonetheless, the productivity of ranching was low, considering the great areas devoted to it, because the forage was scarce. The carrying capacity of the land was determined not by how many head of cattle were supported by one hectare of caatinga, but rather how many hectares of land were required by one beef critter.

Water was a problem for grazing, although it was not as serious as it was for farming. No rain for sometimes eight or nine successive months made the quest for food very precarious, and many animals died. At the beginning of the dry season, the caatinga became transformed into a gray, ashen-colored desert of leafless bushes and spiny plants which extended endlessly into the sertão. Only with the first rains at the end of the dry season was the caatinga immediately transformed into a landscape of vibrant, dense, and green lushness with many multicolored flowers. The occupation of these lands reveals a constant battle for adaptation to the perceived hostilities of the physical milieu.

In the sertão of eastern Northeast Brazil, the cattle fazendas showed some local variations because of their better adaptation to the physical habitat. In areas of severest droughts, the cattle are still tended solto, or on the open range without the limits of fencing. This system derives from the utter poverty of the pastures and the enormous sizes of the fazendas, or from the simple fact that the animals had more value than the land itself.

To counteract the scarcity of water during the height of the dry season, the fazendeiros open up wells and water holes in the dry river beds and build small açudes (reservoirs). Another practice is to round up the animals and drive them to mangas, that is, to turn them out into fields where the maize, beans, cotton, or whatever had already been harvested, so that they could feed on the stubble and waste. The last resort is to leave the cattle to shift for themselves in the caatinga, and to sometimes feed them cactuslike faveleiro or xique-xique, after the vaqueiro has piled them up and burned the spines off them.

Next to the main house of the fazenda is the vaqueiro's house of daub and wattle construction, with a tile roof; the small corrals for goats and sheep; and beyond, the larger corrals for cattle. In the old days (and still today in the remotest areas) it was common to pay the vaqueiro in kind, that is, with part of the increase of the herd under his care, traditionally the sorte system that gave the cowboy one out of four newborn calves. Now the high valorization of beef has made cattle too valuable to be given away so lightly and most vaqueiros are paid daily wages, which, from their point of view, is not nearly as desirable, since many of them actually became fazendeiros in their own right through the sorte system.

In the fazendas one encounters grazing cattle alongside commercial crops, not to mention the subsistence crops destined to feed the local inhabitants and nearby towns. The most important commercial crops are cotton, mamona,

A fifteen-year-old working vaqueiro, framed by intricately woven caatingeira fence. The cost of labor to build such a fence is much less than the price of barbed wire.

oiticica (on a small scale), and agave. The small areas of sugarcane are cultivated on the margins of some reservoirs. The pastoral fazendas of the moister, eastern caatinga near the agreste have characteristic fences, or hedgerows. They are called travessões (fences) of aveloz, and they isolate and protect the cultivated fields on the better lands. In contrast to the type of mixed farming of livestock and crops in parts of the United States and Europe, where the two are intimately associated, in these areas of the eastern caatinga the livestock and agriculture exist side by side but are not integrally associated.

Small-scale farming. Farming on a small scale is found in diverse areas of the Northeast, always occupying the most fertile and well-watered lands suitable for either subsistence or commercial crops on a limited scale. The agreste is the Northeastern zone par excellence of subsistence polyculture. Moreover, it is important to distinguish between the two areas within the agreste: (1) the semiarid zone of livestock raising that has developed alongside subsistence farming, and (2) the more highly elevated areas of cooler and moister climate where the small properties of polyculture abound. In the driest areas of the agreste, livestock raising is dominant, although it is practiced less extensively than in the sertão. Nevertheless, agriculture as practiced by sharecroppers, renters, or salaried workers (under contracts of five years' maximum on the same fazenda) is also important in supplying the basic food supply. Most landowners prefer to be involved only with cattle raising; others stress cotton.

Contrasted with these drier areas are the cooler, higher zones locally called brejos. Favored, like the serras, by higher rainfall, the brejos are distinguished by a hilly relief, soil rich in organic material, and a thick layer of rock decomposition, which makes for excellent cropland. Small properties dominate the brejos, with individual farmsteads or clusters of farmsteads scattered over the landscape. Besides the larger houses of the owners, there are numerous humbler houses of sharecroppers and workers, all of whom carry on small-scale farming.

Agave is the chief commercial crop of the brejos and is considered the "landowners' crop," a holdover from the system absorbed from the traditional sugarcane engenho, which also still operates in the brejos. In fact it is striking to see cane and agave coexisting side by side in the agreste, the cane being the traditional culture and the agave representing the most recent boom crop. Along with the brejos, the lands of the pés de serra, the varzea (floodplains), and the serras have been favored by higher rainfall and are used mainly as subsistence crop areas.

Property in these areas has been subdivided into small plots, many of which are worked by their owners. In the serras, the houses are generally of brick and tile, denoting a higher living standard. A group of fruit trees clusters

Fence separates water hole of cattle, on the left, from crops, to the right. Caatinga in background.

around the house and the livestock consists of only a few head of dairy cattle for local consumption.

Cotton was always a highly valorized crop in the Northeast owing to its resistance to the aridity and ready adaptation to the soil as well as climatic conditions. In fact, cotton requires a prolonged dry season.

Two main types of cotton are used: arboreal cotton (mocó), and herbaceous cotton (herbaceo), both of which are widely dispersed throughout the sertão. The mocó is better adapted to the driest areas of the true sertão, and the herbaceous cotton occupies a zone along the border of the zona da mata within both sertão and agreste zones where there are moister and sometimes cooler conditions. On an area basis, the broad sertão expanses are dominated by cattle raising, although cotton tends to yield a higher return per unit-area because of its intensive exploitation. Because a pastoral mentality prevails, the actual cultivation of cotton is not done by the fazendeiro, but rather by the sharecroppers or renters who, under contract, prepare the land for cotton and then care for it. The most desirable areas are the strips of fertile soil along the floodplains. The durability of cotton depends upon the soil fertility, while the productivity varies with local availability of water.

The primitive farming techniques and the needs of the livestock explain why the animals are left to forage in the cotton fields after the harvest. The forage is necessary for the cattle, even if they destroy some plants.

Extractive activities. This interesting form of land use is most evident in the states of Piaui and Maranhão (the Meio Norte region), where babaçu is gathered, and in Ceará state, where carnaúba palm leaves are valued for their wax. Other products such as maniçoba, the licuri palm, cajú (cashew nuts), pequi, tucum, caroa, coconut of Bahia, all contribute to the Northeast's economy, but only on a relatively small scale.

New crops. With the introduction of new crops, and the accompaniment of new techniques to process them, the traditional agrarian landscapes of the Northeast have become modified.

Innovations have stemmed from a variety of causes, from new domestic markets to international situations brought on by World War II. Agave, tomatoes, mamona, and forage palma are the principal crops and are well suited to the area. Coffee must be mentioned as one of the older crops of the Northeast, although plagues in this century wiped out most of the production except in the serras da Baturité of Ceará.

Also constituting innovations in the farming sector are pineapples and bananas grown on a small commercial scale, different from the quintal (backyard) cultivation of the old days from which people used to (and still do) supply their own dinner tables.

The agave became so important that it can be called a "cycle" stimulated by World War II and by new processing techniques that allowed complete use of the entire plant, including the bucha, or pulp, which has been used locally as fertilizer or for the cellulose in paper making. Although agave can grow in most Northeast states, its ideal habitat is Paraíba in the moist, cool brejos where it has succeeded in displacing some cotton. Even in the zona da mata, agave has displaced some sugarcane. The spread and dominance of agave is a prime example of how the extent of area cultivated has really very little relationship to the physical habitat characteristics but rather relates to what the world market price is. If the market prices are high enough for agave, it will be grown practically anywhere.

With the introduction of agave, the agrarian structure changed. Initially, agave was introduced by tenants and, in proportion to its development, the fazendeiros became less interested in keeping tenants who produced only subsistence crops. There was more potential for the owners in having their lands in agave on a sharecropping basis. Those tenants who declined to stay on as sharecroppers left in search of other lands to rent.

On the other hand, agave required abundant manpower, not only for cultivation but also for separating and processing the fiber; this was why the fazendeiros were interested in keeping their moradores under conditions of dependence (moradores de sujeição). With this transformation, one can perceive the blow that was dealt to subsistence farming as it was practiced by renters. Only during the first years were they allowed to interplant maize and beans with the agave. During the former period of the cotton boom, it was entirely possible and permitted for sharecroppers to interplant maize and beans, and cotton required less labor than agave. Also, if, on the one hand, agave was a more profitable crop, on the other, it was more susceptible to violent market-price fluctuations.

The forage palma was perfectly adapted to climatic and soil conditions in the Northeast, and it succeeded in partially solving the problem of cattle food in many of the driest areas. It is a typical crop of both the sertão and the agreste.

In his book on the origin and introduction of forage palma in the Northeast, Octavio Domingues speaks of tracing the first mention of the use of cactus as forage in Northeast Brazil to 1893.[11] The first two types of spineless cactus were: (1) *Opuntia ficus-indica,* or the great palma or palma da corte; and (2) *Nopalea cochenillifere,* the small or sweet palm. Both of these were probably introduced from the Canary Islands, during the eighteenth-century colonial period, to feed to the cochineal insects that were so highly prized for their red juice, which was used for dyes. This particular plan did not succeed in Brazil, but the cactus came to be used as an ornamental plant. In the early twentieth century, these cacti were used in Brazil for forage; the spineless cactus Burbank was also imported from California, although it is not now cultivated in Brazil. Spineless cactus was obtained by selection of spineless species or strains from spontaneous and natural variation by mutation. The palma was observed growing in Caruarú in 1902 but its effective spread and diffusion over the Northeast, and Paraíba and Pernambuco especially, did not occur until after 1930. There is abundant evidence in the memories of people living in those areas today of the 1930s being the decade of rapid spread of the palma.

The palma was generally planted in areas of extensive pastures, and wherever it is, the

[11] Domingues, *Origem e Introdução da Palma Forrageira no Nordeste.*

montonous and sad appearance of the caatinga during the dry season takes on another aspect, since this cactus stays green because of its capacity to store water. It is over 93 percent water by weight, and the "leaves" of the palma, if one picks them up, are indeed extremely heavy. The cactus also has a high nutritive value as well as being able to retain a large amount of water. It is almost always the crop of the large cattle fazendas and is consumed on the same fazenda, since it is not valuable enough to support the costs of transportation for any distance. It is the only one of the "new" crops that is not commercialized, yet this one plant and its use is maybe the best example of how man has been able to change the significance of his physical habitat. He is no longer as passive, or as helpless in the face of lack of rainfall or the effects of the droughts, not because he has changed the climate but because he has provided alternative sources of water and forage to his cattle.

The pineapple and banana are also "new" crops, in the sense mentioned earlier. The pineapple has had an important growth since around 1950, turning from a sort of backyard crop to a commercial crop. The banana has expanded in response to growing city markets. It takes advantage of the moist valleys emptying into the Atlantic, preferring lands not needing fertilizer. In a few areas banana crops are irrigated. Generally speaking, it is the owners of small and medium farms who grow these crops.

Possibilities for improved land use

While one of the main themes of this book is to place most of the blame for the Northeast's problems and misery upon the social and cultural factors that have conspired over four hundred years to maintain a fabric of human, economic, and social relationships that have not allowed the majority of Northeasterners to improve their lot, there is, at the same time, much possibility for improvement in the kinds and manners of land use. In the foregoing sections we have discussed how the "hydraulic solutions" to the droughts did not work. In terms of land use it is ironic, that although most of Northeast Brazil is very dry, most of the crops grown there are humid-land crops. Maize and beans are crops that require much rainfall, and yet the Nordestinos grow or try to grow them even in the driest-baked pockets of the Northeast, hoping to catch the first torrential shower of the *inverno* (rainy season) and thereby cause germination of the seeds. It is further ironic that one of the most revolutionary ideas for helping the Northeast has been propounded for many years by one of the most senior authorities on the Northeast—José Guimarães Duque. In both his early and his recent writings he has continued to hammer at a theme that is almost ridiculous in its simple logic: that in an area with a dry climate, or a climate with uncertain rainfall, the best crops to grow are those that are naturally adapted to that climate. Duque says, Let us honestly accept the fact of aridity; let us find the perennial plants of commercial value and let us develop those. In his landmark study *Solo e Agua no Polígono das Secas,* which has gone through several editions and was first published in October 1949, he writes convincingly of the errors made by Portuguese colonizers and others who tried to transfer midlatitude farming techniques to the tropics. And when the transfer was attempted to dry tropical climates, the difficulties multiplied.

Duque points out how the soils of the midlatitude and cold climates—cultivated mostly with short-cycle, small grains (wheat, rye, oats, barley) of dense plantings and shallow roots—need to have great chemical richness and a high level of organic material for the chemical breakdown of minerals and for intensifying the rate of organic reactions. Those midlatitude soils tend to have a stable structure because of the equilibrium between the minerals and the organic matter maintained by biological action and favorable climatic conditions. The clay-humus complex acts as the exclusive controlling mechanism in plant nutrition, and it retains in the soil, without dillution in time, the elements that become progressively dissolved much later.[12]

The normal climates, with their regularly repeating seasons and the scientific investigations that have been carried on for centuries, the establishment of crop rotation, fertilizers, and so on, have created in the middle latitudes a stable agriculture that is in harmony with the physical habitat, the technology, and the needs of man. In summary, the soils, the plants, the conservation methods, the techniques, used by the farmers form a closed cycle that is stable, comprehensive, and highly productive.

In the humid tropics, on the other hand, the action of the disintegrating and dispersive forces on the land—such as rainfall, temperature, microbe action, wind—for 365 days of the year, accelerate the dissolution of mineral nutrients that are flushed away by the rains, leaving only aluminium and iron silicates behind. These remaining soils are infertile, have a week absorption capacity, an extremely low index of exchangeable bases, and a scarcity of organic material. In the hot climates, the cultivated plants, the soils, the native vegetation, and the farming methods desperately need a strategy to balance the productive activities with the supposed resources that are more apparent than real. The balanced biological cycle for use in tropical agriculture has generally been sought in a system of interplantings, in a continuous ground cover, in a long fallow period for the soil, and a more effective use of local plants, all this to be accomplished with a *minimum of human energy!* All farming done by native populations in the tropics is based on employing a minimum of labor. Compare this with the wasteful (of human energy) slash and burn system of land rotations in Brazil. Of the total energy spent in clearing forest for crops, in planting and harvesting the crop, a disproportionately high percentage was wasted just preparing the field to be planted.

Some of the recommended measures are moderate use of plowing in low areas, substitution of the plow by the disk or harrow whenever possible, minimum use of burning, use of a green plant cover in the summer (dry season), periodic alteration of crops and pasture on the same fields, and use of contour cultivation in place of straight-line rows running up and down slopes.

Duque calls the lavouras secas (dry crops) those plants that are drought resistant and well adapted to the natural conditions of the drought polygon.[13] Most of these plants grow and yield abundantly within the irregular and even harsh climate; some, because they accumulate reserves of water; others because they normally consume little water, and still others because they absorb part of their water from the atmosphere at night through condensation of the plant's leaves. Examples of dry crops are: mocó cotton, carnaúba plant, oiticica, agave, caroa, maniçoba, umbuzeiro, pequizeiro, faveleiro, and the spineless palma discussed previously. These are plants with strong osmotic suction in their root systems. With the exception of the fruits of the pequizeiro, umbuzeiro, faveleiro (which are edible), and the palma forage plant, the foregoing crops are exportable industrial raw materials that can earn foreign exchange for Brazil.

The reasons the dry crops have not been promoted and developed are vague. They have more to do with cultural traditions and preferences than with economics. The traditional crops of the Northeast are the current crops. The lavouras secas are not traditional; they do not

[12] Duque, *Solo e Agua,* p. 64.

[13] Ibid., p. 101.

form a weighty proportion of the cultural baggage of the average Nordestino farmer.

Another approach to the problem of increasing efficiency and effectiveness of land use is the result of studies sponsored by various research organizations. One such study, prepared in 1960 for the Instituto de Pesquisas Agronomicas, Pernambuco, by James Haynes, an American connected with the USAID mission in Recife, examines a number of possibilities and their priorities for raising farm output in Pernambuco.[14]

The study dealt in gross numbers of population and land areas, concluding that the entire state had an average of only 0.25 hectares per capita of reasonably good agricultural land. It saw some 461,000 hectares as potentially productive farmland if there were greater inputs of technology, and another 200,000 hectares as responding to added technological inputs for "range and livestock management."

The first priority research targets were those classified as:

Group A areas: coastal plain sands of the coast. The target there was to double production on 30,000 hectares, now farmed in cajú and coconuts, and to bring another 40,000 hectares under cultivation. The chief obstacle is a low mineral retention in soils against intensive leaching. Remedy: wind protection and irrigation.

Group B areas: white sand tabuleiros of the zona da mata and

Group C areas: black sand *chãs*. The target was to increase production on 16,000 hectares of D lands and on 10,000 hectares of B lands, and to bring 40,000 additional hectares of B lands under intensive cultivation. Obstacles are the same as in A areas plus the need for greater control of the water table.

[14] Haynes, "Estimates of Physical Resources for Agricultural Production in Pernambuco and Opinions Regarding Possibilities for Increasing Their Productive Use."

One of the most interesting aspects of these areas of B and D is that they are almost flat and would theoretically lend themselves to mechanization. They are also adjacent to the zones of highest population in Pernambuco. The tabuleiros are mostly unused at present, covered with capoeira, but with some mandioca and fruits in a few places. The second priority targets included:

Group M areas: uncultivated lowland sertão soils. The target there is to increase the livestock turnover rate by 35 percent within the 6,000,000 hectares area of sertão. At present the carrying capacity is one beef animal per 5 hectares and it takes it five years to reach the slaughterhouse. Chief obstacle to shortening the period for maturation for market is the lack of a full season feed supply.

Group H areas: agreste soils less than 1 meter deep. The target is an annual production of 300 million kilograms of milk and 15 million kilograms of beef on 1.6 hectares of thin soil. Obstacles: inefficient and uneconomical methods of producing, harvesting, storing, and using forage crops for hay, silage, and pasture.

Group G areas: agreste soils more than 1 meter deep. The target is to increase food and fiber (agave) crops by 50 percent on 200,000 hectares and another 60,000 hectares under cultivation, and to make Pernambuco a surplus-bean producer. Obstacles: present cultivation practices are inappropriate for respective crops, and management is bad for soils. Also bad is the use of the crop-grazing-capoeira sequence instead of continuous use of economic crops. Another difficulty is the lack of disease-resistant species and hybrids in the local climates, and the lack of on-farm storage facilities. The present land use on 220,000 hectares of these lands out of a total of 1,638,000 hectares is cotton, manioc, maize, beans, grazing on capoeira, palma, and in some places, dairying.

These appraisals and recommendations are

provocative since they are based upon a technically competent examination of the purely physical aspects, the management, and the market aspects of the situation. One wonders, however, how much more intelligible they would be if they were combined with a realistic assessment of the cultural and social parameters relevant to their effective application. Whose land is being discussed? What means are there for effecting a change in land use? How receptive are the farmers to a new idea? Can anyone, including the government, really control these people and their behavior?

In summary, the pattern of observable land use in Northeast Brazil is baffling. We can observe some modern efficient operations, such as the tomato plantations at Pesqueira, Pernambuco, but at the same time we can see land-use activities that go right back to the sixteenth and seventeenth centuries. Following a cause-and-effect analysis leads one to realize that the raising of living standards in Northeast Brazil involves (1) an increase in the aggregate productivity of the area, and (2) a more equitable distribution of the benefits stemming from such increased production. The answer to the question of *why* the Nordestinos have not made more efficient use of their land cannot really be answered in terms of land quality or techniques, but must be answered more in terms of human institutions. Where land taxes are low or nonexistant, landowners *can* afford to be unproductive. Where wages for day labor average 50 cents per day, the labor force *can* be inefficiently used. The picture is a grim one, and not one that is easy to understand, much less to solve. We shall look at some of the relevant factors in the penultimate chapter.

Chapter Five
THE ZONA DA MATA

Man has had his way with the zona da mata for over 400 years. It is ironic that such a persistent and dominating influence has today produced the types of man-land relationships that fall far short of ideal. It is ironic that Northeast Brazil, and particularly the zona da mata, is currently recognized as the economic and social nadir of the country, especially when one looks back to Brazil's "Golden Age" of the seventeenth and eighteenth centuries when the Northeast Brazil sugar zone was the flower of Latin American colonization and the envy of many parts of the world.

One student has noted striking similarities between the mezzogiorno of southern Italy and Northeast Brazil, remarking that both areas, distinguished now by their low human and economic ebb, were formerly the zeniths of culture and civilization within their respective orbits; the mezzogiorno at the time of the Punic Wars, and Northeast Brazil in the eighteenth century.[1]

In this chapter we shall ask a historical geographer's question: What does the biography of this landscape reveal of the causes and processes that have produced the present situation? We shall look hard at the all-important early colonial years when the antecedents and precedents for later actions were established. If there were ever an area of Brazil where traditions have persisted, it is Northeast Brazil, so it is toward the early Portuguese experience there that we must look for enlightenment.

[1] Otto Gustavo Wadsted, "On the Structure of Regional Economic Differentials: Brazil's Northeast and Italy's Mezzogiorno."

THE COLONIAL PERIOD

When the Portuguese desbravadores first plunged into the dark matas of the Pernambucan litoral, they were enveloped by the rank verdure. Little did they realize at that time that eventually much of that forest would be destroyed and largely replaced by a manmade vegetative cover—sugarcane.

It is ironic that the Portuguese settlement tended to destroy much of the original landscape, because many of the indigenous cultural artifacts and impedimenta have persisted until today. One is astounded to read a list of indigenous elements still used in Brazil, especially along the coast of Northeast Brazil. João de Mello Moraes has compiled such a list: maloca (simple thatched hut), rede (hammock), remo de cabo (canoe paddle), panelas de barro (earthenware pots), ceramicas envernizadas (polished or glazed ceramics), abano de palha entrançada (woven straw bellows), ralador de mandioca (mandioca grater), tipiti (woven juice extractor for manioc), almofariz de pau (wooden hammer handle), rolo de fumo a feiçao de charuto (tobacco roll used for cigar making), anzol (fishhook), pescaria de barragem (fishing behind small dams), jangada (balsa sailing raft), arpão (harpoon), rede de pesca (fishing net), curral de pesca (fish weir), arapuca (bird trap), caçuá (woven carrying bags), gamela (wooden bowl), cuia (gourds for measuring or cups), esteira de piripiri (woven reed mat), and so on.[2] The cuisine of the Northeast bears a strong imprint of indigenous plants, including mandioca, maize, yams, macacheira (aipins, or sweet manioc—can be boiled and eaten as a vegetable), beiju (manioc cake), mungunzá (cooked maize dish), and other dishes.

Probably the most important legacy given the Portuguese by the Indians was the domesticated plants, manioc and maize. In the early seventeenth century, the celebrated scientist Marcgrav verified that farinha de mandioca was the common food of the Indians.

> They eat it with their hands; they do not use spoons; they place the farinha in their mouths with the two or three last fingers of their right hand. They do not eat at any particular hour, and they rarely drink during a meal. They drink only after finishing the meal. They sleep in hammocks and are lazy. It is remarkable to note that in the middle of a drinking party they rarely fight, except occasionally for jealousy. Men and women spend days and nights on end singing, dancing, and having a continuous drinking party.[3]

The only way we have to try to imagine what the landscape was like in the early colonial period is to read some of the descriptions that have been preserved by contemporary eye witnesses. Many contemporary comments have been collected by Francisco Augusto Pereira da Costa in his volumes *Anais Pernambucanos,* which give a chronological account of various facts and occurrences in Pernambucan history.

It is interesting to note that the word *mata* occurs frequently; it has a qualitative and possibly an emotional connotation that the word *forest* does not convey to the average North American. Mata, as discussed in the chapter on physical habitat, is something *good* in that it is associated with fertile land. Duarte Coelho, the first hereditary donatory of Pernambuco Northeast Brazil, is quoted as issuing a ruling that read in part:

> And then I order the people to help themselves to the said forests for firewood and timber for their houses, and to take advantage of the cleared land to make roças [fields] cultivated and to use palms for making baskets, but from that place on upstream, you are not to cut, without permission from me or my duly recognized officials, because those trees are for other purposes, and under pain of penalty by my ruling, in this way you will regard all the timber and forests which surround the streams and springs.[4]

The tone of the ruling is that Duarte gives and also restricts. In this first citation we note the appearance, still in the sixteenth century, of a general conservation problem, one that is to appear again and again right up to the present.

For example, on March 7, 1609, he wrote:

> Already feeling the pernicious effects of the destruction of *matas* and the cutting of timber for dyewoods and construction purposes; the government of the metropole recommended to the general governor in the "Regimento da Relaçao do Brazil," expedited on that date [March 7, 1607] that he take especial care with the woods and timbers, and that if people continue to slash and burn the forest to make roças or other things, which can be excused in part, then in some captaincies there will be a lack of firewood and timber, and further in the future there will be even a greater scarcity which will mean that no new engenhos can be built, and that the existing mills will have to shut down their sugar operations.[5]

In Book I of the *Ordenações do Reino (Royal Orders)* it was recommended to the camaras municipais (municipal councils) and the corregedores da comarca (coregents of the dis-

[2] Moraes, *Aspectos da Região Litoranea do Nordeste,"* p. 13.

[3] Ibid., p. 13, citing Marcgrav.

[4] Pereira da Costa, *Anais Pernambucanos,* 1:191.

[5] Ibid., 2:275.

tricts) that they actively support the conservation of the forests and woods. The law of March 30, 1623, and the Regimento (Ruling) of September 12, 1652, prescribed the means for stopping the devastation. The Regimento of June 23, 1677, said to guard the matas so that there would not be a lack of firewood or timber for construction.

In a Carta Regia of March 17, 1769, a new type of magistrate was created with the imposing title of Juiz Conservador das Matas, or Forest Conservation Judge.[6] This development is especially interesting in view of the letter written August 2, 1797, from Porto de Pedras by José de Medonça de Mattos Moreira, entitled "As Matas das Alagoas: Providencias Acerca dellas e sua descripção."[7] Moreira may have just heard about the Forest Conservation Judgeship, or he may have simply anticipated it. In any event, he was greatly disturbed by the way the forests were being treated. There was "conservation-mindedness" even in those days. His letter of August 2, 1797, follows:

> The forests here and in the Captaincy of Pernambuco extend 90 leagues to the Caricés or tabuleiros of Goiana. All forests begin in Pescoço 8 leagues north of the Rio São Francisco. . . . All these matas range from 4 to 6 leagues from the coast [24 to 36 kilometers] with brazilwood rarely found very far from the coast. Brazilwood is thought to be practically extinct because it is only cut irregularly now. They [the brazilwood trees] would have yielded the same for the future if these forests had been cared for.
>
> All the 19 leagues from Pescoço to the barra of São Miguel[8] are very abundant in madeira of Secupira, but all the trees are short, slender, and of small dimensions because the lands are arid: They are good only for merchant ship construction. After the closing of the matas of Palmares, and of the ports serving those matas, many ships were built. Those matas should be reserved for the merchant marine. Sections of brazilwood should be closed for the Royal Crown which could benefit from them at a later date. North of São Miguel are the matas of Riachão with 4 or 5 leagues of extent beyond which are the famous matas of Palmares which are as well known for their fertility as for the extraordinary grandeur of their timber.
>
> Opposite Maceió [Alagoa do Sul], the mata extends 10 to 12 leagues inland from the coast. There are many ports there. All these *matas* are very much destroyed because of roçadas [farm plots] and fogos [burnings] which have been introduced. It is these activities which have caused all the construction work to suffer; Royal works as well as merchant marine ship building, which has been done in this comarca since the discoveries of the conquests.
>
> I recommend that His Majesty preserve all matas from the Rio São Miguel to the Rio Una to the Serras. All other forests north of the Rio Una will not serve for His Majesty's construction because they are already highly devastated and already occupied by many moradores [squatters] and engenhos which extend today many leagues back from the beach. Even if one did succeed in finding some tall timber, the distances and the rapids of the rivers would be too much to overcome.
>
> It would appear to be in the greatest interest of the Royal Crown to create a superintendency to regulate and guard the matas; they could be traversed by various patrols of Indians in order that its exclusive use be protected.[9]

It is surprising to hear educated individuals in the colonial period complaining loudly about the destruction of natural resources. It has the familiar ring of today's conservationists' pleas. The situation today, of course, is much more serious because man has the tools with which to destroy his habitat at an even faster rate and also because there are so many more people to multiply the destructive activities.

[6] Ibid., 2:276.

[7] In the opinion of Professor José Honorio Rodrigues, expressed in personal communication to author, Rio de Janeiro, August 1964, the letter was probably addressed to the Governor of Pernambuco, Thomaz José de Mello, who held office from 1787 to 1798.

[8] Remnants of the early mata were still being cut from this area in the middle 1960s and in 1973.

[9] Moreira, "As Matas des Alagoas," pp. 339–45.

The annals of Pereira da Costa show that in 1872 a promotion commission of the Provincial Exposition of Pernambuco called for a Forest Code, making the observation that "arbitrariness was the only law then" pertaining to the use and misuse of forested lands.[10]

In 1841, an engineer named Luis Leger Kutheir, a director of public works, wrote in his report of that year of increased runoff of the Capiberibe and Ipojuca, of the resulting loss of soil moisture, and of transpiration, attributing it to the destruction of the forests.[11]

What we can conclude from these references, and others too numerous to cite, is that the forest was regarded by the Portuguese colonizer as an expendable resource, if not an outright obstacle, and that he treated it as such. It is really quite surprising that the low density of population in the colonial period could be such an effective agent in the alteration of the vegetation cover.

Of course, the way in which man treated the land was closely related to the purposes of his being there, and we should understand clearly the conditions under which the Portuguese entered the zona da mata.

We should remember that the settlement of Pernambuco was actually begun in the period before the creation of the hereditary captaincies and that the initial settlement was tied to the exploitation of brazilwood. And this exploitation was by French as well as Portuguese in the beginning. People of both nationalities established temporary feitorias (factories) and then permanent ones, as on Itamaracá Island. Around the feitorias, the Portuguese began to adapt more or less to the local customs—for example, keeping parrots as pets, and eating manioc and maize, which have persisted until today as two dominant items of Brazilian diet.[12]

With the prospect of denser, more sustained settlement, the question arose as to what was the most effective way to settle the New World colony. The only solution that presented itself was that used by Henry the Navigator on the African islands, namely the adoption of the system of hereditary captaincies. Although some writers disagree, the organization of the captaincies was derived directly from the feudal system in Europe, but it was adapted to the new conditions of territories with a physical and cultural milieu completely different from those under which feudalism evolved in Europe. In Europe the feudal lords imposed their authority on densley settled lands occupied by a people with a strong agrarian tradition. In Brazil the Portuguese encountered a humid tropical climate in a region not only sparsely inhabited, but inhabited by Indians who subsisted on hunting, fishing, and gathering. The serfs in Europe sought to become self-sufficient, while in Brazil sugarcane, destined for export, was cultivated by slaves who had no hope of self-sufficiency. In Europe the humble residents became vassal serfs of the feudal conquerors; in Brazil the sugar growers had to import Africans to work as slaves. Nevertheless, in both Europe and Brazil the feudal and captaincy systems fostered the appearance of two very distinct social classes—the gentlemen and the manual workers (whether serfs or outright slaves)—and produced a society that was deeply antiurban and rural in its roots and outlook.

Beginning in the year 1530, decisions were made that were to determine the formation of the Brazilian nation. In that year Martin Afonso de Souza was sent to Brazil to explore the coast, fight the foreign privateers, and establish the first nuclei of settlement on the coast. He was able to settle the coast mainly to stop the French from doing business with the Indians, and the years 1531 and 1532 were years of fighting along the coast of Northeast Brazil.

It is instructive to inspect the document wherein Duarte Coelho in 1534 was given the land of his captaincy. He received the first letter

[10] Pereira da Costa, *Anais Pernambucanos,* 2:277.

[11] Ibid., p. 278.

[12] Manuel Correia de Andrade, *Economia Pernambucana no Seculo XVI,* pp. 16–21.

of grant (doação) in partial recognition of his valuable services to the Crown in India, in southeast Asia, and in his African shore patrols. The carta de doação (letter of grant) and the Foral (legal letter—carta de lei—which regulated the administration of a place or conceded privileges to individuals or corporations) were expedited in September 1534.

The carta de doação conferred upon the donatory a number of important powers that he would exercise in a territory extending from the Rio Santa Cruz (just south of Island of Itamaracá, near Recife) to the mouth of the Rio São Francisco, including all of present-day Alagoas and much of Pernambuco. From those two points, imaginary straight boundary lines extended directly toward the interior to meet with the imaginary Treaty of Tordesilhas meridian, thus giving the donatory the right to explore, exploit, and settle all the area. Duarte Coelho even had rights over the islands in the Rio São Francisco as well as the islands within 10 leagues from "his" coast. Within this area, which was many times larger than the Portuguese realm, the donatory would have the powers of governor, administrator, and judge, and the right to exploit various income sources. The king reserved for himself some rights, such as the exploitation of brazilwood.

Let us briefly summarize the rights and obligations that devolved upon Duarte Coelho:

(1) He had the power to judge all criminal and civil cases within his jurisdiction, and this power included the right to pass or commute a death sentence. The four serious crimes were heresy (as judged by ecclesiastical authorities), sodomy, treason, and counterfeiting.

(2) He could build villages freely on the coast and in the interior with the condition that they be at least 3 but no more than 6 leagues apart.

(3) He could appoint notaries public.

(4) He could collect fees with interest, tribute, and the like.

(5) He could collect tribute from sugar engenhos, water mills, and salt works, and authorize their construction.

(6) He could separate out for himself up to 10 leagues of coastlands extending from the litoral inland to the sertão, in separate discontinuous lots, without paying any tribute except the tenth, or tithe (dizimo), to the Order of Christ.

(7) He had the right to give a sesmaria to any person able to establish himself, who was Christian, who would not make his wife or son heir within eight years, and who would not sell it.

(8) Of any fish caught along the coast, outside of his 10-league-long lot, he had the right to half of the tenth paid by the fisherman.

(9) To him also belonged a tenth of the taxes paid to the King or to the Order of Christ.

(10) He had the right to one-twentieth (vintena) of the net profit obtained for the King by the sale of brazilwood, which was a royal monopoly.

(11) He had the right to enslave Indians and to export up to twenty-four slaves a year to Portugal.

(12) He established the rights of succession in which direct descendents had preference over ascendent or collateral relatives; males had preference over the females, and legitimate descendents over illegitimate.

(13) He was obliged to keep the captaincy intact, not to divide, sell, or give it away, on penalty of losing it, but if, for any reason, he were to lose it, it would pass to his heirs.

(14) If the Crown were, for whatever reason, prevented from exercising its jurisdiction, or if he (Duarte Coelho) were to commit any crime requiring punishment, the Court would be convened to deal with the matter.

(15) He had the right to take possession of land, with all the rights specified in the carta de doação, while all laws were revoked that applied to the area at the time of the issuance of the original carta de doação.

In the Foral issued also in September 1534, the King established other conditions to be observed:

(1) He established that one-fifth (quinto) of all minerals found in the captaincy belonged to the King and one-tenth of that quinto (or 2 percent of the total value) belonged to the donatory.

(2) He reserved for the Crown the right to exploit the brazilwood and the dyes, drugs, and spices there.

(3) He regulated the trade between Brazil and the kingdom of Portugal and the fees and taxes paid.

(4) He regulated trade of foreign ships, which paid 10 percent tax on any business transacted.

(5) He exempted arms and munitions from any taxes in order to encourage defense of the colony.

(6) He prohibited nonresidents of the captaincy from trading with the Indians.

(7) He gave to the capitão mor the rights to inspect any departing shipment.

(8) He permitted residents to trade with the Indians and the residents of neighboring captaincies.

(9) He ruled that the capitão mor should place ferry boats on the rivers to facilitate crossing them, and to collect fares.

(10) He ruled that the notaries and judges appointed by the capitães mores should pay to them 500 reis per year. (This is a clear case of institutionalization of the "kick-back" for public office.)

(11) He established that in wartime, the capitão mor should count on the help of the residents, who were obliged to help him.

As can be seen, the governing rights given to the donatories were extremely broad. They became practically kings of their donatory realms, but the obligations and responsibilities were also great—comparable in scale to the privileges. It was a lot of work for one man to be, at the same time, administrator, military commander, judge, landowner, and businessman. Because of these great responsibilities, the King was obliged to give great rewards and advantages if prospective donatories were going to be interested. After all, each donatory was expected to invest *much of his own money* in the venture. There were few candidates in the first place, and most of them failed. Most lost their money, if not their lives, in the undertaking. Even Duarte Coelho, the donatory of the only eventual success—Pernambuco—died poor and in debt. The historian Oliveira Lima commented that Duarte Coelho succeeded in conquering inch by inch the lands that had been given him league by league.[13] That captaincy only began to yield profits for the descendents of Duarte Coelho.

It seems almost ridiculous that such minutiae of administrative details would be applied to such a vast area occupied by so few people at that time, yet eventually the system did work, even as it had worked in other Portuguese colonial ventures. And, like it or not, the Portuguese have been the most successful colonizers in the modern world. They started early in the fifteenth century in Africa and are still going strong in the 1970s.

One estimate of the extent of forest at the end of the eighteenth century has been reported by John Galloway,[14] who relied upon the basic census-type document of that time, the *Idea da População,*[15] which gave only a rough idea of the forested areas. The famous French traveler Tollenare, who was in coastal Pernambuco in 1816–18, estimated that within eighty miles of Recife there was still twenty-five to thirty times as much area in mata as in cultivated land. The 1799 map of the "Forests of the Captaincy of Pernambuco" shows a fringe of cultivated land along the coast and nothing but forest behind it. Part of that forest was a timber reserve used for ship construction by the Royal Navy. Its remoteness, and its proximity to the Quilombo of Palmares (a forest encampment of runaway slaves understandably hostile to white men), helped to

[13] Ibid., p. 24.

[14] Galloway, "Pernambuco 1770–1920," p. 24.

[15] Jose Cezar de Menezes, "Idea da populacao da Capitania de Pernambuco e das suas annexas."

preserve it, in Galloway's opinion, although the anguished conservationist pleas of José de Medonça de Mattos Moreira would make it appear that the fact that an area is designated as forest on a map, or that it is a forest preserve, is no guarantee that people are not helping themselves to its useful species.

In the early eighteenth century, the parishes of Santo Antão and Tracunhaém were created in northern Pernambuco, where the zona da mata narrows abruptly, which meant that forest clearing had moved at least that far inland from the coast.

There were two ways of attacking the forest. One was to make a clean clearing for sugarcane or subsistence crops; the other was to make a selective cutting of the most prized species of brazilwood and cabinet woods, such as jaracanda and pau ferro, and a less discriminatory cutting of firewood with which to stoke the fires of the engenhos. The selective cutting is less evident to spot in any zone, whether the mata or the caatinga of today, and the main point is that except for some floodplain areas which were in sugarcane, most of the zona da mata remained in forest.

THE INDUSTRIAL REVOLUTION OF THE NINETEENTH AND EARLY TWENTIETH CENTURIES

The years leading up to the nineteenth century could be characterized as ones of growth and development of sugarcane in the zona da mata, and of increasing population density in both the zona da mata and the other areas where subsidiary and complementary activities were being carried on in conjunction with cane growing. The eighteenth century had witnessed serious problems for cane growing in Northeast Brazil because of the competition from the West Indies (Antilles) where sugar could be produced at lower cost and where the distances to European markets were less. Also, sugar had a new competitor within Brazil, namely the gold rush of central Minas Gerais.[16] Gold had been discovered in the 1690s near Ouro Preto, and diamonds had been discovered around thirty years later at Diamantina, to the north. In view of the dimming prospects for sugar, many senhores de engenhos packed up their families and belongings and traveled with their slaves to the gold fields.

In the first decades of the nineteenth century, however, sugar cane once again looked promising in Northeast Brazil. The prosperity of sugar continued to grow but was, this time, based upon a firm international market and an acceptance of Brazilian sugar in Europe.[17]

Fundamentally different innovations were introduced: caiana cane, the steam engine, use of the pressed cane waste (bagasse) for fuel in the steam engine, new milling machines, a new system of boilers (caldeiras), and, finally, the usina central. What was happening was that the era of true industrialization of sugarcane had begun, and the days of the traditional engenho were numbered.

It comes as no surprise that this happened, because under normal circumstances one would certainly not expect a product to be exploited with the same technology after three hundred years, and three hundred years had passed since sugarcane was first grown in Brazil.

This was the period when the sugarcane cycle, as originally established, died out. The sugar culture had occupied not only an important center of social life, but also of economic production. The influence of sugarcane had been felt in all urban areas, and many of the villages and settlements were an extension of the engenho. By the nineteenth century the singular feudal dominance of the senhores de engenho—which came from their holding key public and administrative offices or having

[16] Kempton E. Webb, "Origins and Development of a Food Economy in Central Minas Gerais," pp. 409–19.

[17] Manuel Diegues, Jr., *O Engenho de Acucar no Nordeste,* p. 4.

their favored candidates hold them—was finally declining. The social and economic groups that the senhores dominated were also political centers, and their influence ebbed.

The city began to appear on the landscape for the first time as a viable, autonomous, cultural feature. A distinct cleft between rural and urban realms was developing, and in the nineteenth century Recife was the flower of Brazilian urban culture. It was the place of traders who, having risen on the fortunes of sugarcane, then turned to become powerful countervailing forces in that the aims and functions of city life were different from those of the senhores de engenho. The channels of upward social and economic mobility became more varied, and people found the roads to success in the cities. At the same time, many of the older sugar families faced economic and social reverses. Freyre observed that that experience in nineteenth-century Northeast Brazil was contrary to European experience. Whereas in Europe it was the tradition to be born poor and to die rich (also a North American operational myth), in Northeast Brazil there were many aristocratic families who were born into wealth but died poor. Trade and commerce eventually came to have a social respectability that they did not have in the colonial period, and the merchants vied with the old rural families.

The cleavage between town and country was repeated, with a different twist, in other parts of Brazil. While the Pernambucan coast was its most developed area, its interior was still wild, yet in Minas Gerais and southeast Brazil the coast was hardly settled, and the zone of greatest progress was around the gold mines.

The decline of the engenho dealt a harsh blow not only to the economic fortunes of the old sugar families of Northeast Brazil, but also to their psychological well-being. The memoirs of a senhor de engenho, by Julio Bello, are most revealing.[18] The general theme is that, with the coming of the modern sugar mill, the usina, "the good life" vanished. He writes, "ja passou a vida melhor do engenho." He views the old sugar engenho as being superior to the usina, and part of his observations suffer from that kind of sentimental hindsight that memoir writers frequently have; in other words, "the old days were always better."[19] The usina ended all the good things. He says that the social and psychic distances increased between the owner families and the workers. He writes of the lyricism between man and the landscape, the forest, the animals, and the rivers; he says that all that is gone. The book is quite gossipy and dull but does contain some interesting commentaries on life in the old days.

Bello purports also to speak for the slaves and their attitudes. Most of them enjoyed their roles, he writes, enjoyed going fishing with the sons of the senhores; what they apparently feared most was to be "sold to coffee [plantations] in São Paulo or Rio." He even ascribes to the usina the changing tastes of the young people; he wryly observes that the young men "prefer to go out with blond girls, but that they continue to deflower the mulattas." Let us listen to his description of what it meant when the usinas took over.

> The man from the city bought the usina and he bought the land. He permeated the canefields and every corner of the engenhos with his commercial utilitarianism and his details of debits and credits, of profits and losses, with that niggardly spirit of detail of the businessman who intelligently investigates everything, notes and approves everything that will increase the production of sugarcane. He bought from the poor people in exchange for the illusory advantage of a small salary, their small fields of manioc and other subsistence food crops. These small farmers stopped farming, which

[18] Bello, *Memórias de um Senhor de Engenho.*
[19] Ibid., p. 16.

ordinarily the former senhor do engenho would have encouraged him to continue. These poor farmers left the engenhos and went off to live in the towns of the interior to live off their small "apparently better" salaries.[20]

Not having a square foot of land to cultivate, these people conformed with the desires of the rich men with a resignation inherited from three hundred years of oppression. Of their salaries, they saved no part for the "rainy day"; neither did they think of doing anything to help themselves. They came to think of selling their services to others, of helping others and not themselves. With the tolerance of the administration, the workers' areas became transformed day by day into focal points of vice and misery. The pitiful wages were frittered away by gambling, which was also tolerated by the government.

Hospitals closed, while malaria, yellow fever, and syphilis increased. The sadness of the people was the fruit of the epoch, of a regime of work and vices controlled by the administration. People rarely found relief and mercy in being given a dose of quinine—or, in local parlance, a few drops of the "Oil of Saint Mary."[21]

Bello does have some valid critical evaluations of the Brazilian's perception of his land:

Unfortunately the intensity of cultivation, after the coming of the usina, and other climatic causes, the multiplication of plagues in lands without protection, and without the least scientific techniques for fighting them, and without government help, to conserve and protect subsistence farming, proceeded to exhaust rapidly the productive capacity of the land.

If our soil had the amazing fertility of our imagination, this country would really be the fabulous country blessed by God and nature, which primary school textbooks and certain other false and fraudulent books gush over. They create, in the imaginations of children and important people who are easily impressed, the notion of Brazil as a Garden of Eden and limitless riches. The Brazilian, without thinking or knowing about it, continues to proudly beat his chest, directing his eyes to where the tears fall, extolling, "the inexhaustible fertility of our soil," and feeling a deep pride for his country.[22]

Accompanying the widespread transformation in the economic and social life of the zona da mata which the usina brought with it in the nineteenth century was the selective but progressive deforestation of the area, and Brazilians continued to remark on this fact, even as they had done in the seventeenth and eighteenth centuries. Enough time had passed so that the secondary- and tertiary-order repercussions of the deforestation were becoming apparent. Vasconcelos Sobrinho, writing about "the natural regions of Pernambuco" states that "when man caused the mata to retreat," using destructive farming methods, he changed the soil that had been painstakingly developed over centuries of vegetation growth. The physical habitat ceased to be favorable to the growing of mata and only the most rugged plant forms that were capable of living with the degradation of the soil survived. By multiplying themselves these hardier plants succeeded in advancing and taking over where the mata was retreating. It was the reverse of the natural phenomenon of the expansion of forest. And it was man who, with his touch of black magic, provoked this perversion of natural laws.[23]

The retreat of the mata proceeded simultaneously from the side of the caatinga and that of the coast. Caught between two consuming fires—literally, because of the slash-and-burn roça system—the mata retreated on two fronts. Thus the municipios formerly situated within

[20] Ibid., p. 186.

[21] Ibid., p. 187.

[22] Ibid., p. 189.

[23] Sobrinho, *As Regioes Naturais de Pernambuco o Meio e a Civilização*, p. 22.

the heart of the mata, such as Gloria do Goitá, became almost totally absorbed by the agreste. The Serra das Ruças was formerly crowned by tall matas, as attested to by a few remnants; today the caatinga stands at the doors of Vitória-de-Santo-Antão. If the pace of deforestation and the advance of the dry zone continue, it will not be long before the flagellado, fleeing the caatinga, will find himself right at the sea coast.

The caatinga, which is sharply differentiated from the mata, has always had its own physiognomy. The coast, however, as we know it today, is only a scraggly remnant of the original panorama, and the existence of deep soil moisture and a dependable rainfall regime will stimulate a return of the coastal mata only if man will permit it.

The middle half of the twentieth century has brought to the landscape of the zona da mata an accelerating rhythm of areal differentiation. Many new forms of land use have been added to those of traditional subsistence agriculture and sugarcane growing. To encompass these more recent changes and to be able to interpret the landscape seen on air photographs around 1940 and 1960, we should review the pattern of greater areal differentiation.

It is most important to understand at the very outset that, although we may speak of the zona da mata as one thing, there is in fact very little of a homogeneous nature to it. The aerial differentiation of the zone has been studied by Lins and Andrade with a view to analyzing what significant differences exist in the ecological setting which relate to man's occupance.[24]

The zona da mata reflects the climatic and soil conditions that favor sugarcane growing, and this zone narrows from south to north at the same time that rainfall decreases from east to west. There is, in effect, a pinching out to the north and a squeezing out to the west of the very conditions favorable for cane. If the cane areas do not have a uniform aspect throughout the zone, it is due to a number of problems, especially soil drainage, which is probably accentuated in certain cases by a history of relentless, destructive deforestation. This deforestation, which has reduced the Atlantic tropical forest of Northeast Brazil to mere fragmented remnants, was due largely to the multiplication and dispersal of the cane fields over the centuries and the insatiable appetites of the sugar mills for firewood.

When one considers the east coast of Northeast Brazil as a whole, one is struck with the first element of diversification in the natural setting—the sedimentary tabuleiros that are found north of Recife and south of Barreiras, and between these two formations the crystalline basement complex that underlies them and outcrops west of them, advancing to the coast between Barreiras and Recife.

There are, then, five structural areas:

1. the southern section of the coastal sedimentary band (the tabuleiros of Alagoas and Sergipe);
2. the northern section of the coastal sedimentary band (the tabuleiros north of Recife);
3. the crystalline areas back (west) of the southern tabuleiros;
4. the Pernambucan crystalline area between the latitudes of Recife and Barreiras;
5. the Pernambuca-Paraíba crystalline area back (west) of the northern tabuleiros.

One of the most significant differences concerns the nature of the water and the soils.[25] In (1), the southern section of the coastal sedimentary band, the stream drainage is perennial in the lower valleys and in the upper tributaries flowing off from the tertiary interfluves. The *varzeas* are constantly subjected to flooding in their lower ends and the terminal channels

[24] Rachel Caldas Lins and Gilberto Osorio de Andrade, "Differentes Combinaçoes do Meio Natural da Zona da Mata Nordestina."

[25] Ibid., p. 15.

are occupied by long lakes. The quaternary soils of those varzeas are mostly clayey and rich in humus. On the tabuleiros there is a sandy layer of varying thickness with a capacity for water storage. Dense capoeirões and the remnants of a dense humid forest remain in the low spots. On the slopes are found erosion processes carving into the poor soils of the tertiary. Erosion accelerates in proportion to the deforestation practiced on the edges of the tabuleiros.

In the northern section of the coastal sedimentary band, (2), the drainage is ephemeral and torrential. It is perennial or subpermanent only in the small tributaries. As one goes north, this regularity of annual stream discharge is reduced and the quaternary varzeas are almost always permanently flooded because of the obstruction by aquatic vegetation of natural drainage channels in the estuaries. These areas are rich in humus but also have a high proportion of sands, which is evidence of a heavy sediment charge in the floods, and of sandy deposits, which are transported down the leeward slopes of the tabuleiros. This presence of sandier soils on the leeward slopes may contribute to and attenuate the orographic effect I have cited in chapter 2, where much sparser caatinga is found on the leeward locations of orographic barriers less than 100 meters high. Also found there (leeward locations of tabuleiros) are clayey patches of acid soils. In the tabuleiros, with their sandy cover of varying depth, there are sparse capoeiras commonly showing invasion by plant associations of the campo cerrado and caatinga, and very few scraggly remains of the original tropical humid forest (or mata seca, depending on location).

In the Alagoan crystalline rocks behind the southern tabuleiros, (3), the drainage is perennial, with greater or lesser variation, in a very dense and ramified hydrographic network. The alluvial varzeas and permanently humid colluvial deposits are plentiful in a well-drained landscape that has clay-humus soils constantly being renewed by mass soil movements.

In the Pernambucan crystalline area between Recife and Barreiras, (4), conditions are basically the same as for the Alagoan crystalline area. A surface configuration of endless, low rounded hills, appearing as a late mature surface, is covered by a continuous red clay.

In the crystalline area in back of (west) the northern tabuleiros, (5), the drainage is ephemeral. Constantly flowing streams occur only in the headwaters of the higher and moister brejo zone. The westernmost projection of the sandy quaternary varzeas is flanked by stony soils of the caatinga. The decomposition of the crystalline formation is relatively intense on the windward slopes of the Piraua massif and of the serra da Copaoba (brejo zone of Paraiba), producing soils that ressemble those of the crystalline areas south of Recife.

What have these different soil-landscape types meant to human settlement? In the colonial period, the Northeast remained for a long time very close to the coast. And cane growing is still limited, in terms of the largest, most efficient producing units, to that same coastal zone. It became established in those crystalline areas between Recife and Barreiras and in the terminal varzeas incised in the tabuleiros to the north of Recife and the south of Barreiras. Cane growing became adapted to a limited number of topographic circumstances within which soil types and different rainfall regimes were to have further differentiation effects.

Three principal historical events greatly influenced the development of the sugar zone: (1) the cotton boom in the nineteenth century; (2) the abolition of slavery in 1888, and (3) the general phenomenon of the Industrial Revolution, which culminated with the establishment of the usinas.[26]

Cotton did not compete successfully with the

[26] Ibid., p. 18.

sugarcane plantations of the red clay crystalline zone south of Recife, but it did substitute many cotton gins for engenhos in the areas of the lower Paraıba and Mamanguape rivers of Paraıba. Cotton markedly affected the existing land tenure system and posed a direct threat to the sugar cycle. It provided real competition for that aristocratic sugar society that had come, bringing its cane and slaves with it, northward from the crystalline zone between Recife and Barrieras to the varzeas of the Paraíban rivers

The abolition of slavery, with all the changes it brought to the economic and social structures of the sugar society, produced both different problems, and common problems in differing degrees, within the areas we are comparing. The resulting shortages of manpower were not everywhere comparable; in some areas the engenhos had reached a climax of high productivity, while in other areas they had reached only modest development and could not operate on the same large scale as in Pernambuco. In other places, such as the zona da mata of Paraıba and the agreste zone, there was already considerable migration of seasonal workers from the interior, the corumbas or caatingueiros from the agreste. But, by way of compensation, in the flooded varzeas of the coastal sedimentary zone, the abolition of slavery, caused the stoppage of the heavy drainage works that were under way. In all cases, the general breakdown in the operations of the engenho heralded the decisive beginning of deruralization of the country.

It was the influence of the Industrial Revolution, although somewhat delayed in Northeast Brazil, that produced the greatest transformation in the sugar zone. Almost all the traditional work relationships were modified. In the crystalline as well as the sedimentary areas the problem continued to be treated in different ways and the marks of these different solutions are also different.

To develop transportation systems, in view of the great volumes of raw material demanded by the sugar mills, railroad trails were spread across the cane fields, always adapting to the terrain, the water drainage, and the soils. On the other hand, the extent to which each usina used mules, ox carts, trucks, and tractors during the harvest, corresponded closely to relief and soil conditions of each area.

The extensive sugar monoculture, carried on by more-modern management rules, tended to promote and disperse new techniques of irrigation,[27] drainage, fertilizer, mechanization, and so on, which were applied with consideration of water supply, steepness of slopes, physical and chemical properties of soils, rainfall régimes, and general soil structure characteristics. One of the effects of the centralization of cane agriculture in the usinas was the deruralization of the countryside and the concentration of people into urban places and the usina centers.

Mario Lacerda de Melo has observed that the projection of the crystalline basement toward and right up to the ocean (the zone between Recife and Barreiros) constituted a fact of great importance, not only in explaining the great diversity of farming methods and land use in the sugar zone, but also in understanding the primacy of Pernambuco in the sugar industry of Northeast Brazil from the early sixteenth century.[28] It is in essence on the crystalline hilly surface south of Recife that the largest and most productive usinas in Northeast Brazil developed. It was also there that the ciclo dos bangues (engenho cycle) was defined in the precise terms of that aristocratic, patriarchal, hybrid, monocultural, landowning, slave-hold-

[27] Irrigation is needed even in a rainy area for the proper maturing of the cane, through control of the amount and timing of the water supply.

[28] Lins and Andrade, "Differentes Combinações do Meio Natural," p. 21.

ing society (Gilberto Freyre) of which only pale imitations are found in those two sedimentary sections along the coast.

In the varzeas (floodplains of the sedimentary sections) there was a competition of other rural activities with sugarcane; there was cattle raising, and the growing of rice, bananas, and coconuts in the Alagoan sedimentary varzeas. There was cattle raising, and the growing of cotton, subsistence roças, and even carnaúba wax trees in the northern sedimentary varzeas. The cultivation of coconut palms in the coastal zone of Alagoas today is competitive with sugarcane within the zones actually controlled by the usinas. Diversified land-use practices of this type have never, until now, interfered with the rigid monocultural approach that the usinas established on the crystalline coast. The usinas continued to spread their cane fields wherever the massapé (soil) was found in numerous varzeas and on the barro vermelho (red clay) of the hillsides.

In any event, from a strictly sugar-industry point of view, the agrarian picture of the terminal varzeas of the coastal sedimentary band suffers from more problems than that of the crystalline area between Recife and Barreiras. Some of these problems of the sedimentary zone are: slopes of poor tertiary soils, flooded varzeas, and the great variety of varzea soils that make sugarcane planting difficult. When the flooding is more persistent, less cultivation can be done with tractors, animal-drawn plows, or even hoes.

To conclude this review of the five basic lands, the crystalline areas west of the northern sedimentary tabuleiro and the southern sedimentary tabuleiros have had a development that is much more recent than the other three areas. The crystalline areas northwest of Recife have been exploited only since the promotional policies of the Instituto do Açucar e Alcohol have been in effect, and which have stimulated the establishment of usinas in places where formerly sugarcane cultivation was very modest. In the latter areas, which had more mata seca (dry forest) than mata humida (humid forest), the history of land use began with the extraction of brazilwood, and was followed by a polycultural system producing cotton, coffee, and bananas—not only sugarcane.[29]

In the Alagoan crystalline area, where the characteristics of the natural habitat are similar to those of the crystalline area between Recife and Barreiros, the spread of settlement was extremely slow and sparse. That is the part of Northeast Brazil where the last remains of the primeval forest stand. At São Miguel dos Campos (Alagoas) they are still cutting down the giant trees.[30] Sugar cultivation there has to take into consideration the greater impact of terrain conditions upon farming methods. Land rotation on the slopes, irrigation problems, fertilization on the varzeas and slopes, are problems that continually demand of the workers a more receptive and progressive mentality, and a more frequent recourse to the rational and reasoned choice of farming methods. In other words, the growing of sugarcane there is not carried out with that tranquil, traditional, lazy routine that, in years gone by, spread out across the Pernambucan crystalline areas south of Recife where the cane worker has always remained generally resistant to new ideas and new ways of doing things.

RECENT LANDSCAPE CHANGES

One of the most useful and yet little used tools of historical geographical research is air photography—using aerial photographs of the same area taken at different periods. This technique of comparing the distributional patterns of houses, fields, forests, transportation routes,

[29] See map 10 in chapter 2.
[30] Field notes, 1964, p. 9, and 1973.

urban patterns, and so on, has been combined with field observations and interviews to provide an accurate picture of actual changes in the appearance of the earth's surface since around 1940. The air photos of the zona da mata, figures 8 through 14, include one group taken by the United States Air Force in 1942–43 and later sets taken by the Brazilians in the late 1950s and early 1960s. An interval of almost twenty years, although it is not sufficient to show much in the way of changes in the physical habitat, even though some stream-pattern changes are evident, is clearly sufficient to determine the nature of areal changes of land-use and human-occupance patterns.

We can summarize the basic outlines of change between 1940 and 1964 as follows: (1) There was much more specialization of land use associated with specific ecological situations in 1964 than in 1940. Whereas in earlier times some roça farming tended to become concentrated upon areas with specific values or lack of values; for example, on the slopes leading down to the floodplains. Conversely, sugarcane occupies almost exclusively the fertile varzea floodplain now, as compared to 1942. (2) There is much greater use of all areas in the zona da mata but the increase of use is very selective. The varzeas are the most valorized of the areas; the tabuleiros are the least valorized. (3) There is a wider diversity of land uses—that is, more fruit trees, more coconut palms, more rural, nonfarm usages—at the same time that the location of these activities is more specifically localized than it was.

Let us compare the "sugar river" floodplain near Santa Rita, just 10 kilometers west of João Pessoa, as it looked in 1942 (figure 8) and in 1959 (figure 9). The floodplain itself shows a patchwork quilt of different fields and land-use patterns in 1942, compared to 1959. The broad, uniform tone and texture on the 1959 photos is that of a sea of sugarcane, which, because of improved market prices in the intervening years, had spread and engulfed many areas, even in the floodplain, that had earlier been devoted to subsistence ariculture. In the 1959 photos we can observe that the roças, the small fields of subsistence crops, and not of sugarcane, have retreated to the lands of lower priority; that is, the slopes adjacent to the varzea. Then there are places, shown on the photograph, where field interviews in 1964 verified that there were many more backyard gardens belonging to sugar workers in 1942 than there were in 1964 when, as the local informant informed me, "the cane now comes right up to the kitchen door." There was no possibility of raising those subsistence food crops that in former days provided much needed sustenance for a family. In this sense, then, diet is probably worse today than in the past. Meat is consumed less frequently, and there is less of a well-balanced diet. The more recent photos reveal a much larger area in roça, or subsistence farming, which is expanding out from the former roças. The areas that are in the mata, or really tall capoeirão, and that have been undistributed for two or three decades, are naturally denser and higher than before, and the characteristic pattern of coqueiro groves (coconut), shown by intensely black dots in a rectilinear pattern, is more prevalent on the recent photos.

A careful comparison of the photos reveals that some of the swampy areas of the varzea were drained and put into cane production. Other changes in the urban zone are probably more striking. One is the astounding areal expansion of the town of Santa Rita and of the roça fields that border the newer residential areas. The livelihood of people in this lower section of the Rio Paraíba valley depends very closely upon the sugar industry, and it is therefore interesting to observe that practically all the varzea land between Santa Rita and Sapé, 32 kilometers to the west and marking the eastern boundary of the agreste, belongs to two large companies that are essentially two wealthy families.[31]

South of João Pessoa, on a very narrow valley that can hardly be called one of the "sugar rivers" and that is deeply incised into the tabuleiro, we find examples of land uses between 1942 and 1959. These photos reveal a striking difference in the situation of the floodplain and adjacent slopes as compared with the tabuleiros. (See figures 10 and 11.) The slopes seem much more cleared and extensively cultivated in 1959 than in 1942, yet flat tabuleiros seem essentially intact and unaltered, with almost absolutely no change. What happened in the varzeas was that some drainage works were built and some sugarcane was added, but the principal change was the addition of roça plots that valorized the area, and this in the absence of any new roads leading directly to the area. On the northern side of the valley the cutting of capoeira has occurred in those areas that were left alone to grow some mato. But, generally speaking, the darker the tone on the photos, the denser and taller the vegetation cover; those lighter areas, particularly south of the valley, which by their very sterility do not support capoeirão of any type are also the areas which people have avoided and which show practically no change in an interval of seventeen years. In summary, the more valorized areas are those that have been subjected to the most change.

The photos showing the area around Goiana (figures 12, 13, and 14), an important colonial city which is now just another sugar factory town, reflect many of the same changes found around Santa Rita. These are the greater valorization of the varzea, reflected by: (1) more extensive drainage systems; (2) greater areas planted in sugarcane; and (3) the pioneering or opening up of new areas on the slopes to be planted in food crops. The actual area of the city of Goiana has not expanded as much, proportionately, as has that of Santa Rita, although the new Recife–João Pessoa highway, started in 1959, cuts across the landscape on the outskirts of Goiana. The undisturbed slopes continue to grow a denser forest cover and, with the passage of time, become more and more desirable as possible sites for new roças. One interesting thing about Goiana is that the straight shipping canal, evident on the 1942 photo (figure 12), had been dug in the 1870s to link that city with the navigable Goiana River canal.[32] This was extremely important for shipping out the sugar. That channel had been dug because of progressive silting of the Goiana River and, even in the old days, was capable of accommodating only boats or barges with a draft of very few feet.

A traverse southward from João Pessoa to Recife provides an excellent opportunity to visit the places shown on the air photos, and the interviews with local residents provided useful interpretations of just what happened in that part of the zona da mata over the last few decades.

At Alagoinha, a small hamlet only 9 kilometers south of João Pessoa, an informant described the local tabuleiro surface as *chã,* explaining that chã meant literally an elevated, flat surface but that it really meant that there was no water available.[33] One had to haul his water; therefore it was bad for farming. This is an explanation in the local vernacular of why the tabuleiros have been so unused for farming. The soils of the chãs are poor for agriculture because they are sandy. Barra, or clay, which is found in the varzeas, is good for maize and beans; it is con-

[31] Interview with straw boss on cane operation 14 kilometers west of Santa Rita, Paraíba, April 6, 1964.

[32] Galloway, "Pernambuco 1770–1920," p. 160.

[33] Field notes, May 28 1964, p. 152.

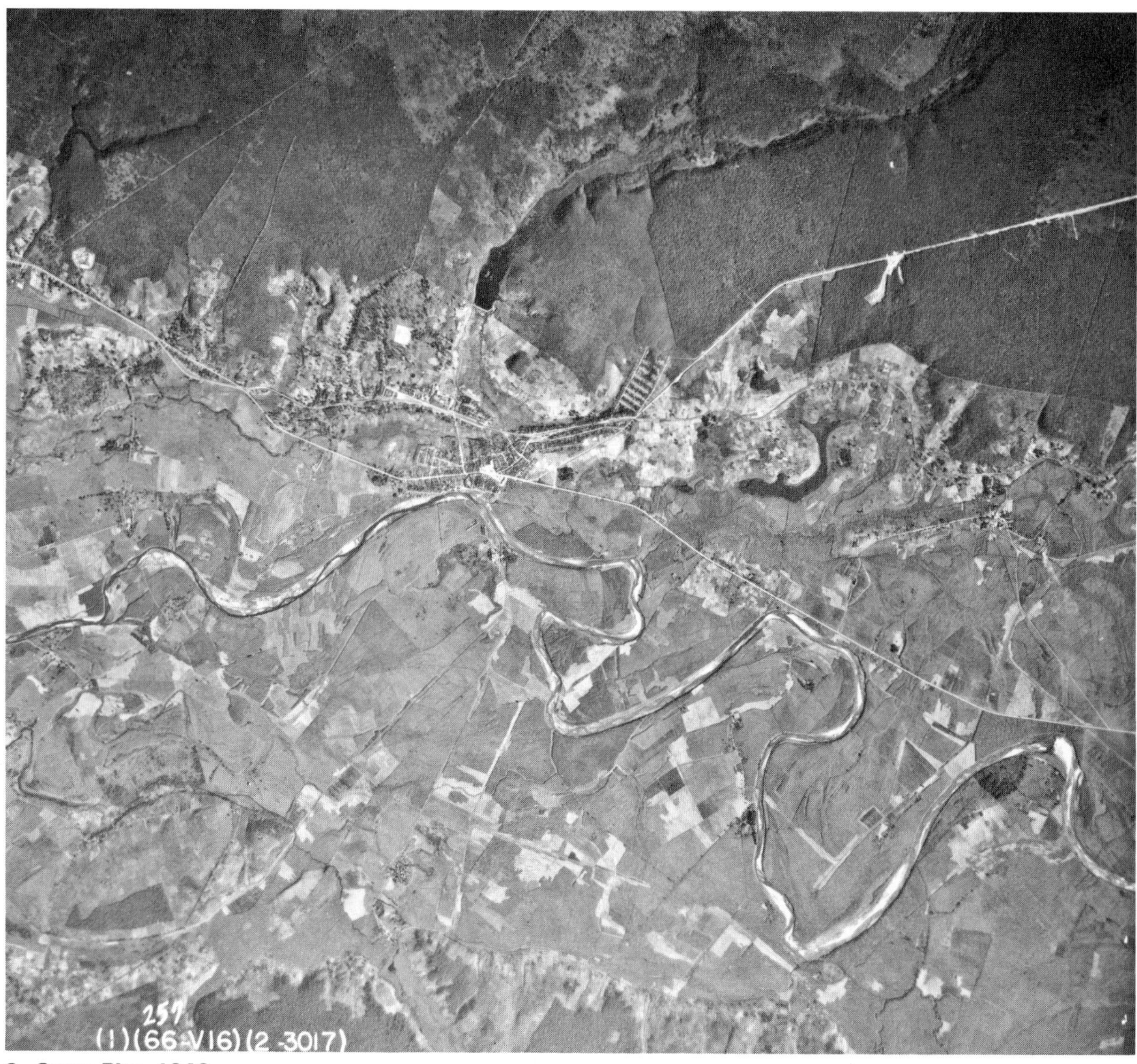

8. Santa Rita, 1942

sidered forte, or a strong soil. Transitional soils that are sandy clays will yield yams, manioc, and sweet potatoes, but not the white Irish potato (batata inglesa). It appeared to the informant that the engenhos were planting more sugarcane in the 1960s than they had been earlier, and that much of it was made into rum, while in the 1950s more rapadura was produced. He confirmed the air photos by stating that there were many more fruit trees in the 1960s "because fruits bring a price." The backland producer of oranges could get a decent price for his oranges at his farm, while in the past there was no sizable market for fruit outside of the cities. The largest properties were on the varzeas and the tabuleiros; the smaller properties were those devoted to food crops and were located on the slopes that connect the

9. Santa Rita, 1959

varzeas with the tabuleiros. This same informant observed that there were many more people than twenty years ago; there were more job possibilities. Many people, like him, worked for the National Highway Department on the construction of roads. This is one factor which is, I think, underestimated: the role of road building in the transfer of population, and the fact that many workers stay and put down roots beside the road they helped to build.

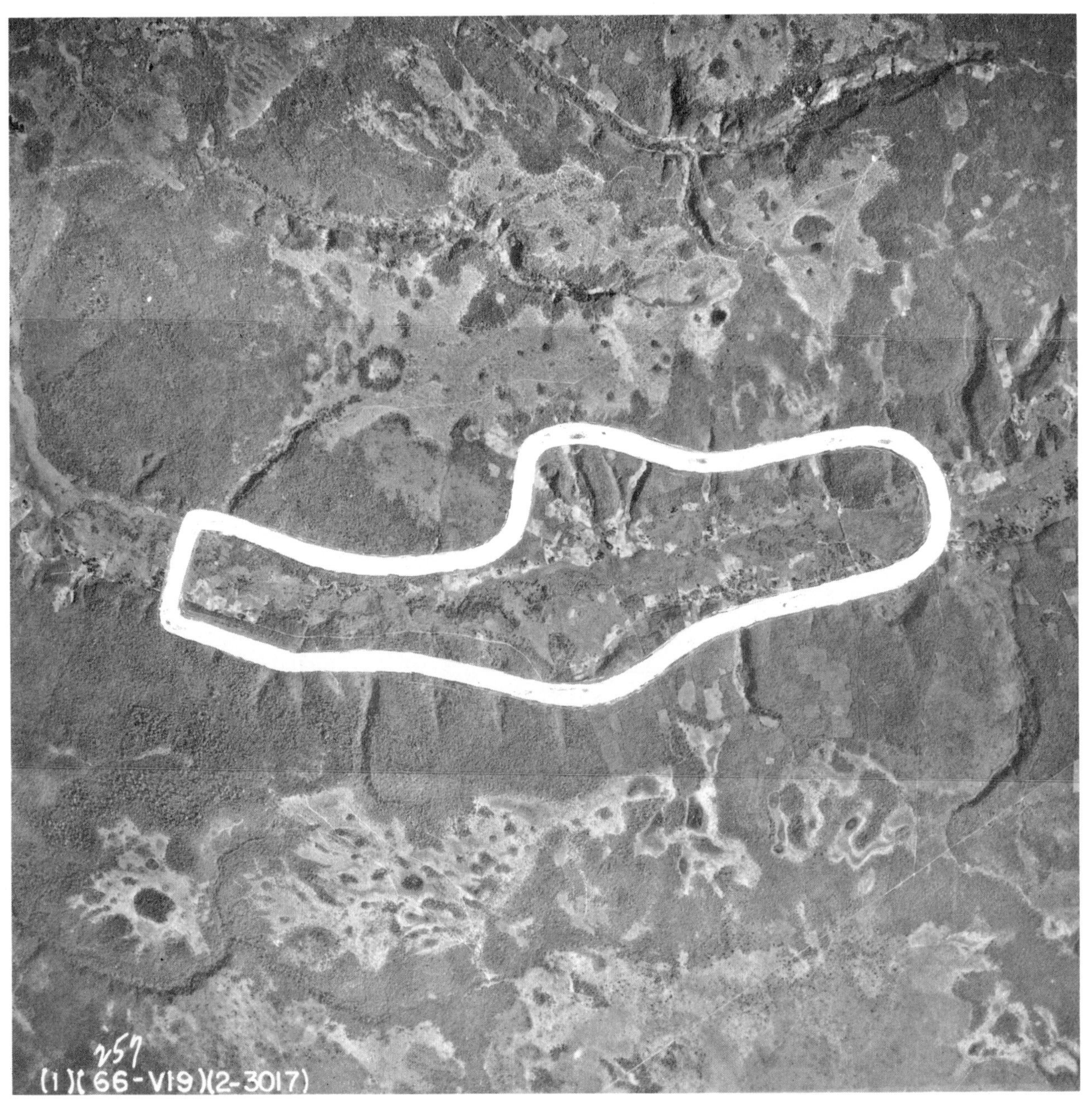

10. South of João Pessoa, 1942

One traditional use of the tabuleiros is as a source of firewood and construction wood. One man was observed working in a patch of mata, cutting down and trimming trees of a 6-inch diameter for use in construction as scaffolding. The firewood can be used directly or—with a great loss in bulk and weight—can be converted to charcoal. The lenhador (woodsman) was paid about 350 cruzeiros (35 cents) to cut and stack 1 cubic meter of wood.[34]

[34] Ibid., p. 154.

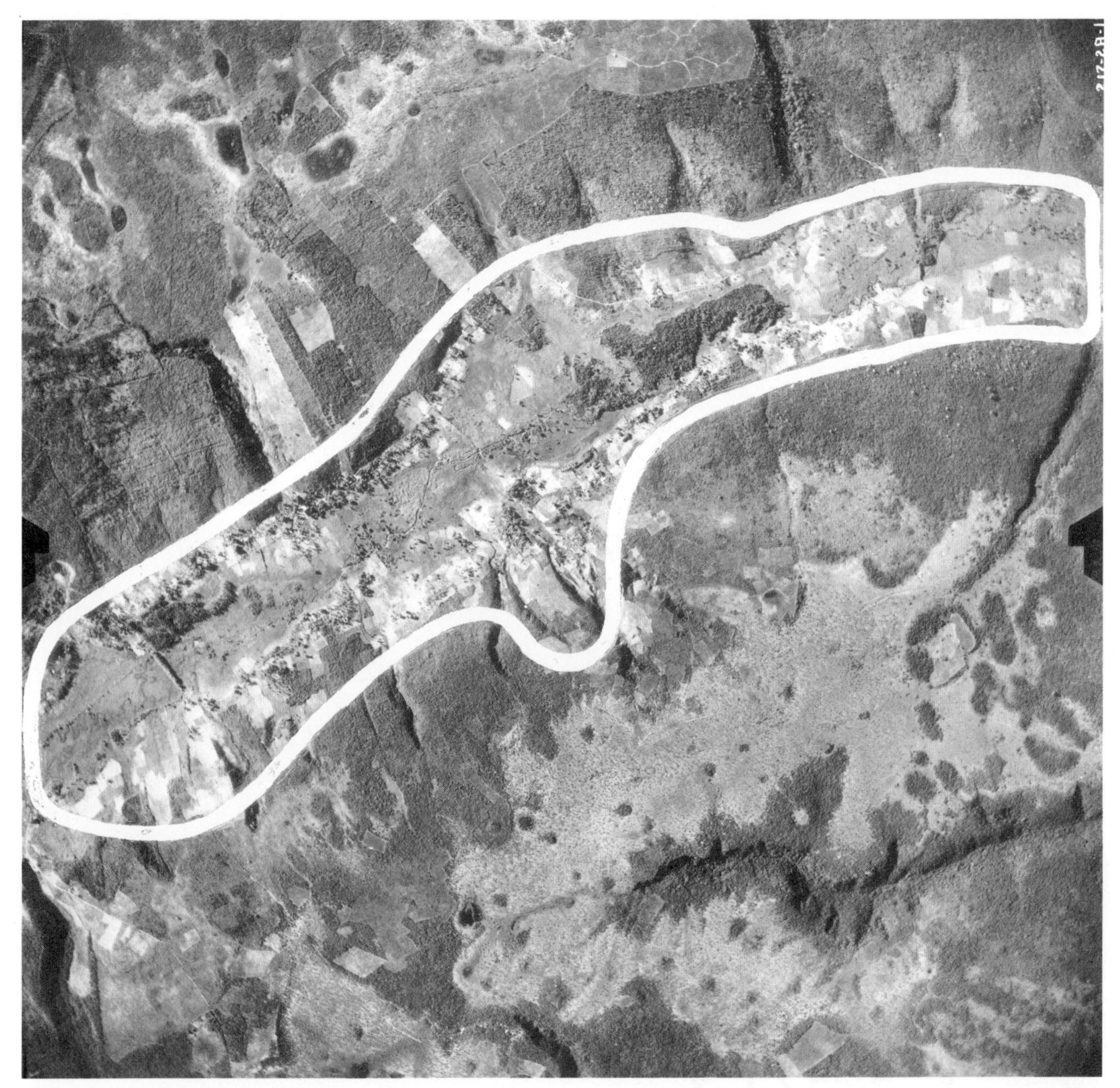

11. South of João Pessoa, 1959

Coconut groves can be seen in the varzeas where formerly there were few; also, there are more bananas, but they have a difficult time competing with sugarcane on the top-priority bottomlands. Some very small agave plantings were also seen, possibly because of locally sandy soils.

Another informant who had lived in the area since 1933 noted that cana amarela (yellow cane) had been planted there until around 1940. After 1940 a different variety, cana damerara, was planted, which yielded up to twice as much mel (cane juice), and other technical innovations were adopted to raise productivity.[35]

[35] Ibid., p. 156.

12. Goiana, 1942

The informant went on to point out the fundamental distinction between the local word given to second-growth vegetation—mato—and that given to thick timber—mata. He noted that much greater areas of land were used then than in the past; moreover, many of the former larger properties had been divided by inheritance. The tabuleiros had changed least because of their unsuitability for most crops—true tabuleiro produces only scrubby cerrado-type vegetation. He remarked that the varzeas and slopes had changed the most. One primary

13. Goiana, 1959*a*

common-size property on the tabuleiro would be 2 or 3 square leagues, whereas a common-sized property on the valley slopes would have only 5 to 10 quadras.

One interesting flashback to the entrepreneurial context of the colonial period was this man's observation that only people with capital can reason for the valorization of the varzeas has been the investment of the state government in financing the drainage of new areas of varzea. There had always been some roça food production on the valley slopes but it was more intensive in the 1960s, and there were definitely more fruit trees. This informant thought that a

14. Goiana, 1959*b*

open and use the varzea—that is, only wealthy individuals, companies, or the state. You will recall that the captains-donatory of the colonial period had to be wealthy in order to invest their own money in Brazil. In that sense, there has been little change in the entrepreneurial function. In the past there were always at least some small areas of varzea planted in maize, sweet potatoes, and vegetables; there was much less in the 1960s, as sugarcane dominated the varzea landscape. As an example of the splitting up of properties, the informant recalled one large landholding that had only one owner in 1934, and that in 1964 had at least twenty owners.

The point is that not only were sugarcane and cane lands more valorized in the 1960s, but *all* crop production was more valorized. Cane production was valorized because of the higher market prices and its commercial value; food crops were more valorized simply because of the greater population in Brazil. The significant distinction is that sugarcane has traditionally enjoyed the best land, whether in 1560 or 1960, and that subsistence food crops have always been relegated to inferior soils.

Another highway department employee said that some people in the area north of Goiana call it agreste; others call it tabuleiro.[36] He defined tabuleiro as meaning weak land, land not worth anything and that does not yield anything. If some manure were applied to it, manioc could be grown, but the land is extremely sandy and soil moisture is not easily retained. This explains the truly xerophytic aspect of the campo-cerrado type of vegetation in the sandier areas. This informant thought there was definitely more dense mato vegetation in former years, but it had been pretty well cut-over for timber and firewood, and no local folk speak of the zone as zona da mata because there is simply no more true mata there!

In this transformed habitat, the realistic, pragmatic farmer no longer seeks true mata because there is no more of it; the areas he seeks are the areas of denser capoeirões in places of lower elevation, with plenty of water and, hopefully, some embaúba trees that indicate relatively fertile soils. Only in a very few places is there denser vegetation cover today than in 1942, and these few places are the result of simple recuperation of the vegetation in an area being reinvaded by forest species.

South of Recife a number of interesting recent landscape changes can be seen. About 31 kilometers south, on the road to Palmares, at the Paváo sugar property in 1964 one could see manioc being grown on former sugarcane land. This use of land would have been unheard of previously, and the explanation is indicative of the times. What had happened was that the sugar workers' union (sindicato) had told the workers to plant roças of manioc in 1962 and 1963. The unions were in positions of ascendancy under both the Goulart federal government and the Arraes state government of Pernambuco. The usinas, or mills, were fined or subjected to a workers' strike if they did not let the workers plant manioc roças. So the actual presence of manioc, that humble subsistence food crop, on prime cane land was a decidely new element on the landscape. It should also be noted that the 1964 revolution represented a swing of government sympathy away from unions, and it will be interesting to see whether or not the growing of manioc on prime cane land has been discontinued.

About 20 kilometers south of Recife is the COPERBO synthetic rubber factory which was under construction in 1963–64. It was a failure in several ways. It was designed to use the alcohol byproduct from the sugarcane refineries as a key raw material, but in the late 1960s other sources of raw materials were being used instead of the alcohol, as originally intended. One of the unfortunate byproducts of the COPERBO plant is the pollution of the river and adjacent sea water; this has, in turn, put many fishermen out of work because of the destruction of the fish.

[36] Ibid., p. 169.

Chapter Six
THE SERTÃO

The meaning of the word *sertão,* like the actual sertão, has a vague, open-ended connotation. One definition is geographic, referring to the dry lowland interior of Northeast Brazil; the other definition means sparsely populated backlands, hinterlands, "the sticks" in American parlance, or the "outback" of the Australians. To most Northeasterners, who live within a few hours' bus travel of the Atlantic coast, the sertão is the vast vacuum behind and beyond everyplace or everything of consequence in Northeast Brazil. The state political capital is regarded as the center of the local universe, and all other places are "interior."[1] For an area such as the Northeast, where all the capitals are clinging, crablike, to the litoral, the distinction is valid. The sertão of Northeast Brazil combines both the above meanings; it is a sparsely settled (in places uninhabited), dry area that is "open-ended"; it appears limitless. One regards it in much the same way one regards the Sahara from any of the capitals of the fringing countries. It is not a question of crossing it, rather, of how deeply to penetrate it before coming back out. The sertão absorbs people, money, animals, and government efforts to change it with hardly any visible difference. It is amusing to contemplate anyone designing an "impact project" for the sertão.

[1] I saw an amusing road sign in Minas Gerais in 1956; the sign just south of the state capital of Belo Horizonte pointed north toward that city and read "to the Capital," and the signs pointing south read "to the interior" and "to Rio de Janeiro."

The first view of the sertão is most impressive, and few people forget it. Two particularly striking traverses from agreste to sertão are from Campina Grande westward toward Soledad in Paraíba, or from Garanhuns northwestward toward Arcoverde in Pernambuco. Upon leaving Garanhuns, the highest point, or the "roof," of the Borborema which is continually touched by low-scudding clouds, or garoa, we travel about 30 kilometers and note a pronounced thinning out of the cloud cover, which is wafted inland by the relentless southeasterly winds. A tall, stately mandacuru cactus stands as a sentinal, announcing the descent to the sertão. Passing the crest of the Borborema where manioc, cotton, and improved dairy pasture lands abound, we descend slightly, noting the increased incidence of barren rock surfaces.[2] From our still-high vantage point, we can see dozens of kilometers to the west through transparent crisp air which is dry and still cool at this elevation (900 meters). We are looking at a vast dry depression, studded with rocky monadnock remnants. We are in the rain shadow of the Borborema and can observe a caatinga vegetation growing on a very thin, sandy soil cover, which is derived from coarse granite country rock. The road cut reveals a soil profile that shows less than half a meter of light-colored soil, covering rotten granite in which the joints and rock itself are deeply weathered. When struck with another rock, the

[2] Field notes, January 1964, p. 11.

bedrock granite gives the dull muffled thud of deeply weathered rock instead of the sharp treble note of fresh unweathered granite. Large crystals of biotite, which tend to decompose first, alternate with large quartz and feldspar crystals. A sandy soil is the product of this weathered granite.

The sertão of Ceará presents slightly different aspects. Very friable (easily broken) mica schists frequently leave weathered sandy surfaces and layers of coarse quartz pebbles. Because of the intense insolation of the noonday sun, the caatinga does not have trees or bushes capable of giving much, if any, shade and the rock pebbles get so hot that you cannot firmly hold one the size of an egg in your hand for more than four or five seconds. There is much bare ground between the plants. The cattle-caused terracettes have contributed to the barrenness of the vegetation. The air is very dry, causing chapped lips and a drying of nasal passages. The leaves of some bushes felt like rough sandpaper. There is dried animal manure all around, unusable for agriculture in such a drying climate. The manure can always be burned as fuel, as in India and other dry wastelands that have been stripped of their firewood.

Cattle trails (terracettes), which aggravate erosion on the sterile, friable soils of southern Ceará. Caatinga vegetation.

MAN-LAND RELATIONSHIPS

Large-scale ranching

A cattle culture evolved in the sertão which was every bit as distinct and persistant as the sugar culture of the zona da mata. In colonial times the powerful sesmeiros (recipients of sesmarias) maintained some cattle corrals in the best areas of their land, but almost always they left the work and responsibility to a vaqueiro who was either a trusted slave or an employee who received, as his payment, one-fourth of all the calves and foals born under his care. Other areas were leased and called sitios; these were usually 1 square league in area, and were rented to the tenants for 10 mil reis per year. The great distances between places and the difficulties of communication made it almost inevitable, in that era, that the people would evolve a civilization that extracted everything possible to serve their needs. Accordingly, in their diet, people used mainly meat and milk (abundant only during the rainy season, or inverno), wild fruits, and a few foods derived from an incipient subsistence agriculture carried out in the brejos, the river floodplains, or riverbeds themselves, and in the caatinga itself during good rainy seasons. Short-cycle crops, such as maize and beans, were enclosed by wooden or stone fences to protect them from damage by the animals.

Most domestic utensils and furniture were fashioned from leather. Capistrano de Abreu analyzed the cultural complex that dominated the region and gave it the felicitous name of "leather civilization." He writes:

> The doors of the rustic dwellings were of leather, the crude sleeping area on the floor, and later the bed used for childbirths; all the ropes were of leather, the waterbags, the lunch baskets, suitcases, feedbag for horses, the hobbles to restrain the animals during rest

stops or trips, knife sheaths, clothes in which to work in the spiny caatinga, the slings and bags in which to carry the cane bagasse and salt; the saddle bags in which dirt for building the dams was carried.[3]

For centuries this system dominated the sertão, and when Spix and Martius explored the Northeast in the nineteenth century, they arrived in Piauí to find—on fazendas which were property of the Imperial Government—the same system of livestock described by Antonil.[4] In Piauí, they found dozens of royal fazendas dived into three inspectories, each directed by an inspector who earned 300 cruzeiros a year. Each fazenda was run by a vaqueiro who was under the jurisdiction of the inspector. The vaqueiro would sometimes work for several years without payment, toward the eventual settlement of accounts when he would receive his 25 percent of the new cattle and horses of the fazenda. The vaqueiros were allowed to raise goats, pigs, and sheep, and had the right to milk, and to produce cheese. Also on the royal fazendas there were escravos do rei (king's slaves) who received only clothing and meat, since they satisfied the rest of their needs from their own small farming and husbandry operations.[5]

During the rainy season, from around December to April, the cows would be rounded up and milked daily in order to make a less perishable product, cheese. After May, with the beginning of the long dry season, the cows no longer gave milk, and they were turned out to graze in the open caatinga. This system of minimal improvements and attention to the animals and pasture was still observed in the 1960s in the remotest areas, such as the chapada de Apodí (on the border between Ceará and Rio Grande do Norte), in Rio Grande do Norte, and in the high sertões (the most interior backlands) of Pernambuco, Piauí, and Bahia.

The cattle trails that linked the sertão producing areas with the coastal sugar zone markets of the colonial period were very long, both in distance and in travel time. The boiadas or cattle drives, had to stop frequently to renew the cattle's strength and allow them to regain their weight. One 1956 estimate of this weight loss was 1 kilogram of loss per day of walking.[6]

Two main routes to Recife have persisted over the centuries: (1) One reached Olinda (later Recife) after passing through Goiana, Espírito Santo (Paraıba), Mamanguape, Canguaretama (Rio Grande do Norte), Papari, São José de Mipibu, Natal, Açu, Mossoró, Aracatí, and Fortaleza. This was a route not only for cattle but also for traveling merchants who replenished their supplies at the coastal cities and then distributed them in the interior: (2) The second classic cattle route lead from Olinda to Goiana, També, Taperoá, Patos, Pombal, Souza, Icó (Ceará), Taua, and finally to Crateus where hundreds of vaqueiros from Piauı gathered before striking out with their lumbering herds in the direction of the sugar coast to the east.

Later, to offset the strong Bahian influence being felt in the Pernambucan sertoes, the government at Olindo built two roads that reached the Rio São Francisco and Cabrobó and Pilão Arcado, the only two Pernambucan parishes in the Middle São Francisco River in the second half of the eighteenth century (1774). One road led from Recife to Limoeiro and up the valley of the Rio Capiberibe, over the Borborema highlands, descending along the Rio Pajeu, passing Serra Talhada, to Floresta and

[3] Abreu, *Caminhos Antigos e Povoamento do Brasil*, p. 57.

[4] Antonil, *Cultura e Opulencia do Brasil e suas Drogas e Minas*. Antonil was the famous chronicler of the colonial period whose overly candid account was banned for many years in Brazil. It portrayed the daily life of that bygone era.

[5] J. von Spix and K. E. P. Von Martius, *Viagem no Brasil*, São Paulo, 1956, 2:418.

[6] Kempton E. Webb, *Geography of Food Supply in Central Minas Gerais*, p. 55.

finally Cabrobó (where the railroad of the Ferroviaria do Nordeste and the central highway of Pernambuco now exist), then on to Inajá, Tacaratú, Jatiña, and Cabrobó.[7]

The cattle from Ceará arrived in Olinda thin and exhausted after their long trek, and, because of the great distance traveled, higher transportation costs had to be paid for them than the cattle from nearly Paraíba and Rio Grande do Norte states. For this reason the Cearenses had begun, by 1740 to export their beef in the concentrated low-bulk form of carne seca (dried beef) and hides. The salt came from the natural salt deposits at Aracati at the north of the Rio Jaguaribe, which has the distinction of having the highest potential evapotransportation in all Northeast Brazil, equivalent to 186 centimeters of water a year in a climate that produces an average yearly rainfall of only 114 centimeters a year. The cattle came from all along the northern coast of Ceará and Rio Grande do Norte and from the broad valley of the Rio Jaguaribe. And thus appeared the oficinas, or factories, for the making of charque (North American jerky) known in the Northeast as carne-do-ceará, or Ceará meat, and which thereby allowed Ceará to compete with Paraíba and Rio Grande do Norte in supplying the sugar zone of Pernambuco with beef and hides. The number of charque oficinas grew at the mouths of other rivers, such as the Parnaiba, Acaraú, Camocim, Mossoró, and Açú. The demand for beef animals by the charqueadas cut sharply into the supply of animals normally destined for work in the Pernambucan sugar engenhos. The few charque oficinas in Rio Grande do Norte had to shut down for lack of animals. The other oficinas continued to work until the Grande Seca of 1790–92, which almost completely decimated the Cearense herds and ended the new charque industry. The collapse of the industry benefited mainly the fazendeiros of Paraíba, and soon afterward the gaucho charqueadas of Rio Grande do Sul, which subsequently dominated the Northeast Brazil markets and has only recently begun to feel competition from charque producers in Goias and Matto Grosso states.

It was in this way that livestock ranching conquered the sertão of Northeast Brazil. It complemented the humid agricultural zona da mata with an economic activity indispensable to the sugar industry and to the food supply of the growing cities. The sertão absorbed the surplus population of the zona da mata during the stagnant periods of the sugar industry, and benefited from the labors and energies of those who, for economic, psychological, or whatever reason, could not integrate themselves into the famous casa grande e senzala sugar culture. Livestock ranching ultimately permitted the formation of what one writer[8] has called "O Outro Nordeste," or the other Northeast of caatingas and cattle that at the same time competes with and complements the Northeast of the clayey massapé soil and sugarcane.

Agriculture

The beginning of agriculture in the sertão came at the same time as the opening up of the interior to open-range cattle raising. Farming was far from the chief activity, but it developed on a very limited scale near the corrals because of the subsistence-food needs of the vaqueiros sertanejo (backland cattlemen) population and because the remote locations of the fazendas made food brought from the zona da mata prohibitively expensive.

Farming occupied only small areas in the most favored moist areas that had deeper soils, such as the floodplains and dried-up lakes; people also farmed the cultivable riverbed sec-

[7] Manuel Correia de Andrade, *A Terra e o Homen no Nordeste*, p. 180.

[8] Djacir Meneses, *O Outro Nordeste: Formação Social do Nordeste.*

tions of the Rio São Francisco and its tributaries after the river level lowered, leaving exposed beaches and islands available for vazante (floodplain farming). People also cultivated the cool serras with manioc, maize, beans, cotton, and occasionally melons. After some time, fruits and even sugarcane also became cultivated in the serras, which comprised wet spots or oases isolated in the vastness of the caatingas.

The preoccupation with cattle raising was of such an order that lands that were true mata, such as the "new" Cariri zone of southern Ceará, were requested as sesmarias to be devoted to extensive cattle raising. It was only afterward, in proportion to the degree to which population was agglomerating, that these larger, wetter areas, such as those of Teixeira (Paraıba), of Araripe and of Baixa Verde (Pernambuco), of Agua Branca and Mata Grande (Alagoas), of the serras of Ibiapaba, Meruoca, Baturité, and the Cariri (Ceará), came to be enclosed by large fences and valados (trenches) called travessão that defined the limit between areas of agriculture and those of grazing.

Within the travessão, agriculture was freely pursued, and livestock could remain there only if they were fenced or tethered. Outside the travessão, it was the crops that had to be fenced and protected from cattle that roamed at will on the open range. The travessão consisted of a trench in some areas (time-consuming to dig, but difficult to remove or alter), a fence of stones, of branches, of cactus, or in present times of barbed wire or aveloz.[9] Sometimes the travessão was permanently fixed, but in other instances it was movable and advanced or retreated with the season of the year or with the will of a powerful fazendeiro (coronel) or an influential political figure. Since around 1910, barbed wire has been used more and more to segregate the better pastures for exclusive use by the fazendeiros' cattle. The barbed wire also restricts the chances for vaqueiros or poor people to raise animals on the open range, in "posse em commum," as was done in the old days.

Around 1800, sertanejo agriculture took a giant leap with the rapid development of cotton. Much of the cotton was consumed regionally as local weavers processed it into materials and fabrics. Most of it, however, was hauled over a hundred leagues (600 kilometers) to be shipped to English textile mills via the port of Recife.

Cotton did not require as many slaves as sugarcane did, and for this reason a demand for salaried labor was established in the sertão. Cotton also did not lend itself easily to slavery because of its short vegetative cycle, which meant that there was not sufficient work to pay for the slaves' maintenance throughout the year. In times of drought, many slaves had to be sold to the coffee plantations in southern Brazil where, in the nineteenth century, demand was high.

A potentially misleading degree of similarity exists between what happened in the sertão and what happened in the agreste. For one thing, the difficulties of communication between the sertão and the mata were much greater than those between the agreste and the mata. The sertão remained always more remote from the elements of innovation and progress that emanated from the more developed zona da mata. Also, within the sertão, the wetter areas that were more favorable to agriculture comprised a miniscule percentage of the total area, in contrast to the agreste, which has ultimately become a polycultural zone par excellence. The similarity stems from both sertão and agreste having been originally settled by cattlemen, and from cattle raising being the initial wedge whereby both areas were settled. With the growth of population, subsistence agriculture developed in both zones, complemented in a few favored areas by sugarcane cultivation

[9] Andrade, *A Terra,* p. 184.

and rapadura production. In the second half of the eighteenth century both zones were overwhelmed by cotton, and around 1840 coffee came into the interior brejos to stay until the 1920 plague. Today, with greater facilities of communication, namely the truck, the agreste has become a zone of polyculture and improved cattle production, while the sertão is becoming transformed much more slowly.

Sharecropping and salaried labor

Livestock raising remains today, as in the past, the most evident economic activity of the sertão; it is practiced exclusively or in association with cotton growing. The fazendas, whose main house and buildings were almost always situated beside or near large streams, extended frequently for leagues back from the riverbank up into the caatinga. The reason for these linear properties is that hereditary succession had divided the properties to such a degree that they became narrow and elongated, having but a few dozen meters of river frontage by kilometers of depth penetrating the interior caatingas. It has always been, and still is, the length of the river frontage in the floodplain that indicated the value of a fazenda—not the area of caatinga.

The whole system of cattle raising on the large fazendas of the sertão has remained fairly stagnant except for some areas of greater progress and innovation, such as the Cariris Velhos of Paraíba, the sertão baixo of Pernambuco, and the sertão of Alagoas. Over vast areas, however, especially the Bahian and Pernambucan areas drained by the Rio São Francisco, and the south and west of Piauí, livestock raising of the most extensive type is carried out on the open range, producing undersized beef animals that weigh less than 135 kilograms (300 pounds) and take as long as six years to reach slaughterhouse size.

This extensive type of cattle raising gives neither large profits nor does it incur large expenses. The fazendeiros live generally in the cities of the sertão that are close to their fazendas and where they can spend their own energies on other economic activities, such as commerce. The fazenda is left to be managed by a vaqueiro, and the fazendeiro lives on the fazenda only from around November to April, during the rainy season, when the caatinga is in bloom, pasturage is good, water is abundant, and the cows are rounded up and milked so that cheese can be made. It is during the rainy season, or, to be more correct, the rainier season, that the fazendeiro oversees what the vaqueiro-manager has accomplished during the past year and gives him orders for the coming year, such as to repair the fences, corrals, and houses and buildings, and to buy scrawny cattle from other areas to fatten and sell by the end of the period of more abundant natural forage.

During the dry season the pasture is not sufficiently plentiful, and the cattle are driven up to the serras (mountains) where there is more abundant food. These serras are believed to "refresh" the cattle, and the existence of the serras is the reason that sertanejo cattle raising exists over broad areas. In the sertão of Bahia, cattle of the valley of the Rio São Francisco are driven to the highland gerais (grassy wastelands) of the border zone shared by Bahia, Piauí, and Goiás. This migration, or transhumance, depending upon the régime and intensity of the rains, usually begins around March or April, and the cattle remain in the serras until around October. The cattle are so accustomed to this annual migration that they frequently make the trip unaccompanied. With the first showers of the rainy season in October-November, the vaqueiros head for the gerais to round up and bring back the herd which has lived in the open in an almost wild state for half a year.

The central worker-figure on a fazenda is the vaqueiro who tends the herd, manages the property, and, during the absence of the owner, issues orders to the workers and agregados (tenants who pay rent with one or more days of labor per week for the fazendeiro). Sometimes, of course, the vaqueiro is paid by quarters—that is, one-fourth of the newborn calves, goats, foals, born under his care—and this takes place on a day when the fazendeiro is present. When the fazendeiro is more liberal, he has continued this traditional form of payment with all its perquisites, allowing the vaqueiro's animals (with the vaqueiro's own brand) to be raised beside his, as if they were animals "of the fazenda." Other fazendeiros, believing that the animals grow better under the eye of the owner, and because they know that they are away most of the time, fear that in times of drought their own animals may be treated with less care than those belonging to the vaqueiro. These latter fazendeiros require the vaqueiro to sell his animals soon after the division of the herd, thereby removing the possibility that the vaqueiro might someday become a fazendeiro in his own right, with his own herd. With the introduction of Zebu bulls of Indian origin, and of more selective breeding practices, and with the rising prices of beef, the fazendeiros are for the most part abandoning the traditional sorte system and are instead paying their vaqueiros a salary that rarely reaches the legal minimum salary. Making allowances for devaluation of the cruzeiro and changing exchange rates, the average vaqueiro's wage was about a dollar per day in the early 1960s plus the use of a house. It has also been traditional for vaqueiros to benefit from whatever milk is produced, although fresh liquid milk has value only near large cities. The more remote fazendas, of course, transformed their milk to cheeses. Cheese with rapadura and goat meat comprise the daily diet of the sertanejo and are higher in nutritive value than the farinha de manioc (manioc meal) and dried fish that prevail among the masses of people who live in the zona da mata.

The vaqueiro's life might appear, at first glance, to be an easy one. It is not. He spends long periods on horseback inspecting the pastures, fences, and water holes of the fazenda. He drives the cattle to the higher, better pastures of the serras during the refrigerio. His family makes the cheeses during the rainy season and he repairs the fences. There is also the arduous task of rounding up the cattle for branding.

But the dry season is the worst. At times the vaqueiro must prepare certain sertão cacti for use as fodder by cutting down the xique xique, mandacuru, and facheiro and burning off the spines. The macambira must not only have its spines removed but must also be cut up into bite-size pieces.

The most serious problem the vaqueiro faces is that of providing water, since sometimes the cattle must be herded for dozens of kilometers to the water holes. They can go for forty-eight hours without drinking while, under emergency conditions, water holes can be dug in the dry riverbeds. The water holes are dug to the depth at which the ground water table lies; they are almost always fenced on one side so that the animals do not trample and destroy the excavation wall. As they mill around the water hole the cattle drink water, urinate, and defecate, thus transmitting their diseases to each other.

Besides the vaqueiros, the fazendas have some other workers paid in money wages, the carreiros (ox-cart drivers). Their importance derives from the use of the traditional carro de boi (ox cart), which is declining in recent years owing to the opening up of new roads and the increase in the numbers of trucks. Actually, since World War II it has been the truck which has been the great conqueror of the sertão, the vehicle which has succeeded in breaking the age-old ways and transforming the modes of life. Still, even now the carreiro, in his leather cape and hat and his long goad-pole over his shoulder, can be seen languidly walking beside his ox cart. He is assisted by his sons of ten years or more of age, who are in this way learning the mysteries of a profession that is transmitted from generation to generation.

The tangerinos or tangedores (cattle drovers) constitute another class that is disappearing, and whose locus of activity is limited to the most remote sertoes—again owing to the competition of the truck, which transports cattle to the most distant cities. The areas today that offer the most work for the tangerinos are those of the sertão of Piauí that focus upon the city of Araripina (Pernambuco); those from northern Bahia (the sertão of Rodelas and the Raso de Catarina) that focus on the sertanejo cities of Parnamirim, Salgueiro, and Arcoverde in Pernambuco; those roads that lead to northern Minas Gerais and southern Bahia and converge upon Propriá, penetrating into Sergipe by way of Simao Dias; and those roads that go from Propriá toward Caruarú, Maceio, and Recife.[10]

The tangerinos drive the cattle herds just as they did in the times of Antonil; they "reside" in the towns and villages, where they have more opportunity to find work, but they really spend their lives roaming the sertões, paid very low wages (on contract), accompanying the herds on foot, perhaps having horses to ride for a few hours during the day.

Sometimes the tangerinos live in a crude shack on some fazenda where they plant roça. At lunchtime the whole family gathers around a large clay pot and fishes out the food with their hands. The standard meal is almost always beans, manioc meal, salt and pepper, and occasionally meat.

When areas of better soils exist on a fazenda, the fazendeiros sometimes let their moradores and people of neighboring towns or villages make roças. Also in those areas the cultivation of mocó cotton has developed. It is planted every three or four years in association with beans and maize. Frequently the landowners hire day-wage workers to make large clearings and plantings with this crop association.

The majority of the fazendeiros, however, prefer to devote their land to the cultivation of cotton and cereals, putting their cattle on the stubble and leftovers of the harvested field during the two driest months of the year. The lands generally are not rented since the owners prefer to have a sharecropping (parceria) arrangement. Of the different parceria variations, the meia (half) is widespread. In it, the owners furnish the land and seed and financing during the preparation and cultivation of the plot, and after the harvest they receive as payment half of the cotton produced and the stubble and stocks left from the plants. The farmer who actually cultivated the land keeps the other half of the cotton, the cereals, such as maize and beans, that were interplanted with the cotton, and the fruta de rama, or squashes, melons, and so on.[11] When the cultivation is done in the river floodplain lands, or vazante, the landowner also takes half of the cereals and of the frutas de rama.

In some areas of the sertão, the terça (third) system of pay is used instead of the meia. In such cases two-thirds of the harvest goes to the landowner, and only one-third to the farmer. In Piauí the system of quarta (quartering) is used not only for cattle raising but also in agriculture.

The sujeição (subjection) typical of the zona da mata is also encountered in the sertão and agreste. Under the sujeição, the foreiros (landless workers) are obliged to give to the landowner one day of labor each week. This is the famous cambão (wage-worker) system against which the Ligas Camponesas fought. The one day of work is in some areas considered a

[10] Ibid., p. 198.

[11] Helio Galvão, *O Mutirão no Nordeste,* Cited by Andrade in *A Terra.* p. 47.

personal obligation or debt that does not allow the foreiro to pay someone else to perform that labor for him. It is like paying a personal homage to the landowner. If we calculate one day's labor as being worth a dollar (1,000 cruzeiros in 1963), we can see that the foreiro provides yearly services to the landowner worth 50 dollars (50,000 cruzeiros), which is a truly exhorbitant rent for the small area of cultivable land and the miserable shelter provided on it. It can be seen then that in the work relationships just outlined, the great disadvantage that befalls the landless farmer subjects him to contractual conditions that are truly exploitative. We should remember also that in these dry sertão areas the farmers are liable to lose their work *and* their shares of the harvest if the inverno (rainy season) is irregular and causes losses. The arbitrariness of the landowner is a constant source of anxiety to the farmer since, as he has no written contract, he has no guarantees or protection on the land and can be sent away at any time for no reason at all to seek work on another fazenda under exactly the same humiliating conditions.[12]

These workers who labor day in and day out for more than ten hours a day receive wages that rarely exceed a dollar a day, salaries that do not provide even a modest living standard. The contribution of subsistence crops, which are cultivated by these moradores and which are given such prominence by defenders of the present social structures in rural Northeast Brazil, is almost insignificant because the plots are so small (one-third or one-half a hectare) and because they are not farmed rationally with fertilizers, rotation, and so forth. Moreover, it should be stressed that there is little or no preoccupation of the government agricultural experimental stations with subsistence farming using better seed selection and better ways of fighting plagues. The traditional preoccupation of these stations has always revolved around large-scale agriculture, export crops, and, on a lesser scale, fruits.

POCINHOS: A CASE STUDY OF MAN IN THE SERTÃO

Let us examine in more detail the nature of man's occupance of the driest part of Brazil—in this case the municipio of Pocinhos, which is 30 kilometers northwest of Campina Grande on the Borborema at an elevation of around 600 meters and which receives some 650 millimeters of rainfall each year. Gerard Prost has carried out field research comparing Pocinhos, a sertão town, with Esperança, a representative agreste town, and we shall present the results of those studies in these chapters on sertão and agreste.[13]

The Cariri, extending more than 100 kilometers west of Campina Grande, and which crosses Paraíba state from north to south, is the driest part of all Brazil with an average annual rainfall of 250 to 300 millimeters. During the summer its barren caatinga is the yellowest of the entire state, and the waters in its reservoirs are salty. The area has traditionally been little used, and its towns have been insignificant. Over the past centuries the two economic bases were (a) extension cattle raising, with about one animal for each 15 hectares of land, and (b) small cotton fields.

Everything has changed during the years since World War II; within a radius of 50 kilometers of Campina Grande the region was transformed by the introduction of the new plant, agave. Until the war, most of the landscape was untouched except by a few cattle; now it is half-covered by crops.

Agrarian structure

Within this relatively homogeneous physical milieu of the Cariri, the different forms of land tenure provide the basis of all areal diversification. Let us examine this data in greater detail.

[12] Andrade, *A Terra,* p. 200.

[13] Gerard Prost, "Dans le Nord-Est du Brasil."

The cadastral data. Of the twenty-seven properties surveyed, which covered a total area of 5,250 hectares, only three were very large—that is, larger than 500 hectares.[14] Nevertheless, those three properties occupied half of the entire area studied near Pocinhos. See table 3, adapted from Prost, for a breakdown of these twenty-seven properties.[15] These figures confirm what one observes all over the country: a small number of favored owners who occupy the greater areas of the best land, while the majority of farmers occupy a large number of small and middle-sized properties.

For types of occupant, let us turn again to table 3. The first group in this listing, called minifundios, comprises properties of between 5 and 20 hectares; they are really too small to absorb all the energies of their owners, who must therefore find additional work on other farms. The second group, owned by sitiantes, or peasants in the European sense of the word, are small, independently owned farms of between 18 and 40 hectares. The owners live on the property, work there, and only occasionally are employed outside. The third group comprises fazendas of 70 to 1,300 hectares; one has less than 100 hectares, three have from 200 to 300, another has 670, and the largest has 1,300 hectares. This group is the most heterogeneous; their owners live in Pocinhos but supervise the daily work on their fazendas. These are the owner-operated fazendas. The fourth group has three properties of from 75 to 95 hectares, three from 200 to 370 hectares, and one of 700 hectares. Their fazendeiros also live in town, but they visit their fazendas only once a week. These are owner-administered fazendas. The fifth group is composed of one absentee fazendeiro who rarely visits his property.

The area surveyed covers almost 5,500 hectares. As indicated in table 4, again taken from Prost, a little less than 2,900 hectares is covered by caatinga; a little less than 2,000 hectares is planted in agave; 180 are in roça or annual subsistence crops; 160 are planted in forage palma (cactus inerme); and 160 were cleared but not planted. Of the total 5,250 exploited hectares, 55 percent are occupied by caatinga, 37 percent by agave, 3.5 percent by roça crops, and 3 percent by palma. Table 4 shows the distribution of land-use types by size of property and type of farm owner.[16] Let us discuss further the three major uses to which this land is put.

[14] Data gathered by field interviews using air photographs and municipal tax records.

[15] Prost, "Dans le Nord-Est du Brasil," Extract, p. 3.

Land uses

Caatinga. The area of caatinga pasture is enormous, but it supports only a few dozen cattle most of the time, and at any one time no more than a maximum of two hundred head. During the inverno, or rainy season, the animals graze in the open caatinga, but after the rains they feed on the remnants and scraps of the cotton and bean fields and ultimately are fed in the corral by vaqueiros. Since around 1945 the palma forage plant has gradually gained acceptance. This plant is perfectly adapted to a dry climate since it is originated on the arid Barbary coast of North Africa. Most fazendeiros also feed their animals cottonseed cake. The low density of cattle (around one per 5 hectares of caatinga) reflects the climate as well as the fact that the primary interest now is in agave and not livestock raising.

Agave. This plant, originally introduced from Mexico, is also perfectly adapted to the dry conditions of the semiarid Cariri. It can be planted during the dry season, which is the slack work season, and has to be weeded only during the first two years. Only the harvesting and defibering of the "leaves" require any further labor. If the market price is low, the agave grower can wait while the plant continues to grow. It "stores" or preserves itself.

[16] Ibid., p. 6.

Table 3. Classification of properties

Category	Number of properties		Area covered	
	Number in each group	Percent in each group	Of each group (in hectares)	Percent in each group
By area (in hectares)				
less than 20	4	14.8	50	1.0
20 to 50	5	18.5	140	2.8
50 to 100	5	18.5	375	6.2
100 to 200	5	18.5	665	12.8
200 to 500	5	18.5	1,350	26.0
500 to 1000	2	7.4	1,370	26.2
more than 1,000	1	3.8	1,300	25.0
Total	27	100.0	5,250	100.0
By type of occupant				
Minifundio operators	5	18.5	52.5	1.0
Small farmers (sitiantes)	8	29.7	472.5	9.0
Owner-operated Fazendas	6	22.0	2,835.0	54.0
Owner-administered fazendas	7	26.0	1,785	34.0
Absentee fazendeiro	1	3.8	105.0	2.0
Total	27	100.0	5,250.0	100.0

Because of agave, there is no more famine in the area. The economy has also changed abruptly: the cotton plantations have been almost entirely eliminated, and half the newly cleared lands have been planted in agave. Most of these clearings date from the years of World War II. The caatinga is cut down, burned, and the agave shoots are planted; the rows are always planted up and down the steepest slope. In the same row, the plants are spaced one meter apart, while 2.5 meters separates the rows. This spacing permits around 4,100 agave plants on each hectare of land. The leaves are cut and defibered in the third year. The fibers are dried, and the pulp is spread out on the agave fields as green manure.

The yield is about 1,100 to 1,200 kilograms of fiber per hectare. This first cutting is double, followed by constantly decreasing yields. The income around 1965 was about 100,000 cruzeiros ($100) per hectare per year for work involving only ten or eleven days per year after the more time-consuming first two years.

Roça, or annual subsistence crops. Roça agriculture occupies only 7 percent of the cultivated lands, and is found in the wetter bottomlands. Generally the roça crops are in permanent fields that are not rotated. In January or February, one month before the probable beginning of the rainy season, the land is prepared with occasional use of a motor-cultivator. Only one farmer had a disker pulled by a tractor. Seeds of maize and beans are planted in the same field when the first rains come. The field is weeded two or three times a year and it is the most arduous work of the year. Maize is harvested after sixty days; beans after forty-five to ninety days. The few farmers who plant herbaceous cotton harvest it in October. In October or November the roça is turned over to cattle for grazing during the dry season. Their manure and the old weeds constitute the only fertilizer the land receives. Only two farmers applied additional manure from their corrals. The same cycle is repeated yearly, except for the cotton which is replaced every five or six years.

The smallest sitiante had seeded his three hectares with 15 to 20 liters of maize each year. He harvested 120 liters one year; he harvested 300 liters in 1965. His bean yields also fluc-

Table 4. Land use

Category	Percentage in Caatinga	Agave	Palma	Roca, or subsistence crops
By area (in hectares)				
Less than 20	8	67	—	25
20 to 50	35	45	—	20
50 to 100	28	55	2	8
100 to 200	40	50	4	6
200 to 500	55	45	—	—
500 to 1,000	70	30	—	—
Larger than 1,000	60	25	8	7
By type of occupant				
Minifundio operators	13	52	10	25
Small farmers (sitiantes)	45	35	8	12
Owner-operated fazendas	62	30	4	4
Owner-administered fazendas	55	45	—	—
Absentee fazendeiro	60	30	2	8

tuated widely. In 1965 his family's needs were covered; in 1966 he had to begin buying maize and beans in November.[17]

The prospects

Prost attempts to assess the prospect for each of the four major groups studied in Pocinhos. Summaries of his assessments follow.

1. The situation of the small, independent farmer is generally satisfactory. His land nourishes him well; all he has to buy is occasional maize and beans, manioc meal, sugar, coffee, meat, and lamp fuel. These expenses amount to around 0.5 million cruzeiros ($500) a year while the income from his agave, grown on from 15 to 30 hectares, is 1.2 to 2.4 million cruzeiros ($1,200 to $2,400) per year. This means that in good years this average small farmer can undertake certain improvements of his property (building a storage building or reservoir, redecorating or repairing the house, etc.), although in bad years, such as 1966 when his income fell to 0.7 to 1.3 million cruzeiros ($700 to $1,300), he cannot.

The difference in family living levels depends also, of course, upon the number of people in the family. Four men, working 60 hectares, can support a family of ten very well, but 20 hectares cannot in any way support a family of twenty.

If the sitiante can intensify all his farming methods, notably by seed selection, and can sell his products at a good market price, the future is open to him.

2. The case of the fazendeiros is different. They are really gentlemen farmers who have one or more economic activities in town and who retain a fazenda for tradition's sake or for the supplementary income it provides. Their well-being does not depend exclusively upon how well the fazenda is managed. They can afford to be inefficient! Only the owner-operated fazenda boasts a true farmer whose existence depends entirely upon his skills.

In 1966, the agave revenues fell by around 50 percent and they approached the costs of the fiber production. Agave owner-operators found themselves in a difficult situation. It possibly made some fazendeiros consider the benefits of a more diversified productive base that would be less susceptible to fluctuations in the world market price of sisal fiber. Two fazendeiros intended to branch out into dairying. What would happen to the area if sisal prices re-

[17] Ibid., p. 15.

mained low and no other economic base was promoted? In 1966 there was no more clearing of the caatinga, no more planting or harvesting of agave; the price of sisal did not justify it and, as recently as 1964, interest rates were as high as 50 percent per year. Can the "town fazendeiros," who regard agave as the only crop worth growing, be considered as positive elements for the future of the region?

3. There are slim additional resources available to the landless, salaried farm workers. These people who lack any real independence seem to be disappearing from the Pocinhos area. It is interesting that their salaries were well maintained despite the fall in the sisal market in 1966.

4. Agave is the object of all discussions and preoccupations. It has brought wealth and dependence as well. After twenty years of growth, the crisis of 1966 stopped the expansion.Will agave continue to be a dynamic factor in the agriculture of Northeast Brazil? The response to this crisis will determine the future welfare of this recently emerged boom corner of the sertão.

RECENT LANDSCAPE CHANGES

The remoteness of the sertão from the large cities and zones of concentrated population along the coast continues to relegate it to a place of secondary importance in terms of innovations and new enterprises that have expression on the landscape. In short, the sertão has experienced the least amount of landscape change during the past twenty to thirty years. The little change that has occurred has been limited mostly to zones that have already been exploited. This selective areal modification has been limited to the varzeas and along the roads; the varzeas because they have the most productive soils of the area, and the roads because of their role in getting products to markets and feiras (fairs). The vast expanses of caatinga-covered sertão, which are located leagues from any road and which boast little water or good soil, cannot hope to attract the investment of money that would improve the areas and make them more productive. The agave areas described above actually represent only a minute fraction of the entire sertão.

The first pair of air photos (figures 15 and 16) is of the area just south of Joazeirinho in Paraiba and is one of the few examples where one can see, with a binocular stereoscope, increases in the area of bare rock exposed. The more recent photos show a small but decisive expansion in this area of rock. Despite its darker tone, the 1942 photo (figure 15) shows a denser growth of caatinga vegetation. There are very few new areas of agriculture. Most of the clearings for farms remain in the same places. It is interesting to observe how many farm plots are attracted to those areas surrounding the bare rock outcrops. The probable reason for this is that those barren surfaces tend to concentrate around their margins the water from any rain that falls on them. Therefore, the areas around the bases of those exposed rocks would have larger amounts of water available for crops. This is evident on the photographs.

The next pair of photos (figures 17 and 18) is taken farther to the east, between Farinha and Soledad. These photos again show very little areal change. The areas of caatinga continue to be areas covered with caatinga, and the areas cleared for crops are essentially the same. There has been the addition or loss of a field of manioc here or there, but it is an insignificant change. One can look for the areal changes to be located along the varzeas, along the stream beds where there is more water available, and along the roads. On the newer photo one can see some straightening of and adjustments to the major east-west road. The caatinga also shows a less dense aspect, although allowance has to be made for the technical differences in tone and texture of the two photographs.

East of Farinha, which really marks the beginning of the sertão west of Campina Grande, at the bottom of the back slope of the highlands and one of the driest places in Brazil, we see on figures 19 and 20 a reasonably thick covering of capoeira or caatinga or mato around the pedras, or areas of barren rock. The older photo (figure 19) appears to show many areas with indeterminate land use; the new photos clearly show areas in crops, in pasture, or fallow. Fallow would show capoeira in varying stages of recuperation. On the newer photos there are definitely larger areas of barren rock exposed; there is much wider use of aveloz fences. These fences can be seen as straight dark lines because of their shadows. One interesting way in which the passage of time can be observed on these photos is by the increasing height of the aveloz hedgerows whose shadows cast longer shadows on the newer photos. In figure 21, one can even see an area of loteamento, or house lot subdivision. Photos of this and of neighboring areas show this zone to the east of Farinha to be about 70 percent fenced agriculture. The area in general, being only 25 kilometers west of Campina Grande, has had more intensive land use during the last two decades because of its greater valorization by agave, as described in the preceding section. This is a response to the urban markets of Campina Grande, João Pessoa, and Recife, and is a consequence of its position along the major east-west highway. With the presence of more aveloz hedgerows, we find a reflection of greater organization of land and greater specialization of land-use functions. Many other pairs of photos could be shown in which the areal changes would be minimal, but it is perhaps more interesting to give emphasis to the places with change. The fact remains, however, that most of the sertão looks very much as it did twenty or thirty years before. The only exception is that the covering of caatinga vegetation is less dense owing to the cutting of wood for firewood, construction purposes, and making charcoal.

The cutting-over of the sertão's caatinga for charcoal is a generalized phenomenon or process that finds its main focus in the urban markets of the coastal cities. In one operation, 70 kilometers out of Arcoverde, the lenha, or firewood, was hauled in by ox cart from up to 7 kilometers away.[18] This was a very sparsely inhabited area until the 1920s and 1930s, but by the 1950s and 1960s it had become more settled, with the growing of cotton, subsistence crops, and the increasing cutting of firewood.

The lenha is stacked to a height of 3 meters inside the closed brick ovens, then burned in the near absence of oxygen for four to five days, during which the mass is reduced to a meter-high pile of charred remains. After the oven has cooled for one or two weeks, the charcoal can be removed and packed into burlap sacks weighing 30 kilograms. One oven produces about forty to fifty sacks; they are shipped to Recife where, in 1964, they were sold for about 70 cents per sack.

In that dry area, the only certain activities are cattle and goat raising. People take their chances with maize, beans, moco cotton, and even rice. Of course, one change that is more difficult to read on air photos is the increased importance of cattle raising. The continually rising prices of beef in the cities has made cattle raising profitable, and the larger herds in the sertão would be more difficult to identify on air photos than, say, an increased acreage of cotton or other crops.

In the area around Pocinhos, as has been noted in the previous section of this chapter, we are close to the boundary between agreste and sertão. One farm worker, 4 kilometers east of Pocinhos, allowed that properties are larger there "because it is the Cariri"; because it is drier there, it is worse for farming compared to

[18] Field notes, February 14, 1964, p. 15.

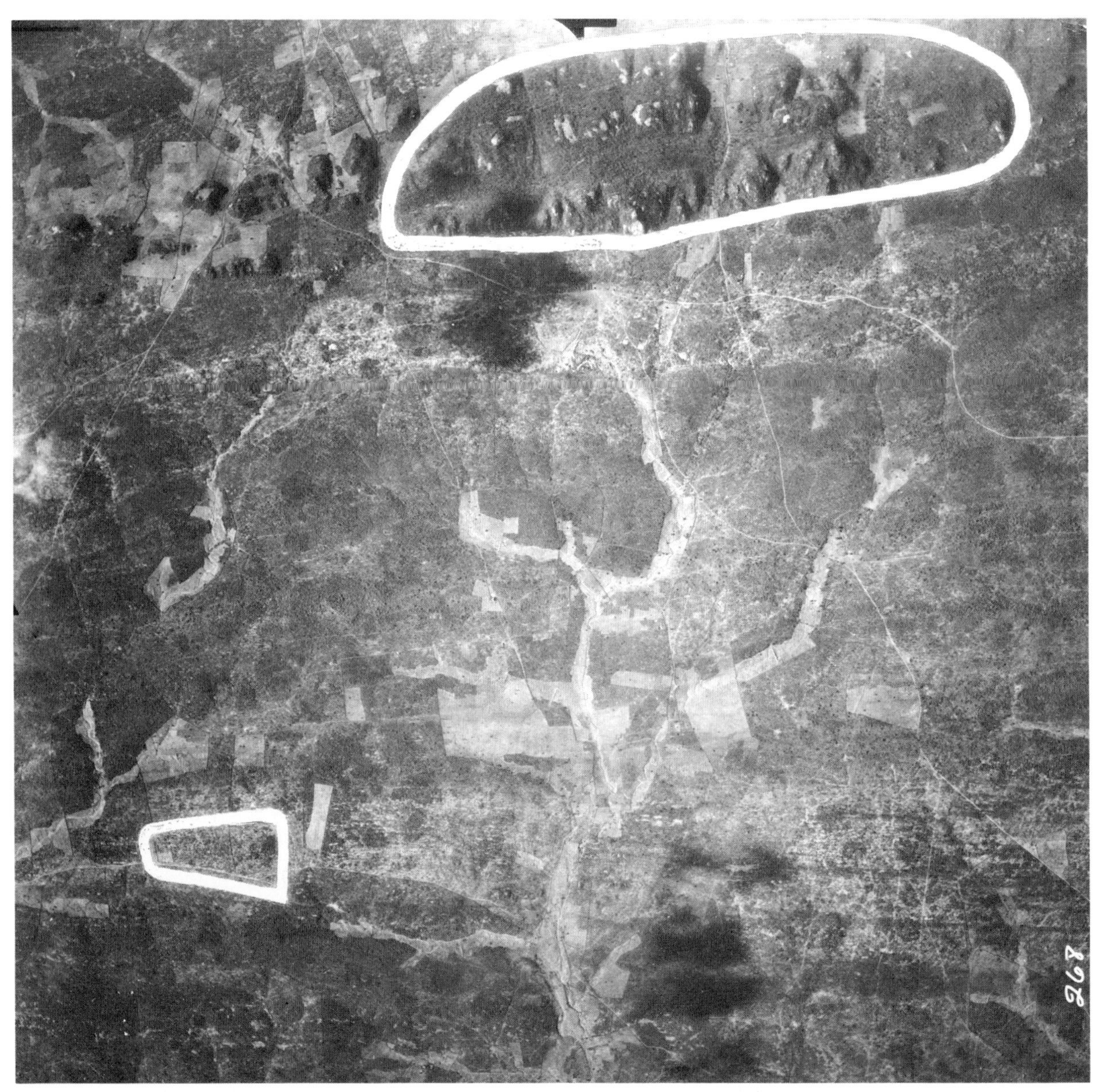

15. South of Joazeirinho, 1942

the areas to the east, such as Puxinanã.[19] He said that the Pocinhos area was formerly devoted to maize and beans, but that since 1963 agave has taken over on a large scale because of the handsome market prices paid. The people in the town of Pocinhos generally agree that the Cariri begins at Pocinhos and continues westward as far as Joãzeirinho. Most of the property owners, confirming Prost's study, live in the town and have several moradores on their properties in the environs. Just west of Pocinhos the road passes immediately into caatinga, after a narrow transition zone of agave plantations. The characteristic trees and plants of the true

[19] Ibid., April 1964, p. 51.

16. South of Joazeirinho, 1959

sertão are seen, such as the facheiro, caatingueiro, xique-xique, and so on. There is an abundance of coarse quartz pebbles, the soil is dry and crunchy under foot; one sees goats and the whole characteristic sertão association of plants, animals, and land-use patterns.

Near Farinha there are some more-recent landscape changes that do not show on the most recent photos because they occurred after the photos were taken and before 1964.[20] This is the conversion of some of the caatinga-covered areas to agave plantations. One infor-

[20] Ibid., p. 58.

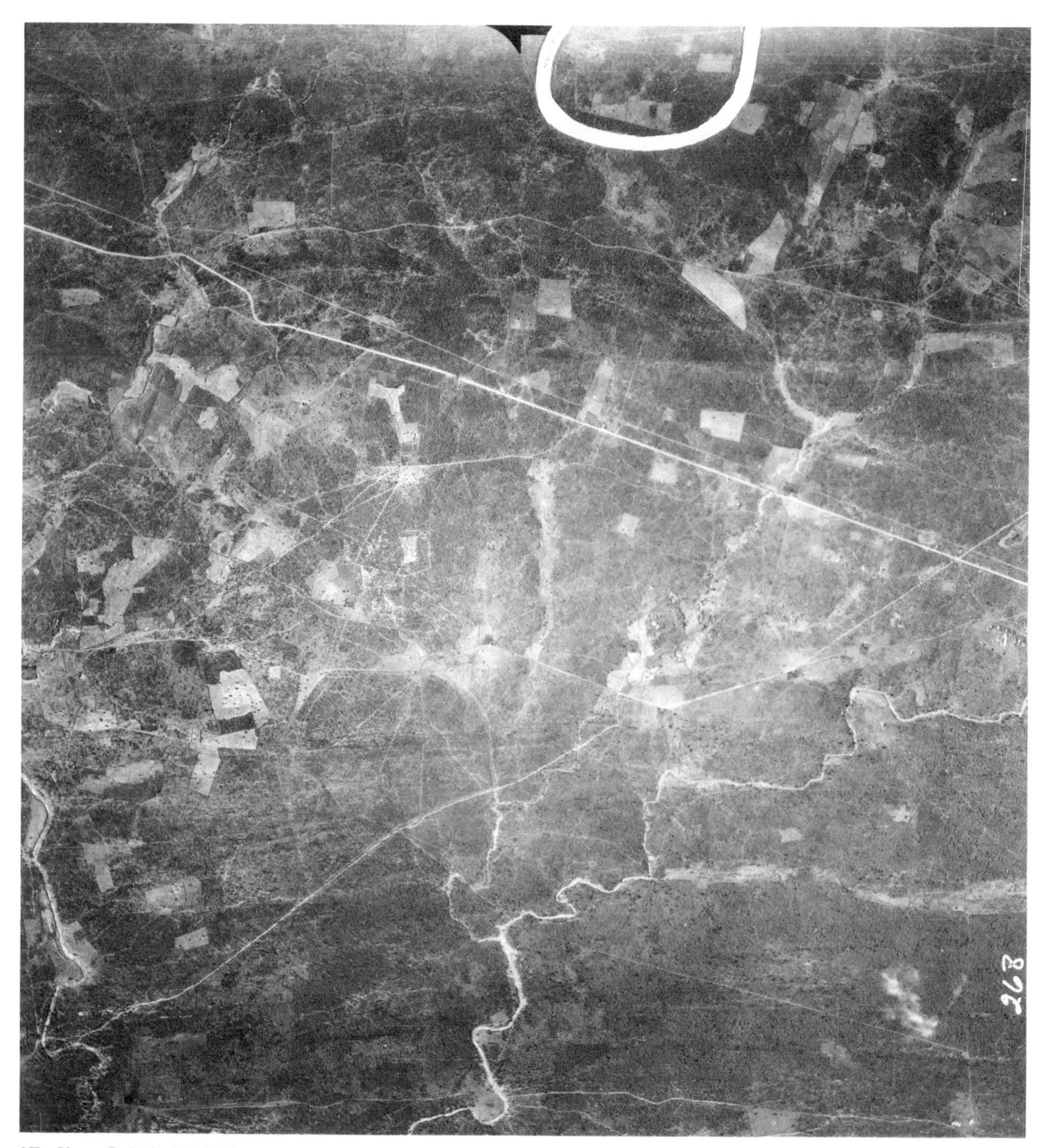

17. Near Soledad, 1942

mant from Alagoa de Roça said that he would plant agave for the first time after he takes care of his "cereals" (maize and beans). Agave will grow in this leeward site that marks the transition from mata seca to caatinga, and of which the facheiro and other xerophytic plants are characteristic. The natural or original vegetation was caatinga but more areas are planted today.

A visit to São João do Cariri takes one to the

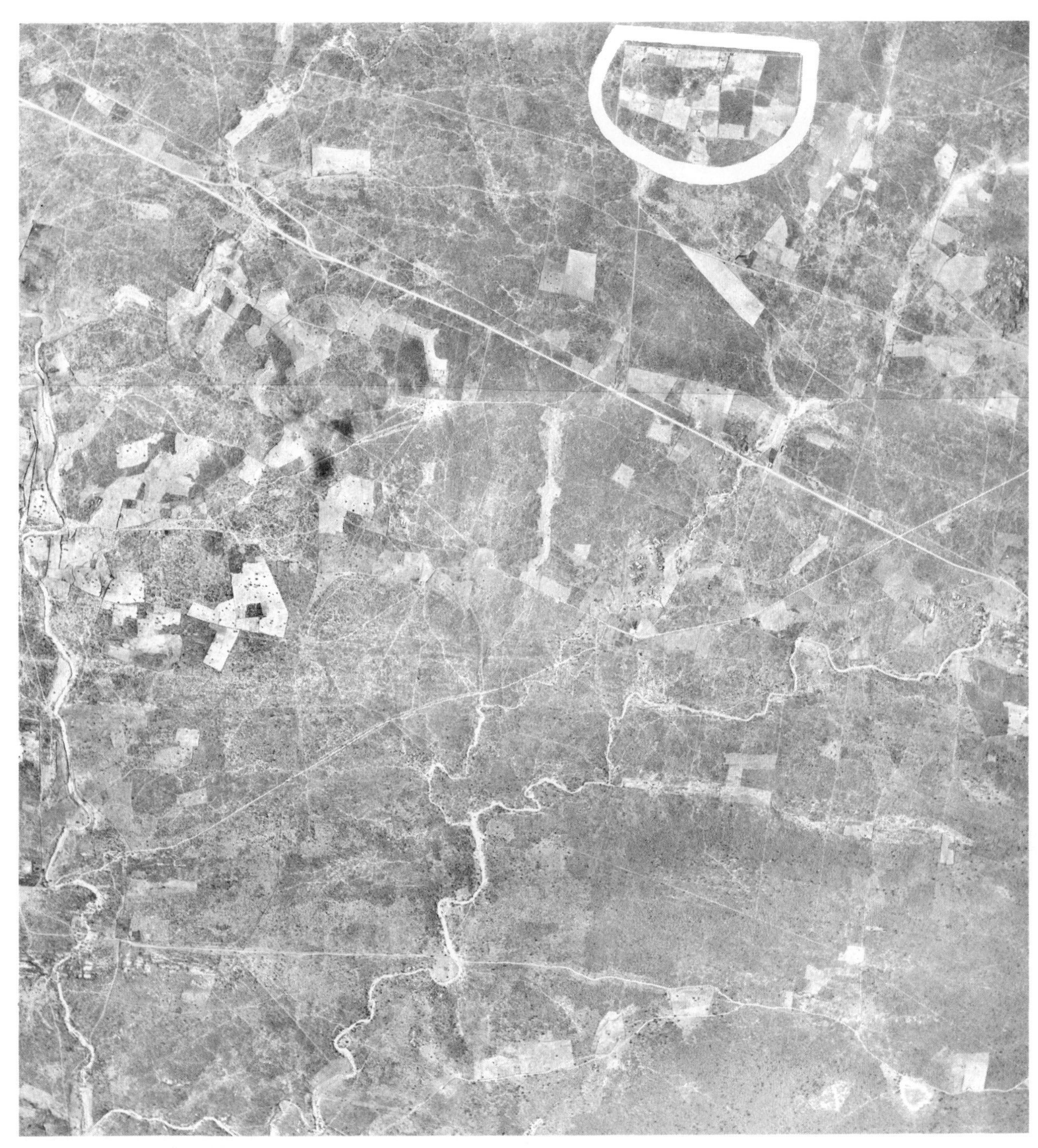

18. Near Soledad, 1959

driest part of all Brazil. One informant who has lived for forty years in the area 16 kilometers southwest of Farinha (Paraíba) said that the zone had not only more timber in the mid-1920s, but that the vegetation was taller and denser and the trees a lot thicker.[21] He said that the area had always been planted in a few subsistence crops with the coming of the rainy

[21] Ibid., p. 68.

19. Near Farinha, 1942

season, especially in the lower places, but that the dominant land use had traditionally been extensive cattle raising. Another informant stated that the entire zone had been unfenced open range in the 1920s. Subdivision of property has occurred; where a piece of land had one owner in the 1920s, it belonged in the 1960s to five or six owners because of the division of the old fazendas by inheritance. The division of property occurs when the head of the family dies; the law provides that 50 percent of the land goes to the widow, if there has been a

20. Near Farinha, 1959*a*

civil marriage, and the remaining 50 percent is divided up by the children. If the man and woman have not had a civil marriage, then all the land goes to the children. The judge or court decides the disposition of the property after an inventory has been made and thirty days have passed. The caatinga of the 1920s was much more closed, although there were still some wood lot reserves. Some fazendeiros live on the fazenda, others live in town. Some fazendeiros

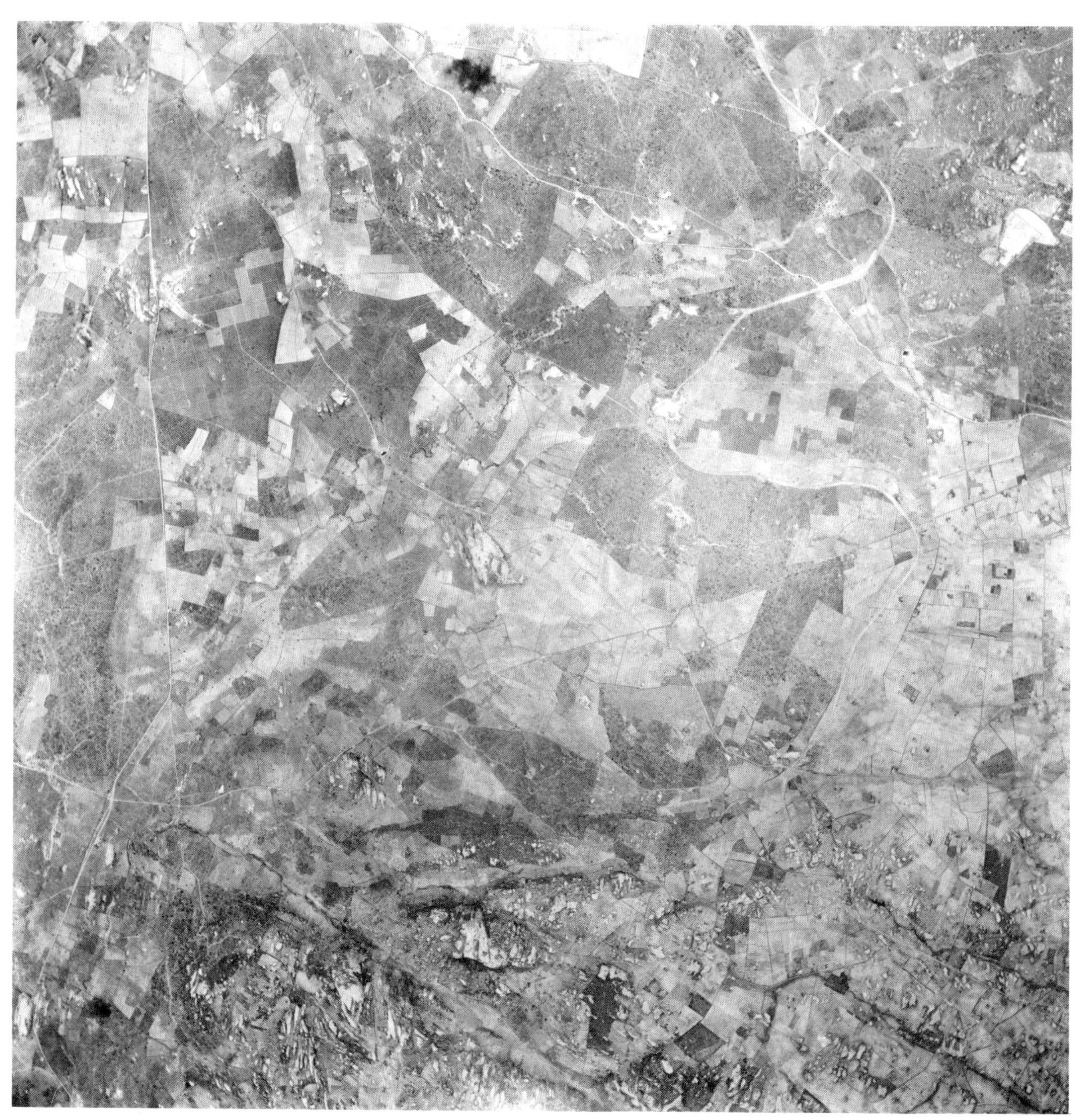

21. Near Farinha, 1959*b*

have no moradores, others have four or five. The animals here are relatively tame; they do not require the care of many vaqueiros. In the 1920s the vaqueiros were paid with the sorte; today practically all are salaried. They have a certain degree of security, but there are upper limits to their ambition. Today agave is the boom crop and its influence extends to some areas in this caatinga. Palma (spineless cactus) is also planted where it was not formerly grown.

In places like São João do Cariri, there are few possibilities for employment. One possibility is fence construction. An interview with three boys from Malhadinha revealed that they were paid 300 cruzeiros per day (30 cents) with lunch included, or 500 cruzeiros (50 cents) if they packed their own lunches. For that wage each boy was expected to build a 3-meter length of sturdy wooden fence per day.[22]

Along the road just south of Campina Grande and that lies still within the Cariri zone there are properties ranging in size from about 50 to 1,500 hectares. According to the Agente Fiscal located 47 kilometers south of Campina Grande, this area began to be fenced as recently as 1940.[23] The fences were first built by the owners to protect their own forage from the grazing of other fazendeiros' animals. Division of the land has continued through inheritance, although many sons have sold their shares to their brothers who have remained as managers. Some of the children move to the large cities in southern and central Brazil. In one family with ten children, three now live in Rio de Janeiro; they return for a home visit every six to thirty-six months. A place such as this home is closely tied to the regional center, Campina Grande, by two buses daily in both directions. It is interesting that agriculture now forms about 50 percent of the economic base of the area—due to the agave boom which began here around 1947—with cattle providing the other 50 percent. Previously the cattle raising dominated.

In summary, the landscape of the sertão is changing slowly and selectively. Most of these changes are linked to greater or lesser accessibility to urban markets and to the roads that lead to those markets. The valorization of commercial cash crops, such as agave or cotton (formerly), and the valorization of beef cattle, are having their impact in the sertão. And yet, because the sertão is located so far from these markets, the most immediate impact is felt in the zone closer to the coastal cities, including not only the zona da mata, but especially the agreste with its more varied panoply of landscapes.

[22] Ibid.
[23] Ibid., p. 69.

Chapter Seven
THE AGRESTE

To the observant traveler in Northeast Brazil, the agreste gives a strong impression of being very distinct from the humid zona da mata on the one side and the dry sertão on the other. But even more striking than the physical differences between the agreste and its neighboring zones is a certain almost undefinable quality of life.

As one proceeds upwards in elevation along the piedmont slopes of the Borborema massif in Pernambuco, for example along the road from Palmares toward Garanhuns, he drives for an entire morning through a sea of green sugarcane, and when the cane is high one is almost lost, overwhelmed by that immense green vastness. In the zona da mata one moves as though through a blind alley, never seeing clearly all the horizons in all directions or even the more immediate features of the landscape.

Past Palmares one begins to climb and to feel a drop in temperature; he can see the surrounding landscape and look back down upon the incredibly vivid green patchwork quilt of the mata landscape.[1] It seems that he is literally on top of the world. There are more people on horseback; these people seem to have a more independent air about them. They seem more prosperous than the people of the sugar areas, or rather less poor. The horizons are more open and accessible. It is an exciting and esthetically pleasing landscape. One feels literally and figuratively on top of the world because he can look down on all sides. This is the part of the Northeast Brazil where there are more small independent farmers. They are poor, to be sure, but what little they produce they can keep for themselves. There is a greater diversity in the kinds of land use and in the systems of land tenure here. It would be well to look into the work relations and systems of work found in the agreste today.

[1] Field notes, January 1964, p. 5.

LAND AND LABOR

We have already noted that the transition area of the agreste possesses characteristics clearly distinguishing it from the mata and the sertão. There are diversities in the types of land use and, consequently, in the systems of labor. We shall stress here the regional importance of the small property and of the economic and cultural levels of the small landowners. From there we shall comment on the tenure systems of the sugarcane, agave, and livestock zones, and finally say something about the coffee and tobacco zones.

The small property is of primary importance in a discussion of agrarian problems in the agreste. More than 86 percent of the farms in the agreste are properties of less than 20 hectares, although they comprise only 14 percent of the total area.[2] These small properties form a rural middle class that has a standard of living

[2] Manuel Correia de Andrade, *A Terra e o Homen no Nordeste*, p. 152.

View of agreste farmland from the heights of the moister Serra do Oratorio. Note rows of maize and dense aveloz hedgerows.

well below that of the large and medium-sized properties but, at the same time, they have an economic and social situation that is still much better than that of the landless workers. Among these small landowners there is an accentuated economic hierarchy that is determined not only by the size of the property but also by its location and soil fertility. Locally, people call the larger properties *sitios,* while the tiny lots of less than one hectare (2.5 acres) they call *chão da casa,* or house lots. Land use and the living level of these small-farm owners also vary from one place to another. In the Brejo of Areia in Paraíba, for example, they practically imitate the traditional senhores de engenho, cultivating sugarcane and agave, but between the agave rows they also grow the traditional subsistence crops of maize and beans. They often also hold jobs as masons, carpenters, mechanics, and so forth, which guarantees them some income. These are artisans, artistas locally, who have a trade that stands them in good stead against hard times.

In the coffee areas of the Pernambucan brejos, the properties are also greatly subdivided. There are sitios in brejos, such as that of the Serra do Vento in Bom Jardim, or the brejo of the Serra Vermelha in Caruarú, and there are the brejos of Bezerros and Camocim of São Felix, in which the small landowners grow a little coffee a few cajú nuts (the cajueira tree shades the coffee), a little black pepper, and some fruit trees, such as orange, mango, avacado, jaca—all in the same field. There is a true vegetal promiscuity in land use from which the owner, using but a small area, seeks to maximize his use of it even though the income yield is small. These owners do not know or use proper soil conservation methods and do not have the money to buy fertilizers; therefore they have a small production that provides an income but that is not sufficient to support a family. The farmer supplements his small income by working as a wage worker on the large and middle-sized properties nearby, or else he may emigrate to the sugar zones to work in the sugar mills, leaving his wife to look after their small property during his absence. And so it happens that around September a great army of landless farmers and small-farm owners migrate to the zona da mata, returning to their agreste homelands with the first rains.

The small landowner of the agreste is also concerned with his self-sufficiency, seeking out those areas in which he can plant some aipim and manioc, some maize associated with beans and fava, and can also raise a few animals. The animals usually include a milk cow or young heifer, which grazes on a tether. The cow furnishes milk to the family and gives birth to calves that can be sold, and the proceeds spent for clothes and other items not produced at home. The heifer is almost always bought at a cattle fair, at one or two years of age, and is fattened and resold at maturity. It is also common for each family to raise pigs, which are usually sold at the end of the year to pay for the extra expenses of Christmas and New Year's festivities. The other animals include, above all, goats to provide milk when there are no cows available.

As to the work relations that apply to landless workers, it should be noted that the broadest areas have the association of land-tenure aspects that are linked to cattle raising and associated cotton and cereal production. In the agreste cattle are raised on fazendas that are much smaller than those of the sertão. The fazendeiro generally divides the property into different enclosed areas, some for the cattle during the rainy season, others for them during the dry season. During the greater part of the year the property is divided into small lots and rented to farmers who receive the land in March with the obligation to return it in December and January. There is no need to have many hired hands or a large number of moradores, as there is on essentially agricultural properties. The standards of livestock raising cannot yet be considered truly intensive, although the level is higher than that of the sertão. The fazendeiros defend themselves and their herds from the droughts by using seasonal migration of cattle to better pastures, by giving supplementary rations to the cattle, and by letting the cattle graze on leftover stalks and remains of the harvested fields of maize, cotton, and rice.

The seasonal migrations used since the eighteenth century are still made between the mata and agreste when the landowner owns property in either one or the other region, or between the caatinga and the brejos of altitude in the agreste itself. In the first case the cattle are driven to the mata area in September when the cane harvest begins, at a time when the agreste pastures are dry, and when there is an abundance of sugarcane remains for forage. With the first rains, in March, the cattle are returned to the caatinga where they spend the "green" season,—that is, the period when the pastures turn green with fresh shoots of milhã and capim raiz, which are local grasses. In the old days, it was common for the senhor de engenho to have a fazenda in the agreste where he would pass the "winter," or rainy season. Today this custom is disappearing. One reason is the high cost of land and the intensification of farm work on the sugar properties, along with the recent expansion of cane areas because of the constant increase in the productive capacities of the usinas. A similar movement occurs between the caatinga and the brejos of altitude. This transhumance movement has already been described in the preceding chapter.

The improvement of the quality of cattle and the rationalization of management techniques caused the fazendeiros to seek plants to serve as forage for cattle; for this reason, since World War II there has been an intensification in the planting of palma and pasture grasses. Palma is widely dispersed in the semiarid areas of less rigorous climate, such as the Paraíban and Pernambucan agreste and in the Alagoan sertão.

The planting of palma requires considerable manpower. Hundreds of hectares of palma can be cultivated, however, without large capital outlays since it is a permanent crop that yields for twelve to fifteen years. The moradores cultivate it in areas the landowners have handed over to them already cleared and ready for planting, together with the *raquetes,* or young palma plants. The farmers are obliged to plant the raquetes and to keep the field weeded; they can grow maize, fava, beans, and cotton for themselves, between the rows of palma. For three to four years, while the palma is still not mature and needs only two to three weedings annually, the farmer takes care of both it and his own crops without any capital outlay required of the landowner. When the palma is ready to be cut, it casts considerable shade over the adjacent areas and hinders the growth of the interplanted crops; at this time the farmer leaves the property, leaving the land and the palma entirely to the landowner. From then on, the owner has only to pay a daily wage to workers to weed the field once a year.

Cattle raising actually requires few people. The vaqueiro today is simply an employee who is trained to handle animals, knows how to cure them of illnesses, how to rope and brand them, and how to care for them in every imaginable way. In the preceding chapter we saw something of the demanding life the vaqueiro leads. One estimate is that two good vaqueiros can handle up to two thousand cattle under ideal conditions. The beef animal that has been raised in relatively small fenced areas, coming to the corral frequently to be vaccinated, branded, cured, or fed is always tame and more easily led by the vaqueiro than the half-wild beasts that are left on the open ranges of the remotest sertões. For this reason, the vaqueiro today is an administrator, or assists the owner in administration. He checks and repairs fences, drives animals to be sold at the fairs, drives them in their seasonal migrations, supervises the milk deliveries, and gets paid a salary of between $5 and $10 a week in addition to having a house and a garden plot. That old custom of paying the vaqueiro with one-fourth of all newborn animals under his care has been entirely abolished in the agreste since the cattle, having been improved with new strains of zebu, holandes, and schuwytz, now command very high prices. In short, cattle are too valuable to give away as presents or wages. The vaqueiro, then, is relatively worse off since he no longer has any hope of actually becoming a fazendeiro himself, which he could have become under the quarta, or sorte system of remuneration.

The utilization of the stubble and chaff of the subsistence crops by cattle causes the fazendeiro to maintain economic relations with a large number of farmers. These are the renters who usually live in the cities, towns, and villages nearby—or even on their own small properties, since many renters work a larger, rented field but still own a "house lot" or minifundium where they live with their families. Today it is rare for a landowner to allow the free use of land in exchange for grazing privileges on the stubble and chaff, since the number of farmers wanting land is great and the available area is limited. The lands are almost always rented for prices varying with their quality, the distance from consuming centers, and from busy roads. The annual rent for a quadra (12,100 square meters) is between 500 and 6,000 cruzeiros (in 1962), or between $5 and $60. The rent is paid in money or in kind (cotton). The farmer has no guarantee of renewal of his contract, nor any written document that legalizes the agreement; he remains at the mercy of the landowner in any emergency. Generally the land is delivered to the farmer in March, with the first rains. Once the land is plowed, he plants maize and beans; in May he cultivates herbaceous cotton; in June and July he harvests the beans and part of the corn, still green, for use in the June festivities of São João, and so on. (The agricultural calendar is shown in figure 22.) The harvest of dry maize is made in September, and is used for feeding both man and animals. The harvest of cotton begins in December and extends through January, at which time the land is returned to the landowner so that he can graze his cattle on the remnants of chaff and stalks left by the other crops. In March the whole cycle begins again and the land is turned back to the farmers. Those farmers are the same ones who, during the month of September, have very little to do in the agreste; they therefore migrate to the sugarcane areas—to work in the mills, which begin to function during September—making the seasonal migrations typical of Northeast Brazil from Rio Grande do Norte to Sergipe. The family is left behind to weed and care for the small farm plot, harvesting the cotton and using the dried maize for food.[3]

The high population density of the agreste and the precarious conditions of life there have transformed the region into a center of emigration; many people have abandoned the

[3] Ibid., p. 162.

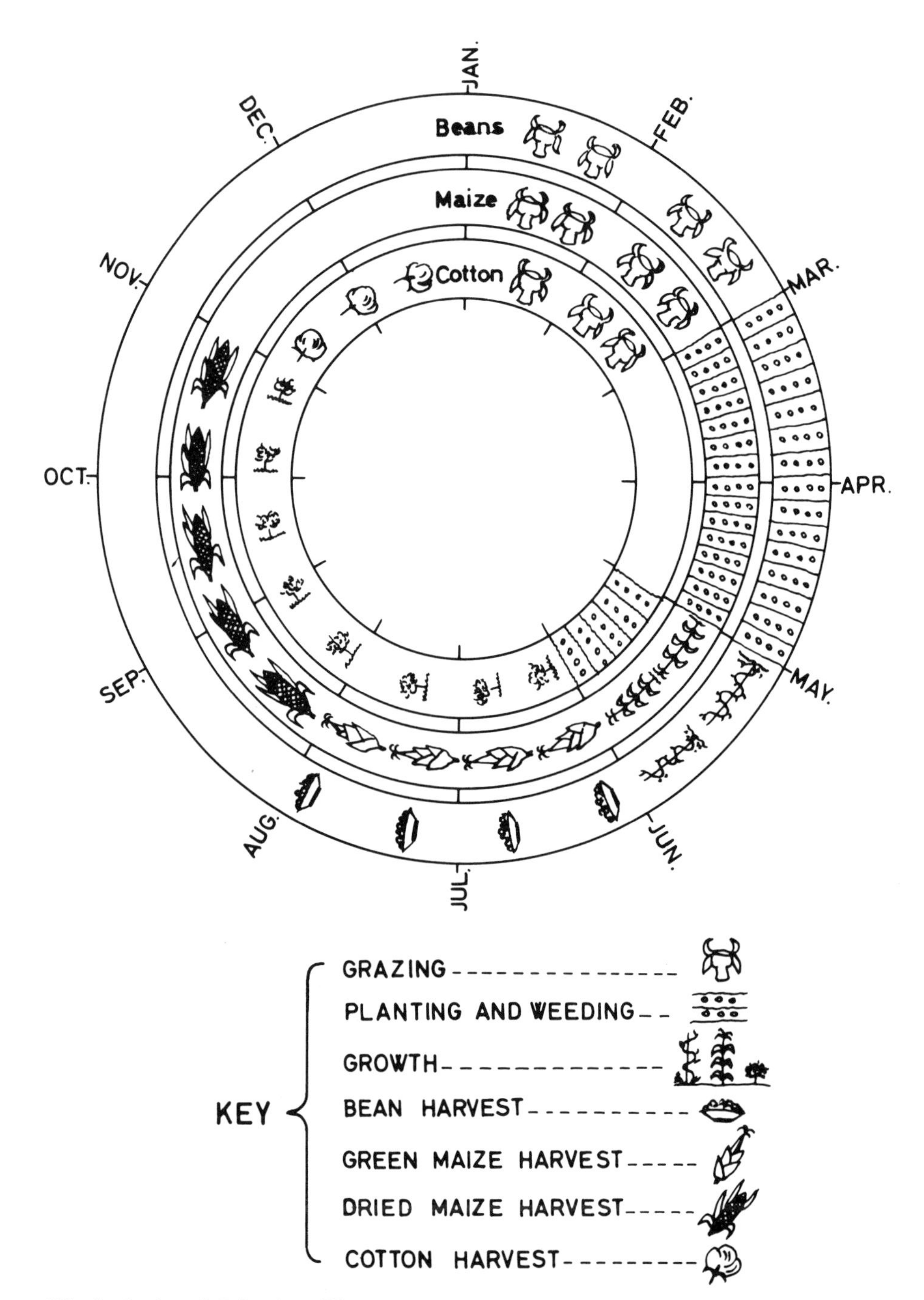

22. Agricultural Calendar—Diagram

area and moved to the larger cities, either to the coastal state capitals of the Northeast—Recife, especially—or, by way of the long arduous routes of the paus-de-arara (trucks that transport people), to Rio de Janeiro, São Paulo, Brasilia, and northern Paraná. This migration of workers to central and southern Brazil has disturbed the sugar property owners who are feeling an increasing lack of manpower to work in the cane fields and mills.

In the Paraíban *brejo*, especially in the municipios of Areia, Serraria, Pirpirituba, and Alagoa Grande, the rural work relationships take on a different aspect, since there sugarcane is dominant, followed by agave. We shall have more to say about the brejos in the following chapter. Nevertheless, in the brejos we find typical plantation agriculture, on a more modest scale than in the zona da mata, occupying large and middle-sized properties. The numerous salaried workers devote their energies to two export crops (sugar and agave) which are subject to the fluctuations and vagaries of external markets. In this sense the brejos have strong economic similarities to the zona da mata.

Another crop that generates specific work relationships is coffee, and although the coffee plagues have dealt a crippling blow to coffee production as of the 1920s, there is still a small amount produced. The large and middle-sized properties have moradores who, as in the Paraíban brejo, receive a house to live in and a small farm plot for growing subsistence crops. It is rare for land to be rented there since the landowner seldom has cattle to take advantage of the crop stubble. In general, the morador gives three days of service each week to the fazenda and receives a salary of less than the legal minimum wage. The three days of obligated work can be increased or decreased depending upon the exigencies of the agricultural work season. In Alagoas it is customary for the worker when he does not live on the fazenda property, to receive in addition to his small wage the midday meal, consisting of beans with charque or with salted fish. The harvest of coffee begins in August and lasts until November or December. It is done slowly, by collecting only the ripened coffee beans and leaving the green ones for later.

In the tobacco-growing areas, there is another type of work régime. These areas form an important zone in the sandy lands of the agreste, the most outstanding of which include the municipios of Bananeiras in Paraíba, Gravatá in Pernambuco, Arapiraca in Alagoas, and Lagarto in Sergipe. These four states produce about one-tenth of the national tobacco production. To-acco growing is extremely labor-intensive, and is cultivated by renters or sharecroppers and by small and middle-sized landowners.

The planting of tobacco is done in the rainy season, beginning in March, followed by two transplantations, and the final harvest in August. Thirty days after the first cutting of to-bacco growing is extremely labor-intensive, and Wages are low, and much of the extra manpower needed during the busy harvest season is furnished by day-wage workers from adjacent areas.

The tobacco leaves are hung up to cure in drying sheds for twenty-five days, or else they are rolled up for ninety days to cure into fumo de corda (plug tobacco). Tobacco requires special care, fertilizers, and treatments before it reaches the market.

Because it is a crop of short vegetative cycle, other crops can be rotated with it to benefit from the fertilizers that were applied for the tobacco. In Ubá, maize is rotated with tobacco, while in Arapiraca it is herbaceous cotton, planted in July in the middle of the tobacco field to be harvested in January. In this way the landowner and the sharecropper (meeiro) derive corresponding profits from two crops grown in the same field. A small amount of subsistence food production also comes from maize, beans, and fava. The fact remains, however, that tobacco is not a crop that supports large areas or large numbers of people in the Northeast or even in the agreste; it is more a specialty crop that touches the lives of few people in a few very limited areas.

ESPERANÇA: A CASE STUDY OF MAN IN THE AGRESTE[4]

Let us turn again to Gerard Prost's field research comparing Pocinhos and Esperança.

Esperança is 25 kilometers north of Campina Grande and lies close to the "continental divide" of the Borborema highlands at just over 600 meters above sea level. The agreste around Esperança is a densely settled region of exclusively small properties, of subsistence food crops. There are no pastures or speculative crops, but solely open field areas broken only by aveloz hedgerows or rare residual forested areas. The crops cover the land with their green mantle during the rainy season, but the landscape is a brilliant white during the dry season because of the white sandy soils. The layer of sands is 0.5 to 2.0 meters deep and rests on clays. The 700 millimeter of rainfall come from February-March to July-August.

The small differences in the distribution of soil moisture are carefully exploited by farmers. The sands of the higher places hold their moisture for a shorter time, as the water filters to the lower areas. In any one season the crops of the baixios, or lower slopes, are always greener and more luxuriant than those of the altos, or upper slopes. The flat bottomland varzeas are rarely cultivated because they are swampy during the rainy season and salty during the dry season.

[4] This account of the agreste area around Esperança is a summary of the detached study by Gerard Prost cited in chapter 6.

The planted slopes are divided into a multitude of fields, or roçados. The word roça, which is generally used throughout Brazil to mean slash-and-burn agriculture, means in Esperança only a field planted in manioc. The small whitewashed cottages are scattered among the fields, surrounded by a few trees. The small patches of intensive crop cultivation around each house give the agreste of Esperança the distinctive air of an authentic peasant farming area, and this has existed there for around forty years.

Crop associations and the agricultural calendar in an intensive subsistence agriculture

The example shown in table 5 (and taken from Prost)[5] is that of an average sitio (small farm) that supports one family and uses both an alto and baixio zone.

We can see that the fields on the lower slopes are almost always used; maize, beans, potatoes, cotton. The ridges support the more delicate crops, notably the sweet potatoes; similarly in the baixos a few select square meters are permanently planted in vegetables, such as squash and pumpkin. The upper slopes do not hold enough soil moisture to grow vegetables or many potatoes (Irish potatoes, or batata inglesa). Manioc is the characteristic crop of the altos.

These small fields of intensive food-crop cultivation are located among the agave fields that furnish a cash income to the farmer. A few square meters may be in palma and some elephant grass, which give several crops per year that are used as forage for the three or four cattle in a corral on the baixio. During the rainy season, all the animals except for one milk cow are sent to graze in the open caatinga, on a fazenda in the Cariri to the west. This agreste

[5] Gerard Prost, "Dans le Nord-Est du Brasil," Extract, p. 34.

Table 5. Agriculture calendar—Esperança

Month	Baixio (lower slopes)	Alto (upper slopes)
January	Clear land	Clear land
February	Prepare the cleared fields	
March	Plant: winter (rainy season)—maize, beans, potatoes	Plant: winter (rainy season)—maize, beans, or potatoes, manioc and maize.
April–May	Do two weedings	
End of May–June	Harvest (except for manioc)	
	Prepare and plant for the dry season:	
July	Potatoes, beans	manioc
August–September	Do two weedings	
End September–October	Harvest beans and potatoes	
November–December	Harvest cotton	
March		Interplant maize with manioc
April–June		Do two weedings
July–August		Harvest maize; do two weedings
September–November		Harvest manioc

of Esperança offers an interesting association of intensive polyculture—with limited cattle raising—in a tropical climate with a dry season.

Cultivation techniques

Much of the laborious work occurs in the dry season. The farmer builds the ridges or mounds and levels the soil; he makes the "bed," he cuts the unwanted weeds with a hoe and buries them; they are never burned. If the field is going to be planted with potatoes, a thin layer of manure is laid down, and the mounds are divided into quadrants. The ideal is to apply four truckloads of manure per hectare.

After several weeks the rains begin. The mounds serve many purposes and are not typical at all of the rather slipshod techniques of the average Brazilian roça farmer. If the "winter" is too rainy, the mounds keep the plant roots from rotting. They facilitate weeding and provide a place in the trenches or rows to discard the weeds and dead plants. On the upper slopes the mounds are built along the contour to retain the moisture; on the middle and lower slopes the mounds run up and down the slope to facilitate drainage. Some of the mounds even take into account the direction of the rain; if the mound is oriented at right angles to the direction of the wind and rain, it will be destroyed or greatly diminished. For this reason they are generally laid out east-west, parallel to the winds, even if it means they trend up and down the slope. The furrows are 40 centimeters wide; the mounds are 80 to 90 centimeters wide and 30 centimeters high.

There is no shifting around of the fields, as with slash-and-burn agriculture, nor is there crop rotation on the same fields. The choices of land use are largely determined by the natural conditions: potatoes can only be grown with the fruits, in the baixos; and manioc can only be grown on the altos. For most of the farmers, the crop requirements for certain land qualities prevent all possibilities of crop rotation.

It is interesting to gauge the length of work time necessary to farm in this area. One hectare of baixio, with its two farming periods, and 1 hectare of baixio, with its first period of polyculture followed by manioc, *each* require eighty to ninety days of work of which fifty to sixty days are spent weeding. In the second year, the manioc field will require only thirty days of labor.

Let us consider a property of 3 hectares of land that has 1 hectare of baixio and 2 of alto, of which the first alto hectare is planted in manioc one year and the second is planted in manioc the second year. (Manioc takes eighteen months to mature here.) The total number of work days is increased to 210 (90 plus 90 plus 30), which corresponds to the number of working days in nine months. This means that an active man can handle 4 or 5 hectares. In one exceptional case a vigorous farmer who had owned his land for only two years was working 7 hectares, but he had a family of four young children to feed, and was well motivated![6]

Yields

Yields, given below in kilograms per hectare, vary widely according to the quality of land management and the climatic variations:

Potatoes (batata inglesa)	2,500 to 5,000
Maize	250 to 1,000
Beans (mulatinho)	500 to 3,000
Manioc (farinha or meal)	1,000 to 5,000
Cotton	150 to 500
Sweet potatoes	about 3,000

Problems and prospects

The two characteristics of this part of the agreste, its complete occupation and dense population, are relatively recent developments. Before 1920, the line that separated the zones of open pasture from the cultivated zones (the travessão) passed about a dozen kilometers to the east of Esperança. In the present agreste, there are only small fields that are well enclosed to protect them from animals. As the old residents would say, "It was a real Cariri," or, in other words, it was wild caatinga in the old days.

[6] Ibid., p. 37.

Beginning in 1915–18, some people from the nearby brejo, to the east, bought land here and proceeded to clear it. By 1940 there was practically no caatinga left. Thus, within two decades, a sparse population that was adapted to life on the fazenda had been replaced by one of the densest rural populations in all Brazil. This growth has produced overpopulation and soil exhaustion. Manuring is required now, but no one has sufficient cattle to supply it. It is a vicious circle: the more the population grows, the less land each family has per capita, and the less money it has to buy sufficient manure to maintain or raise the productivity of the soil. Therefore, the soil becomes exhausted.

The owners of minifundios are in the tightest bind; of a total of 118 sitios surveyed, 74 (or 66 percent) had land whose extent was *6 hectares or less!*[7] On the other hand, these owners of small properties are in another way better off than many Nordestinos because of the healthier social structure within which they live. They are not isolated, they can see a number of neighbor's houses from their own front door; their children go to school; the people enjoy a certain community of existence and interest that is absent in most other rural areas dominated by the large land holdings.

THE BOUNDARY BETWEEN THE SERTÃO (CARIRI) AND THE AGRESTE

The Cariri of the Paraíban sertão and the agreste of Esperança comprise two relatively homogeneous and distinct regions. In the Cariri, the agave fields and cattle grazing in the caatinga dominate the landscape, and the population is sparse. The agreste, on the other hand, is distinguished by its small properties,

[7] Ibid., p. 43.

intensively cultivated, and densely populated. Why was the recently established boundary between these two regions fixed where it now is, and not elsewhere? Are the reasons physical or are they cultural and historical?

The boundary and the physical habitat

Map 11, again after Prost (as is map 12), shows the crest zone of the agreste near Esperança where the distribution of the contour lines of 650 meters, 700 meters, and 750 meters can be compared to the distribution of farm properties. The coarse dotted line marks the western and northern limit of manioc and potato cultivation, and coincides closely with the orographic climax of the crest area. The picture is quite simple; the pattern of small fields and crops in the agreste is closely linked to the higher moisture of the windward slope of the Borborema; the larger properties of the sertão are found to the leeward western side of the crest, generally below 700 meters elevation.

A more detailed examination, however, reveals that the physical factors do not explain completely the advance of some small properties toward the west. We must seek other reasons. On map 12, which shows phases of land clearing, there is a striking coincidence between the present boundary and the limit that separates the two zones cleared in different periods. To the east, all lands were cleared between 1920 and 1940, while in the west most of the lands were cleared after 1942–45. We can say that the "hinge" period, 1940–45, was the time of the fixing of the boundary. Let us examine the cultural processes and actions preceding and following that period.

Development between 1920 and 1940. Two developments stood out during that twenty year interval between 1920 and 1940: the definitive establishment of the fazendeiro families toward the west, and the breakup of the large properties to the east. Many fazendas in the sertão were bought up as pieces of larger fazendas when the larger fazenda was divided, usually when the old fazendeiro died. The wave of small farmers from the east proceeded little by little with the clearing of the caatinga, whereupon the agreste replaced the Cariri with a type of cultural landscape more characteristic of humid zones: the small property replaced the large.

The fazendeiros sold their land for various reasons, such as the dying out of old families locally when many children moved away, and the need for money. They sold their land either to a sole buyer or, more commonly, in pieces to several buyers. Beginning around 1915–20, the fazendeiros encountered an abundance of farmers desiring to buy land and thus the pioneer front of small farmers advanced westward at the expense of the traditional cattle fazenda. Around 1940, the westward advance of the agreste had progressed to the zone where we observe it in the mid-1960s.

Development since 1940. The westward advance of the small property proceeded very slowly after 1940; nevertheless, the numbers of people desiring land grew, thus producing the pressure of population on limited land areas that led to the minifundios.

The fazendas to the west of the boundary have retained their territorial expanses despite the buildup of pressure from the east. One reason is the markedly drier ecological conditions of the sertão (Cariri). The other was the historical accident of agave introduction in the 1940s, which allowed the fazendeiros to make large profits by planting agave on former caatinga lands and, in the meanwhile, watch the land values of their extensive holdings rise rapidly. The holding of land for speculation has been not only a fact of life in urban Brazil, especially since 1950, but also in rural areas.

11. Crest Zone of Agrests near Esperança
1. Contour lines; 2. Northern and western limits of the manioc and potato cultures; 3. Approximate property limits

In some cases, fazendeiros took back lands they had formerly rented out to tenant farmers and planted agave for their own accounts.

The present boundary separates two very different domains: that of the large property covered by caatinga and cattle with abundant recent agave plantations, and that of the small intensively cultivated property of the small farmer. In the areas to the northwest of Esperança these small farmers had already reached

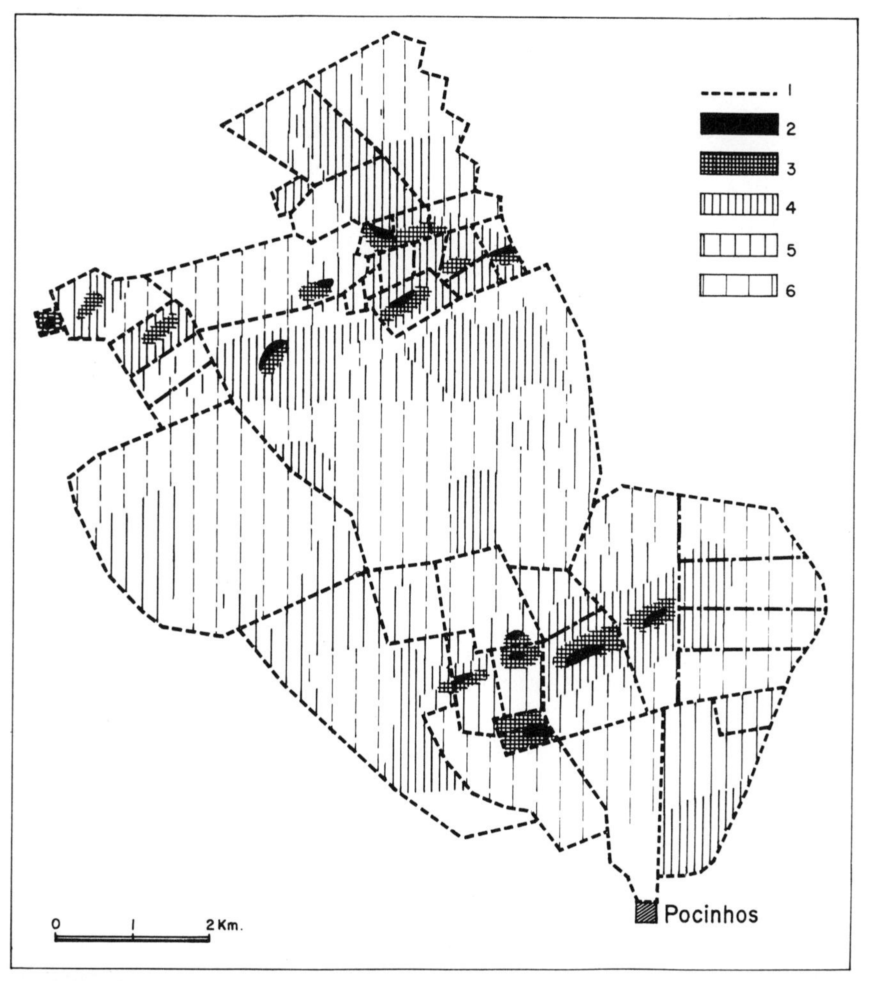

12. Phases of Land Clearing
1. Property limits; 2. Lands cleared 1880–1920; 3. Lands cleared 1920–40; 4. Lands cleared 1940–60; 5. Lands cleared 1960–66; 6. Caatinga

their ecological limits by 1940. In the south, the small farmers would have advanced another 20 kilometers to the west if agave had not given a new vigor to the fazendas there, blocking their advance and the advance of their subsistence food crops as well.

This equilibrium, however, rests solely upon the world market price of sisal, and in 1966 an agave crisis developed that resulted in a stoppage of almost all planting and harvesting operations. Rather than sell some of their large properties, the fazendeiros awaited the hoped-for resumption of the upward spiral of land values and sisal prices. Some of them transformed their fields into planted pastures, which both assured them an income and required less labor.

It appears, therefore, that the present boundary between the Cariri (sertão) and the agreste of Esperança does not really correspond to a bioclimatic limit, but more to a pioneer front of small cultivators stabilized there for over twenty years. The development of agave plantations was responsible for this stabilization. Whether or not the boundary will remain in the same place depends upon how the fazendeiros adjust to the agave crisis. If they hang on to their large holdings and wait out the crisis, the boundary will remain; if they begin to sell out to small farmers, the westward movement of the sertão/agreste boundary will resume.

RECENT LANDSCAPE CHANGES

Landscape changes in the agreste over the past thirty years can be summed up in two words: aveloz and agave. The hedgerows of aveloz have become almost synonymous with the agreste region, and signify increasingly throughout this century the further subdivision of the agreste into properties of growing intensity of land use. Agave is the commercial crop that has brought an economic boom to not only the agreste, but to broad areas of Northeast Brazil. It has affected the valorization of areas hitherto considered—in the prenineteenth century—as land suitable only for extensive cattle raising, or, in the early twentieth century, as land suited only to subsistence crops mixed with grazing and some cotton growing. One can see the long hedgerows, extending in some places for several kilometers in straight lines back at right angles from the stream banks. In this respect—the obsession for land with river frontage—there is a resemblance to the sertão.

A dominant theme of recent landscape change in the agreste is that of intense and growing population pressure. This is the part of Brazil where the minifundio exists. Why has the minifundio occurred? It has been partly because of the attractiveness of the area as one of the last agricultural frontiers within the settled zones of Brazil where small, independent farmers can establish themselves. The rush for the remaining land along with the high birth rate has resulted in fragmentation of properties to sizes too small to maintain a family with even a minimal standard of living. Until the early nineteenth century, the same extensive type of man-land relationships existed in the agreste as in the sertão: a few men, more cattle, and land without end. The early twentieth century has witnessed the areal diversification of the agreste wherein subsistence crops and the cash crops of cotton and sugarcane varied the scene. Air photos of 1942 show considerable areas of capoeirão and mata seca of respectable size, as well as many grazing lands and croplands. More recent air photos of the agreste and my fieldwork in 1964 and 1973 revealed very little forest reserve or anything that could be called mata. Not only have the areas of capoeirão or mata seca been cleared, but also the areas devoted to cattle raising have shrunk, and almost the entire zone is devoted to more intensive production of both commercial and food crops. The land hunger of people who have grown up in the agreste is such that they have carried their characteristic agreste-type agriculture westward into less costly lands in the sertão. We find areas of subsistence crops is association with agave that have pushed into the sertão. The transmission and dispersal of agreste cultivation and culture westward, toward the dryward side, does not at all alter the basic fact that progressive desertification is proceeding in the opposite or easterly direction as more and more sertão plant species invade and take over the subhumid and semiarid areas of the agreste.

Figures 23 and 24 illustrate the range of different landscapes seen in the agreste. Figure 23 is an oblique view, looking toward the northwest, of the crest of the Borborema—not far from Esperança, Paraíba. One can see on the same photograph the agreste foreground with its minifundios, remnants of denser vegetation cleared for crops, and the sertão background of open caatinga of the driest Cariris Velhos zone, which in 1942 was still largely unfenced and undifferentiated open range. The foreground catches the orographic moisture on the Borborema crest; the background is the dry leeward rain shadow of the Borborema. To see these views on the same photograph is quite unusual, and further illustrates how sharply the physical gradients vary within short distances in Northeast Brazil.

Figure 24 shows the pattern of hedgerows and property lines extending back at right angles to the stream bank. Successive land divisions, through inheritance, have fragmented the original properties, which may have started out as sesmarias with 1 league of frontage by 3 leagues of depth. Subsequent divisions have occurred parallel to the original lines and at right angles to the rivers. Hence the long, narrow strips of land, often bordered by aveloz hedgerows.

Recent landscape changes in an area around Correntes, in the agreste of Pernambuco 42 kilometers southeast of Garanhuns, reflect a higher valorization of the zone in which maize, beans, and cotton are planted as a means of clearing land for cattle.[8] Ten years are left for a fallow period, then for five or six years cattle are pastured on the land. The land-use cycle can be either of two plans: (1) clearing the capoeira, planting crops, exhausting of the soil by the crops, turning over the land to cattle grazing, then allowing the capoeira to come back while the cattle are there, letting the land lie fallow, clearing the land, and repeating the cycle; or (2) clearing the capoeira, planting pasture grasses, and letting the cattle in directly without any intermediate crop stage.

In another area, west of Recife and as one drives toward Caruarú, one can identify the agreste by the appearance of small, diversified properties. In that part of Pernambuco, the agreste begins just west of Vitória de Santo Antão, at the bottom of the serra das Russas, and continues westward as far as Arcoverde, the "gateway to sertão."

In terms of landscape content, the agreste is much more diverse. Not only is there a greater variety of crops, and of activities pursued, compared to the zona da mata or the sertão, but also there is a greater number of these properties per square kilometer. It seems a kind of microcosm of rural life in a developing society, compared to the zona da mata or the sertão.

As one heads west from João Pessoa toward Campina Grande, he enters the agreste and sees his first aveloz hedgerow and first drying sisal fibers just west of Sapé and some 42 kilometers west of João Pessoa. With the appearance of these two cultural features there is an accompanying and striking decrease in sugar cane fields.

Farther west, at Riachão do Bacamarte, the area was called sertão by a local boy, but an older man stated that it was really agreste and, furthermore, stated that the definition of agreste is the crop association of cotton, maize, beans, and the like—a cultural definition.[9] This may have been true where the area was previously "sertão" in that it was mainly devoted to cattle raising, but now, owing to increasing population pressure on the land, the more recent occupation has brought in the characteristic agreste crop association, as mentioned above. This dispersal of agreste culture proceeded to the west and to the east as well. It is an area where there has been a rapid increase of population. One reason was the asphalt-laying crews of almost five thousand men, some of whom built barracas (huts or shacks) beside the road during its construction and then decided to stay there. The informant above was one of them. Other people of the area are members of local families who have settled on their fragments of the divided plots of their ancestors, and still others have migrated from Rio Grande do Norte, João Pessoa, Campina Grande, Recife, Rio de Janeiro, and other such cities. People tend to travel to wherever there are jobs, and the mammoth road-building programs in Brazil since 1955 have, indirectly, shifted many thousands of people.

In the higher altitude agreste, 20 kilometers

[8] Field notes, January 1964, p. 7.

[9] Ibid., April 1964, p. 43.

23. Oblique View of the Agreste-Sertão Border, 1942

east of Campina Grande, one fifty-six-year-old informant said that there were many more people there than when he was a boy. The majority of the properties have less than 10 hectares and are operated by their owners. There are very few moradores in that area.[10] There are many more fruit trees today because people can now sell their excess fruits, vegetable, potatoes, in Campina Grande. There was more mata, or forest in 1924 as compared to 1964, and in the subsequent decades people took advantage of the fertile forested soils, cleared the trees and planted their roças of maize, potatoes, manioc, and beans, and also raised pigs and chickens.

In the area of Lagoa Seca, just 9 kilometers north of Campina Grande, there are also more fruit trees now than in the 1930s and 1940s. This is because there is a market for fruit, for

[10] Ibid., p. 53.

24. Agreste Hedgerows

garden crops, for tobacco and agave, although manioc and beans remain the basic food commodities since they are the foods that people can fall back on for their own subsistence. In general, most maize is consumed at home. Most farinha de mandioca (manioc meal) is sent to market to be sold. In the 1940s, local farmers sold farinha de mandioca in their own home towns. Higher prices and the presence of a famous and growing feira drew them and their manioc meal to Campina Grande. Of course, improvements in transportation have allowed people to take their produce directly to market where they can get a better price by avoiding at least one middleman.

In the same area near Lagoa Seca, another informant said that in the mid-1930s there were still large stretches of forest, and that there were many more cattle in the 1930s than in the 1960s.[11] These three decades have brought striking changes to this part of the agreste. With increasing mobility, many families try to educate their children. Families that would have remained on the fazenda years ago now try to move to town and leave a manager to look after the fazenda. Why? So that their children can go to school beyond the fourth grade, hopefully even through the colegio, or high school. It is financially difficult to leave a small fazenda where the productivity is insufficient to support both the absenteeism and the added expenses of town living, clothes, and tuition for secondary school—even when the sons of the fazendeiros want the modern life—but the large properties can generally remain more intact, as one son commonly stays on as resident manager. This informant farmer's situation was, admittedly, good as he had 60 hectares to work. He believed that the farm workers are worse off today than during the nineteenth century, particularly in the zona da mata, since the senhores de engenho fed the slaves well so that they would work well. Today everyone is theoretically independent and they go to the areas where they can live better. This informant's grandfather had sought land of his own and had come from the zona da mata where he had been a tenant farmer; then the agreste came to be a zone of convergence of many settlers from both the sertão and the zona da mata.

Lower down, along the eastern escarpment of the Borborema, just north of Juarez Tavora, there is a different situation. There, most of the slopes are covered with light capoeira brush, generally larger properties, and a fairly sparse population. Some of the aveloz fences extend in a straight line for almost 5 kilometers. The cycle there is to cut the mata, burn it, plant cotton (very little in recent years), plant maize and beans.[12] No manioc is planted because it requires one and a half to three years to mature and the landowners want only one year's occupance of their land. The moradores plant maize in January and harvest it in three months. Cotton is harvested after five months and must be planted every year. Cattle are put into the farm plots to feed on the stubble-and-chaff remains after the crop harvest. The cattle naturally benefit the fields by contributing manure to the soil. With the coming of the first rains of the inverno, the crops are planted again. This is an area where agave has had success. There was much more forest in the 1940s than the 1960s. Much of the land here is rented. Each hectare (500 braças) rents for around 1,500 cruzeiros ($1.50) a year. The advantage to the tenant of renting the land is that the entire harvest belongs to him. There are no moradores in the area because the fazendeiros do not want to furnish houses for them nor do they want any commitment to them. The tenant farmers generally live in town and commute or else they maintain a hut in the field where they sleep during the work week, returning home only on weekends.

One important change on the landscape that strikes close to home with the average farmer is that, following the cutting of the forest, the possibilities for finding construction timber become slimmer and slimmer. One informant remarked that twenty or thirty years ago one had only to go out and cut down his own trees whenever he wished to build a house or shed. Now he has to pay hard-earned cash for lumber from a town several kilometers distant.[13] The chances are that that lumber probably comes

[11] Ibid., p. 62.

[12] Ibid., p. 66.

[13] Ibid., p. 69.

from the rapidly vanishing araucaria forests of Santa Catarina in southern Brazil.

The widespread distribution of aveloz as a material for fencing and property division obscures the fact that it is largely a twentieth-century phenomenon on the landscape. Residents in Pocinhos recall that aveloz began to be planted there around 1930.[14] One informant near Sumé, Paraíba, claimed that aveloz did not enter there until 1946, and then only to a limited extent.[15] The history of the spread or dispersal of not only aveloz but also palma would be interesting to know because they are examples of plants that were readily accepted throughout the interior of Northeast Brazil and that have served highly useful purposes.

Some farmers are discontinuing their use of aveloz as a "living fence."[16] Aveloz arrived in Gurinhaem around 1940, at a time when agriculture was still not very important, but now more people use barbed wire because they claim that aveloz can blind animals and stain their hides. A few people also have supposedly been blinded by the plant's juice. Some enterprising and thrifty farmers use both aveloz and wire. For example, the farmer can put up barbed wire until the aveloz gets to a sufficient height, then he can remove the wire and use it to enclose another field. Gurinhaem is, by the way, an example of a settlement that started out as a fazenda in the nineteenth century, after which the fazenda became the nucleus of the community of Gurinhaem. In 1958 Gurinhaem officially became a city.

In another agreste area west of Recife, on the road to Caruarú, an informant affirmed that as recently as 1950 there was much less sugarcane and many more subsistence roças (maize, beans, manioc, sweet potatoes) than earlier, and that in the 1960s he earned the minimum wage of 1,100 cruzeiros a day or 7,700 a week for six days' work. He had three children in school and had to buy books and school supplies for them. In the sense that he therefore has to stretch his money further, he may now have less materially, but at the same time his children have the opportunity to get an education which, years ago, they might not have been able to get.[17] His family did not eat much charque, because 1,100-cruzeiros-a-day wages bought only 1 kilogram of that dried beef but, bought several kilograms of manioc meal, beans, or even rice. In 1973, these same wages (of about a dollar a day) bought only one-half kilogram of charque.

Continuing westward toward Caruarú to a point about 14 kilometers west of Vitoria de Santo Antão, one observes a landscape with a cut-over aspect. The original vegetation there must have been something resembling a caatingao, or dense caatinga, but the area has been intensively cultivated and worn out. There are only a few roças left on the uppermost slopes. The only coconut palms are in the lowest bottomlands where there remain some vestiges of forest; there are also fruit trees planted in the wetter spots. This area is called agreste by the local residents. One informant said that the first-priority farmlands are varzea, or floodplain; the second-priority areas are the summits or highest zones where more orographic moisture is available; the lowest priority areas are the intermediate slopes, neither the pé da serra nor the summits.[18] The southern or windward slopes of the serra are generally better for crops, and the local name given to the vegetation is caatinga. This informant noted the presence of much more running water in the 1940s; there was also much more capoeirão then. One property that had 500 hectares then is now owned by three families. The number of cattle has decreased as the more intensive crop activity in-

[14] Ibid., May 1964, p. 102
[15] Ibid., April 1964, p. 71.
[16] Ibid., May 1964, p. 167.
[17] Ibid., p. 115.
[18] Ibid., p. 117.

creases. The few cattle there are kept in check by fences and tethers. There are more people now, but fewer moradores. Most of the properties are small, and many of them are operated by tenants. This section is on the main line of road traffic between the interior of Pernambuco and the capital of Recife so that any food production has ready access to markets. The recent improvement of the main trunk highways helps to explain the valorization of this and many other such areas. Some of the fruits produced locally are mangoes, jaca, pinheiro, oranges, and pineapple.

By way of summary, the agreste can be thought of as experiencing its greatest amount of landscape change from 1940 onward. These have been qualitative as well as quantitative changes. This is the area that has felt the impact of the growing coastal cities. Not only has there been a net increase in the gross output, or production, owing to the prevalance of owner-operated farms, but there has also been a more widespread distribution of this added income. For this reason, there has probably been a greater relative proportion of gain for the greatest number of people in the agreste, as compared with the zona da mata and the sertão. Certainly the agreste has the prospects of continuing to be the most dynamic area of change in all of Northeast Brazil. It is an area that has been subject to neither the dominant sugar culture of the mata nor the cattle culture of the sertão. Its strength and resilience are the results of its diversity, and for this reason it is well equipped to answer the challenges of the remaining years of the twentieth century and may ultimately provide some of the answers to many of the problems of the Northeast. In the agreste we can find the examples, antecedents, and precedents of a number of forms of man-land relationships that may have a bearing upon problems of the adjacent zones of the mata and sertão.

Chapter Eight
THE BREJOS AND SERRAS

The brejos and serras are further elements of areal differentiation within Northeast Brazil and, more important, are areas that, however small in size, have great importance to the life and livelihood of many Northeasterners. These brejos and serras are the wet spots or oases of greater agricultural opportunity and productivity that punctuate the vast dry interior of Northeast Brazil. They are magnets that have attracted farmers for centuries because of their superior soils, their dependable water supplies, and generally amenable living conditions. I consider these areas of equal importance to the zona da mata, agreste, and sertão. Their qualitative importance makes up for their diminutive size.

One of the most interesting aspects of both brejos and serras is that they are associated with rugged terrain. The highlands, which rarely exceed 1,000 meters, and their slopes present a wide range of land-use options to the man with a hoe. These areas benefit from what I call the "smorgasbord effect" common to all dissected highland areas, especially in the low latitudes where the vertical zonation, because of the decrease of temperature with elevation, permits a more varied diet and panorama of land uses than would otherwise be possible if the area did not have different elevations. In the Andes, for example, the progression from the tierra caliente up through the tierra templada and tierra fria is an extreme example of this phenomenon. In Northeast Brazil only the tierras caliente and templadas are encountered, and the areas of tierra templada are extremely limited, being essentially those areas with an elevation of over 800 meters above sea level. In this chapter we shall try to differentiate brejos from serras, locate them, and assess their importance to the economy of Northeast Brazil.

One preliminary conclusion is that these areas share, with the general region of the agreste, a healthier social and economic environment, both because of the variety of sizes of property and of the kinds of land use, and because a higher percentage of the people who work on the land are actually landowners themselves. It is ironic that much of the landscape of the serras and brejos is not easily observable by the traveler who moves quickly through the countryside. Serras, by definition, are remote and in the faraway mountains slopes, while the brejos, by the same token, are also off the main roads in hilly terrain. On air photographs, however, they show up clearly.

BREJOS

The commonly understood meaning of the word *brejos* is a swampy or flooded area or even a low place whose sediments store a great deal of water throughout the year.[1] This, of course, does occur in the humid zona da mata but it also occurs in the open, semiarid areas of Rio Grande do Norte and the floodplain brejos of the Açu and Apodi—which are broad floodplains in the subterminal courses of the Açu and Apodi riv-

[1] Gilberto Osorio de Andrade and Rachel Caldas Lins, "O Brejo da Serra das Varas," *Boletim do Instituto Joaquim Nabuco de Pesquisas Sociais,* p. 4.

ers, where the floodwaters absorbed by the alluvium are permanently available to the windmills, water pumps, or motor-driven pumps. The word *serra* is used in much the same way as the word *brejo* is in the Northeast. The majority of the northeastern brejos, and all the brejos of Pernambuco, are features related to the local surface configuration. It is necessary, then, to separate the ecological concept of brejo from the connotations of the word serra. Serra means crest or a system of crests rising above the surrounding surfaces and, because of this, with two diverging slopes. But when there is a brejo there, the humid zone does not occupy both slopes, but always the windward slope, or barlavento. In common terminology, many serras are nothing more than escarpments of a planalto (plateau) or the escarpment of a flat chapada, and the presence or absence of brejos depends upon the factors of exposure to humid air masses. Other serras are only isolated mountain massifs in the midst of the Northeastern pediplains, or they may be the remains of old dissected sedimentary basins, or the remnant hills of the progressive erosion of ancient pre-Cambrian landforms. Of all these diverse serra relief types, we can designate only a few as having the truly brejo kind of ecological conditions.

It is known that increasing altitude tends to reduce the air temperature and to increase the amplitude of diurnal and annual temperatures. It is also known that these amplitudes increase proportionally with the distance from the coast —that is, with the increasing effects of continentality. In tropical climates, both these effects are relatively minor, but they cannot be ignored. And thus it is, for example, that the climates of more highly elevated areas are characterized by measurably higher precipitation and lower temperatures.

In the characterization of northeastern brejos, although we do not intend to minimize the effects of altitude, we would be naive to try to understand the brejos only in terms of elevations—which never exceed 1,060 meters and are generally below 600 meters of local relief. This is true of the Serra Negra of Floresta and of the Serra da Baixa Verde of Triunfo. One must take into account the available supply of atmospheric moisture that furnishes the rainfall responsible for these wet places. Moreover, these sources of humid air are located far to the east. The clear air of low relative and absolute humidity, of the surrounding sertões, could not provide the volumes of water that are susceptible to condensation at such a modest altitude.

What we are looking at, then, are true complexes of circumstances whose end product can be ultimately expressed and explained in terms of *exposure;* exposure to the flow of advective (horizontally moving) air masses, or the dispersal of moist convective (vertically active) air masses. In sum, the crucial factor is the geographical location of places in relation to the source regions of these air masses, and of their placement in terms of the general directions those air masses move in throughout the year. It is therefore necessary to understand the mechanisms of atmospheric circulation in Northeast Brazil generally, and particularly the circulation of Pernambuco and Paraíba, as has already been described in chapter 3.

It is the eastern slopes of the Borborema where most of the brejos of this study area are located. That windward-facing slope comprises the orographic barrier against which impinge the moisture-laden easterly winds blowing in off the Atlantic Ocean. These warm, nearly saturated air masses are "refreshed" or chilled in their passage over the occasional cool antarctic air masses that move northward in December-February from high southern latitudes and, as they are forced to rise, they become unstable and condensation and precipitation result. Another way of thinking of the brejo is that it represents a discontinuous extension, or outlier, of the zona da mata; that is, it represents a superhumid or perhumid zone that outcrops at higher elevation farther inland as a result of the forced ascent of the humid air described above. To look at brejos more systematically, we should reserve the name for those isolated humid areas within the subhumid or semiarid areas of the agreste and sertão. Some of the brejos are highly localized: people speak of the brejo of Camocim of São Felix or of the brejo of Bom Conselho.[2] If, in these cases, there is an abrupt transition from the humid zone to the agreste, it occurs because both places are at the extreme interior limit of coastal influences. They are, nevertheless, projections of the zona da mata, although without natural continuity through space.

Historical context

The word *brejo* and its adjectival form have long been part of the language of Northeast Brazil. The early characterizations of land and landscapes make clear the association of more desirable farming conditions with the brejos. In Pereira da Costa's *Anais Pernambucanos,* reference is made to an entry of September 8, 1761, regarding the zone of Tacaratú. Tacaratú would also be called a serra; it is a massive highland area rising over 500 meters above the sertão surface just north of the Rio São Francisco in southern central Pernambuco. The record reads:

> The freguesia of Tacaratú originated from a pastoral fazenda located in a broad valley formed by three hills near the right bank of the Rio Moxotó which empties into the Rio São Francisco. There was already, with the settlement of Tacaratú, a relatively advanced population nucleus. The slopes of the aforementioned hills facing toward the east and southeast form a vast hilly area extending as far as the inhabited plains, and always manifest an opulent, luxuriant vegetation that resembles the zona da mata. In the environs of Tacaratú there are very fertile lands watered by perennial springs, and much agriculture and cattle raising are carried on there. On the moist lands [nos terrenos brejados] sugarcane is grown; on the lush serras, cotton is grown on a large scale. In its forests there is timber for all uses, and in the nearby areas, livestock raising thrives on the abundance of water and pastures, and there are many cattle fazendas.[3] . . . .

Here we see in the eighteenth century the definite association of brejos (and serras) with fertile farmland.

Elpidio de Almeida, in his work on Campina Grande, has uncovered some early references to the so-called brejos in the environs of that city. The present-day Serra de Bodopitá is an important supplier of fruits and vegetables for the growing metropolis of Campina Grande, and the role of that serra was appreciated in the seventeenth century by the early settlers of that zone. Referring to Teodósio de Oliveira Ledo, Elpîdio de Almeida writes, "Exploring the surrounding lands, he [Teodósio] discovered in the serra called Bodopitá a brejo de canas bravas [a moist zone of urubá-de-cabóclo, or plants of the family *Marantaceas*] and matas [forests] in which there was a water hole [olho de agua]," which appeared to him "capable of producing subsistence crops [roças] and other vegetables necessary for the maintenance of the Portugese war against the Tapuia Indians but also for the sustenance of the residents of that sertão."[4] Teodósio requested a sesmaria of land 4 leagues by 1 league in size, which was granted in a Royal Letter (Carta Regia) of December 7, 1697, but it was awarded with the conventional dimension of 3 leagues by 1 league (still a considerable area, of about 50 square miles). As with the successful explorers of any continent, Teodósio had an eye for landscapes

[2] Rachel Caldas Lins and Gilberto Osorio de Andrade, "Differentes Combinações do Meio Natural da Zona da Mata Nordestino," *Cadernos da Faculdade de Filosofia de Pernambuco,* p. 17.

[3] *Anais Pernambucanos,* 6:219.

[4] Almeida, *Histbria de Campina Grande,* p. 37.

and the ability to judge the capacity of the land to support people; it was to his credit that he recognized the life-sustaining capacities of these oases in the middle of backland wastes.

While some observers associate brejos with certain physical characteristics, others tend to associate them with a certain kind of land use. Nilo Bernardes, in an unpublished manuscript on "Estudo Sobre a Utilização da Terra no Nordeste," prepared for the Banco do Nordeste, considers the brejos as part of the general category of agreste.[5] He cites three types of agreste: (1) *agreste seco* (dry agreste), with stony, thin soils where open-range cattle grazing may still occur, as on the sertão; (2) the *subhumid agreste,* with deeper soils, and where crops and cattle must be fenced; and (3) *brejos,* meaning zones of perennial cultivation with deep soils. The brejos are the great concentrators of people, and Bernardes cites two kinds: *(a)* brejos of altitude, which owe their higher moisture to the orographic function, and *(b)* brejos of the valley, which are rarer and which get moisture from ground-water availability. In both of these, the original vegetation was mata, of which little if any remains today. Brejos are famed for their production of fruits (mangoes, pinha, arocado, goiaba, oranges, jaca) and of shade-grown coffee. Manioc is also typical and is interplanted with maize, beans, and fava.

The comments of Philipp von Luetzelburg are interesting not only because they were written by an eminent botanist in an area where there were few of them, but also because of their historical value. Around 1920 Luetzelburg wrote that the brejo cities." meaning cities in or near the brejos zone (Remigio, Campina Grande, Esperança, Arara, Benaneiras, Alagoa Grande, Guarabira), all had intensive trade with the coast (zona da mata) and the interior (sẽrtão).[6] In the higher areas of the brejos, manioc, coffee, and tobacco were grown, while the lower elevations were clothed in sugarcane. There were abundant springs and natural reservoirs that were good for rice. Near Areia was what amounted to permanent natural irrigation. The most significant thing Luetzelburg cited was that during the droughts the brejos were guaranteed zones of agricultural survival. And in Northeast Brazil, where few things in life are guaranteed to most people—except death and probably lifelong misery—it is comforting to know where one can go to find water and a predictable agrarian landscape.

"In remote times," Luetzelburg wrote, "there must have existed in that region true forests. Today there are only small vestiges of mata and a type of capoeira. Later, with the passage of time, plant species of the caatinga entered the area and remained. Of the remaining vegetation encountered in 1920, 10 percent was composed of plants from the zona da mata, and 90 percent was of plants from the caatingas to the west. The characteristic vegetation of the brejo is called *arisco* by local folk."[7]

Luetzelburg speaks of "capoeira brejada," implying a second-growth vegetation cover growing in a well-watered zone.[8] Bananeiras he mentions as being in an area of caatinga brejada, and that city marks the northern limit of the brejo. He should have known where the dry zone began, since he mentions having headed west from Bananeiras and subsequently running out of water. He also noted the high incidence of rattlesnakes in that dry area. His summary statement on the brejos is that they comprised a vast, true mata in pre-European times.[9]

One of the most interesting of the early regional divisions of Paraíba was proposed by Luetzelburg,[10] who divided the state into three dry areas, each with its supplying brejo: (1)

[5] Bernardes, p. 46.

[6] Philipp von Luetzelburg, *Estudo Bontanico do Nordeste,* 2:11.

[7] Ibid., p. 12.

[8] Ibid., p. 14.

[9] Ibid., p. 19.

[10] Ibid., p. 53.

the eastern semiarid zone, which receives its agricultural products from the brejos of the Borborema massif, and whose influence extends as far west as Patos; (2) the central area supplied by the serras of Teixeira, Caatingueira, and São Mamede; (3) the western area, which gets its food from *(a)* the fertile lowlands (pe da serra) of the Serra da Baixada Verde, and *(b)* the lowlands (varzea-brejo) of the Rio do Peixe and its tributaries. Again, the author stresses the importance of the brejos as a granary to supply the basic subsistence needs of an area that is otherwise poorly endowed with good farmland.

Luetzelburg describes the aspect of the brejo as of around 1920 in the following words:

> The brejo region was formerly a hygrophylous megathermal true mata, as the historical records have shown. The dissected mountainous slopes of the Borborema still exhibit the sad remains of the true mata today [1920] in a few low spots and in inaccessible protected slopes. These poor remnants of the mata will also disappear if the government does not intervene. The amenable climate [average annual temperatures of around 22°C], the abundance of springs and streams, and the rich humus forest soils attracted the early colonizers who did not want always to remain on the coast. Thus the matas shortly gave way to vast areas of cultivated land with only a few remaining species now evident as testimony to the luxuriant splendor of the long-since sacrificed forests. Crops, planted over vast areas, sprang up from the soil but soon afterward, once the soil was exhausted and not able to produce anything useful, it was abandoned to weeds. In those abandoned fields was formed a thinner layer of humus which was impoverished by heat and the scarcity of moisture. Thus, the nearby caatinga encountered a soil suitable to contaminate with its seeds. Those caatinga seeds and shoots which did not encounter suitable habitats did not germinate. Others took root with greater or lesser success. In this way the caatinga brejada was formed. The caatinga brejada is nothing more than a capoeira with a heavy proportion of caatinga elements, and the more those elements dominate, the more the vegetation resembles the arisco. Thus we have two types of mixture: (1) caatinga brejada is one part capoeira and three parts caatinga, (2) arisco is one part capoeira with six parts caatinga.
>
> To the east of the brejo there is a vast plain of brejo-like character with a rich humus layer due to the Borborema streams which deposit annual sediments there. All the mouths of these streams are blocked by sands and bordering mangrove vegetation. In that soil, rich in organic substances, and guaranteed the necessary yearly natural fertilization through floods, the Paraiban farmer prepares his vast sugar cane plantings which guarantee him an abundant life.[11]

Other classifications of brejos have been made by other students of Brazil. In 1961 Correia de Andrade wrote that the brejos can be divided into three main types: (1) *brejos of altitude and exposure,* situated on the highest crests which are most directly exposed to southeasterly winds; (2) *brejos of the valleys,* located in depressions trending northwest-southeast, occupied from top to bottom by the most diverse crops; (3) *ciliary brejos,* which circumbscribe a narrow band along the edges of rivers and streams that descend from the crests toward the principal rivers.[12] In those narrow zones of "hairlike" pattern one can find a subsurface layer of permanent water throughout the year, water that maintains sugarcane and other crops and fruit trees without fail.

In certain agricultural aspects, the Pernambucan brejo differs from the Paraíban brejo. In addition to the common short-cycle crops observable in both states, in Pernambuco we encounter areas. of specialized production. This is true of coffee, for example, which has taken advantage of both the highest and wettest lands of the Garanhuns massif and of the brejos of Bezerros and Caruarú.[13] Mandioca, which is also a longer-cycle crop, occupies mainly the

[11] Ibid., p. 19.

[12] Manuel Correia de Andrade, *A Pecuaria no Agreste Pernambucano,* p. 179.

[13] *Grandes Regiões,* p. 307.

intermediate levels of Borborema slopes, while tomatoes are concentrated around Pesqueira. Other characteristic brejos in Pernambuco are those of Triunfo, Ororoba, and Mimoso.

In Paraíba, this superspecialization does not occur because of greater relative climatic uniformity. In Paraíba the brejos form a zone of which the brejos of Areia, Remigio, Alagoa Grande, and Teixeira make a part. In all the areas the land is intensively cultivated.

One notes in Paraíba the association of agave with sugarcane, while in Pernambuco subsistence crops predominate; in Triunfo there is sugarcane with the subsistence crops, and in Teixeira agave accompanies the subsistence crops.

The agave plant came to the brejo and adapted rapidly, especially in Paraíba. It is common to find agave and sugarcane growing on the same property in the Paraíban brejo. Both are harvested in the verão (dry season) and both require much manpower, which is why some landowners have so many moradores on their properties.

These moradores work their allotted plots but are obliged to give two or three days of work each week to the landowner, which is why they are called moradores de sujeiçao (residents of subjection). To a point, these individuals are tied to the land because of the subsistence crops they grow for their own family consumption, but also, they are usually forbidden by the landowner to grow more lucrative crops, such as agave or sugarcane.

The meeiros (sharecroppers) are better off than the moradores. The meeiros correspond to the class of renters or tenants found in the drier areas where the cattle-cotton association predominates. However, within the brejos, and as compared to other areas, the class of meeiros is economically and numerically insignificant. They, also, are forbidden to grow agave because of a traditional attitude inherited from the sugar-growing zones.

In the brejos, sugarcane does not constitute a monoculture; because of the varied terrain and ecological conditions it is practically impossible to occupy and plant all of the land. Conversely, there has been no need for the subsistence crops to occupy all the land. In this way, the brejo regions have always been receptive to the introduction of new crops and elements.

The sugar engenhos of the brejo specialize in the production of rapadura and rum, as do the engenhos of Triunfo in Pernambuco, and of the Cariri zone of southern Ceará, and they supply the markets of the interior sertão. Rapadura and rum represent a further reduction in bulk over refined white sugar, and they can therefore support the added transportation costs throughout the interior.

Through the years, cane cultivation has not declined in the way that cotton cultivation has, since cotton has suffered the impact of agave cultivation on those subhumid and semiarid areas that suit both agave and cotton. Many years before the introduction of agave, around 1940, coffee penetrated the brejos as a profitable new crop that thrived on the moist, well-drained brejo soils. After about forty years of prosperity, coffee suffered a plague in 1920 and never fully recovered its former status.

The sugar cycle came to the fresh, cool serras of the sertão as it did to the moist brejos of Paraíba—as though it were a miniaturized rendering, removed in time and space, of the sugarcane civilization of the zona da mata.[14]

Those improvements and innovations originating in the zona da mata arrived in the brejos and serras of the sertão only after dozens of years of delay. Sometimes the engenhos of the brejos and the humid pockets of the sertão were actually mounted with mills, boilers, and pots that, after long years of service in the en-

[14] Manuel Correia de Andrade, *A Terra e o Homen no Nordeste,* p. 185.

genhos of the zona da mata, had been replaced by more powerful modern equipment. But the old machinery was good enough for the engenhos of the interior, and in some remote areas today you can still see cane milled just as it was two hundred years ago.

One of the most dramatic approaches to the brejo of Paraiba is made along the road leading from Remigio eastward over the escarpment toward Areia.[15] Remigio is still dry, as it lies in one of the drier parts of the agreste; it is on the hinge of the Borborema zone where the adiabatic heating processes reduce the relative humidity leeward of the crest of the escarpment. Heading eastward from Remigio, after a distance of 2 or 3 kilometers, the soil turns a deep red, and is topped by 1.5 meters of humus; there are some remnants of mata vegetation, and the atmosphere turns suddenly very oppressive with high humidity. This is one of the critical crest points. The change in relative humidity is striking. Within five to ten minutes one passes from an area where one's lips and nasal passages are dry to an area where the atmosphere feels like that in a Turkish bath. The landscape of the brejo from the top of the dissected border of the Borborema, as one looks eastward, is one of cane fields on the bottomlands, dense capoeirão (resembling mata) on the back slopes, palm trees and agave on the upper slopes. One is struck by the strong resemblance to the zona da mata, except that in the brejo the growth occurs along an enormously differentiated mountain slope. One can hear the familiar long, sustained squeak of the carro de boi (ox cart) as its wooden wheels turn on its wooden axle without benefit of lubrication. One also notes a much higher proportion of black people, since the original slaves and their descendents have always been associated with sugarcane areas. The air becomes sticky. The wind wafts in the heavy alto-cumulus clouds from the east, striking the mountain slopes that form a natural amphitheater. The presence of numerous embaúba trees is evidence that the original forest vegetation has been cut over many times. There are functioning engenhos. Cane is found mostly on the best bottomlands.

Areia is a characteristic brejo town.[16] The relative humidity ranges from 71 to 86 percent and for seven months of the year it is above 80 percent. Average monthly temperatures range from 21°C to 26°C, and the wind always blows from the southeast. The evaporative power of the atmosphere ranges from 11.7 millimeters of water in June to 28.9 millimeters in January. Rainfall averages 1,200 to 1,300 millimeters per year but varies from 800 to 2,000 millimeters. This is the kind of place where there are great problems of mold and mildew.

Sugarcane has been the traditional crop of the area. The caatinga interrupts the otherwise mata aspect of the landscape of Areia in the process already described (citing Luetzelburg) in chapter 3. It was only as recently as 1850 that engenhos began to be important in the brejo. Cane growing represented a new economic cycle in a new area. The sugar growers around Areia have family roots in the coastal zona da mata, as might be expected. Other crops are the standard subsistence staples of maize, beans, and manioc. Some coffee was grown there, but production stopped in 1926 because of the combined effects of insects, loss of soil fertility, and the red coffee bug. Coffee had been grown on the well-drained slopes but was replaced by agave on those same slopes after 1940. The years between 1920 and 1940 were ones of economic depression that was broken only after the agave boom began to be felt in the 1940s. The first agave pioneers began planting in 1935. Agave begins to yield fibers three years after planting, and then continues to yield

[15] Field notes, April 14, 1964, p. 63.

[16] The following information is based upon interviews with the staff of the Escola de Agronomia in Areia, Paraíba, which was founded in 1936.

for five additional years. One difference between today and the old days is that there are more diseases and plant plagues present today, and they are very expensive to eradicate. Diseases travel faster today than they did forty years ago because they move on trucks and other rapid conveyances. This is a point that probably few people considered, but it is certainly true.

In this brejo zone, the economic size for a sugarcane property is 150 to 200 hectares, although cane is grown on properties ranging from 70 to 500 hectares. But as one morador emphasized strongly, "o engenho e indivisivel," or "the engenho is indivisable." The reference is to the fact that a sugar mill requires a certain area of land from which to feed its hungry machines. There must be a functional relationship between the productive capacity of the engenho and the area of cane fields from which to supply it.

Another characteristic municipio of the Paraiban brejo is Alagoinha, some 15 miles east of Areia (elevation 535 meters) and itself lying at an elevation of about 450 meters. There, the brejo is considered the zone extending all the way from the pé da serra (piedmont) to the summit or top of the escarpment. All the area from Caiçara to Alagoinhos was sugarcane at one time, but by 1964 agave was booming. People in this area in 1964 were buying their maize and beans with cash, whereas twenty years earlier they produced their own subsistence crops. This change indicates in some measure the affluence that agave has brought. Cotton has also been grown in the area; agave began to be planted around 1944. All six engenhos that were operating in Alagoinha in 1964 produced rapadura and rum. It is obvious to local residents that there were many more forested areas in 1945 than there were in 1964. It is a zone where the population of both rural and urban areas is growing, and the reason for the prosperity is agave. After my fieldwork of 1963 and 1964 the price of sisal fiber dropped, much to the consternation of all people in these recent boom areas. By 1973, the price had again slightly improved.

The brejo of the serra das varas: a case study

Brazilian geographers have studied some of the many brejos and have pointed out the great diversity in each of them. In one study directed by Andrade and Lins we have the results of investigations—carried out in the early 1960s—of a brejo in central Pernambuco.[17]

Just southeast of Arcoverde is a zone of brejo wherein the municipios of Pedra and Buique rise from 550 to 800 meters above sea level and tower above the flat sertão surface draining southward to the Rio São Francisco. On these slopes there are two windward brejos that are most characteristic of Pernambuco: the serra of Cabo do Campo in Buique, and the serra das Varas between Pedra and Arcoverde.

These serras are parts of the great escarpment that all motorists traverse when they cross the locally named Serra do Mimoso, some 19 kilometers east of Arcoverde. The escarpment, oriented southwest to northeast from Buique to Belo Jardim, leads up to one of the oldest erosion surfaces in Northeast Brazil, the 850 to 900-meter level upon which rest probably Cretaceous summit landforms of around 1,000 meters elevation.[18] It is a lithologic escarpment, given prominence because of differential erosion of intrusive granites that have resisted weathering better than have the adjacent gneisses. It is not necessary to go into all the physical details of this brejo except to mention that these serras are crystalline areas of differing resistance to erosion, upon which a highly differentiated agricultural landscape has evolved.

All of this brejo is polyculture, associated

[17] "O Brejo da Serra das Varas,"
[18] Ibid., p. 3.

occasionally with cattle raising on a very modest scale.[19] The basis of farm production is maize, beans, and manioc, followed by sweet potato and macaxeira, the manioclike tuber that can be boiled and eaten like potato. Mamona and cotton are grown in some of the zonas agrestadas (drier zones). Fruit cultivation finds its greatest commercial expression in the goiaba, which is grown to supply the goiabada fruit-preserve industries of Arcoverde, Pesqueira, and even of Petrolandia. Mango trees abound in the narrow varzeas; banana plants prefer the deep humid hollows along the streams; there are also caju, jaca, avocado, orange, papaya, and pineapple. Everyone talks about how good the land is for coffee, but the few observable coffee plots are mismanaged and used only for local consumption. House gardens produce lettuce, tomatoes, peppers, onions, carrots. Most people have gardens, and those who do not excuse themselves by saying that "it's a lot of work."

The systems of farm work are those same age-old routines of caboclo agriculture, with the ever-present burning stage preceding the planting of crops. Farmers harvest their maize and beans after three or four months and the manioc after one and a half to two years; they replant only after two or three years of letting the land lie fallow. One planting variant consists of planting manioc only after the bean harvest, then harvesting the maize and replanting it. In only one out of fifteen properties was any use made of chemical fertilizers (such as superphosphate or amonium sulphates). On the other hand, manure was used by nine out of fifteen farmers, especially on the vegetable gardens.

With expressly commercial agriculture farms, only three properties grew maize, beans, and manioc. The other commercialized products were mamona, goiaba, and most fruits and vegetables. All other farm production revolved

Farmer of the moist highland Serra da Baturité (Ceará) holding manioc root and maize. The moist serras produce fruits and vegetables such as bananas, coffee, papaya, and oranges.

around subsistence agriculture, with the selling of any surplus there was. In good years, a farmer could sell three-fourths of his maize and bean crop. In poor years, there was barely enough to eat.

Cattle raising, when it was carried on, occupied the equivalent of between half or up to double the area planted in crops, with wide variation between these two extremes. There was no systematic selection of breeds. There were Creole cattle, Holandes, Turino, Zebu, and Guserate, with a great degree of intermixing. No property had Jersey bulls.

These, finally, are the main lineaments of the organization of agrarian space in the Serra das Varas. That area has, in common with the other brejos discussed, an absence of monoculture and a great preponderance of polycultural forms of land use. Also, a higher proportion of farm workers own their own land, which, though small in area, and not affording a healthy income, did at least provide a better living standard than the wages of salaried workers or sharecroppers in other areas of the Northeast.

[19] Ibid., p. 9

THE SERRAS

The serras, or mountain crests, have been defined and distinguished from the brejos in the preceding section. Many of the same comments regarding the significance of brejos to human occupance can be applied with equal validity to the serras. The serras have always enjoyed a more amenable climate because of higher rainfall and the resulting luxuriant evergreen forest (mata), contrasted to the sparse caatinga cover of the sertão. The distribution of population clearly shows the attraction of people to the mountainous zones of Northeast Brazil. Other "concentrators" of population are the piedmont areas and the larger river valleys.

Some of the outstanding agglomerations of rural population in the Northeast are at the base of the escarpment of the Ibiapaba (or Serra Grande, border area between Ceará and Piauí), and the famous Cariri zone at the base of the Chapada de Araripe in southern Ceará. Both areas benefit from the numerous springs gushing out from the base of the standstone reservoir rocks of those serras. Among other serras are those of Meruoca, Baturité, Pereira, and Uruburetama in Ceará; the serra of Baixa Verde on the northern border of Pernambuco, the serra of Teixeira along the Paraíba-Pernambucan boundary, and also those of Triunfo, Tacaratú (Pernambuco), and Agua Branca (Alagoas). These serras are islands of agriculture, or rather *oases* of agriculture, where the altitude is responsible for a combination of conditions that are conducive to farming.

Generally speaking, crops permanently occupy all the serra lands, seeking the most favored soils and producing incomes that are reflected in an environment of relatively greater well-being. The houses tend to be well constructed. Agricultural activity dominates almost exclusively, while cattle are relegated to the low sertão and are not allowed past the pé da serra (piedmont zone). Sometimes a few dairy cattle are kept, but they have to be fenced or tethered. They furnish milk for household consumption and also supply an incipient home industry for making cheese and butter to be sold. The crops most commonly grown are for subsistence; maize is always grown with beans —the bean plants use the drying maize stalk as a pole to climb up; manioc and sugarcane (for rapadura and rum) complete the list of principal crops destined for the sertão markets.

The main farming system is still the primitive land rotation, or roça system, with its inevitable slash-and-burn initial phase. Capoeiras in different stages of recuperation complete the landscape.

The properties in these highland areas are highly divided; a man may own several small but noncontiguous plots. The renting of farmland is paid with money, not labor. However, in the serras of Tacaratú and Agua Branca, for example, the cattle are fed palma in the rainy season; in the dry season they are fed the remains of the field crops. This forms another partial payment of the tenant farmer, by allowing the cattle of the landowner to take advantage of the palhada (straw scraps).

In the Pernambucan serras there are few, if any, unoccupied lands; the activities there are exclusively agricultural; even in steeply sloping areas, crops such as maize, beans, manioc, and coffee are grown, interrupted here and there by small sugarcane fields.

The greatest problem in these mountainous zones is not so much the impoverishment of soils as it is the intense effects of soil erosion. Evidence of this is seen in the small rock walls built along contours to slow down the erosive work of running water. The hilly relief hinders the use of animal-drawn carts or wagons; the animals encountered in the serras tend to be pack animals.

Hogs are raised because of the edible residues from the sugar engenhos and the abundance of fruits, unsuitable for sale, that can be fed to them.

CULTURAL DEFINITIONS
EARLY LAND-USE PERCEPTIONS

It is interesting to find early references to conservation problems, particularly erosion, in the serras. Attention was called to this by another botanist and contemporary of Philipp von Luetzelburg, Alberto Loefgren, who carried out some important studies during his years with the IFOCS. He remarks in his botanical notes (1923) upon the intense erosion in the mountains of Ceará state, especially the Serra de Ibiapaba. He observed that the detritus formed a sort of transition surface between the matas of the serra and the caatinga of the lowlands, meaning that the nature of the weathered and decomposed rock materials built up on those slopes had produced a regolith capable of supporting a transitional type of vegetation somewhere between the dense matas of the serra and the caatinga. He says that

> . . . the incessant devastation of the forests and the frequent burnings of the caatinga and, to a certain degree, the widespread keeping of goats, has transformed these lands into a vast zone of caapueras [old orthography for capoeiras or sparse secondary vegetation] in which tall timber is extremely rare.
>
> On the mountains or hills of the interior, whose lower surfaces are more undulating, such as the serras of Uruburetama, Mananguape, Baturita, and Machado, the primitive vegetation must have been entirely virgin forest. Today [i.e., 1920], however, the general vegetation cover is capoeira and in the more protected places capoeiraõ [denser secondary growth vegetation] with still a few trees of maçaranduba, ipe, louro, pao d'arco, jatobá, and other large-sized trees; but we have not succeeded in seeing any truly virgin forests [around 1920] despite the fact that all of the original vegetation of those areas was of humid tropical origins.[20]

Loefgren continues his observations and calls for conservation measures to be taken, as much a hopeless plea in 1923 as in the 1970's:

[20] Alberto Loefgren, *Notas Botânicas*, p. 12.

> The restrictive measures against the continuation of the denudation of certain threatened lands and against the destruction of the forests are very difficult to effect. In the first place, one has to overcome ingrained customs and to combat the lack of understanding which, in many cases, would be in the interest of most people, in order to succeed in demonstrating the advantages of conserving the forests, of covering the soil with useful perennial plants, and of creating wind breaks by planting economically useful trees, and at the same time producing a profit, although it may not necessarily be a short-term gain.[21]

Loefgren goes on to call for laws prohibiting the burning-over of areas outside the roças, or farm plots; he would levy severe penalties for the burning-over of pasture lands. As a matter of fact Brazil does have laws that do prohibit burning but, as anyone flying in a low plane over eastern Brazil during September can plainly see, the visibility is greatly reduced because of the numerous fires—one can see as many as fifty at a time—burning on cleared roças in anticipation of planting with the first rains of November. Loefgren's comments are especially interesting because they are directly applicable to today; there is nothing new; there was a need for conservation in the 1920s and there is an even more urgent need today. Much has been learned of the problems, but practically nothing has been done about them.

Luetzelburg, also writing around 1920, mentioned that the area around 20 kilometers south of Campina Grande, the Serra da Fagundes (also called Serra do Bodopitá), still had some areas of virgin mata.[22] The vegetation of the serras was mata seca, composed largely of angicos (a type of tree from the wood of which a red dye is extracted and used in curing leather). The serras had pure caatinga elements up to an elevation of 300 to 400 meters, then, as one ascended higher into the cooler, moister zone, he found

[21] Ibid., p. 28.

[22] Luetzelburg, *Estudo Botânico*, 2:31.

bromeliaceas, orchideas, and *bromelias* completely covering the ground. Luetzelburg noted at that time that on the slopes of the Serra de Fagnundes there were the remnants of a mata into which were introduced caatinga elements. On the central massif of the Borborema, however, Luetzelburg encountered what he called the caatinga brejada, as around Pocinhos, for example. On the summit of the Serra de Fagundes he found pure caatinga with serrano (montane) elements, and on the windward slopes he found true mata.[23]

From my own field observations, it is clear that this same basic distribution still exists, although the five decades between have seen an increasing intervening pressure from the hand of man and his ax on this vegetation at all elevations. There is a gradual upgrading of vegetation from the more drought-resistant plants at lower vegetations to the less drought-resistant plants at higher elevations in that particular serra, south of Campina Grande.

The intrepid traveler, Luetzelburg naturally visited the hill town of Triunfo. He noted then that the town had an intense commerce with nearby towns, such as Rio Branco, and exported much cotton, coffee, and sugar. He noted the abundant water and even waterfalls of the Triunfo zone. Today there is possibly even more stream flow because continued use has tended to erode more of the topsoil and to create greater runoff, which would tend to raise the amount of stream flow since less rainfall is soaking into the soil.

The land use of the serras has attracted the attention of geographers, such as Nilo Bernardes, who points out that the famous crystalline serras and sedimentary chapadas have exerted a powerful indirect agricultural influence in their roles as islands or oases in the middle of the sertão.[24] Both these landforms constitute orographic barriers. They capture more rainfall; they tend to be shaded by a denser cloud cover that decreases the evapotranspiration on the surface of the highlands; moreover, some water enters the soil by infiltration and condensation from the atmosphere without rainfall. The olhos d'agua, or water holes, are more characteristic of the chapadas (the Cariri zone of southern Ceará is an example). The serras tend to guard and retain water more easily in their clayey soils (feldspar minerals of granites and gneisses decompose readily into clay), and for this reason the serras also originally tended to favor forest or mata vegetation. Other zones of agricultural attraction are the pés da serra at the foot of the serras where the ground-water table tends to surface and provide abundant water for crops. There is, of course, a striking difference between the moisture conditions on the windward (wetter) and leeward (drier) pés da serra.

There are also serras secas and serras umidas. The dry serras do not have sufficient elevation to condense and precipitate moisture. These serras have the same farming cycles as the humid serras, although not the same crop associations. The agave plant appears to be well adapted to the somewhat marginal conditions of the dry serras.

Bernardes "insists on the calamitous aspect of soil erosion in the agricultural areas of the serras, even in the humid serras." The serras have always been sought out for subsistence farming; they are now experiencing accelerated use owing to population growth in rural areas. The main point here is that the serras, by virtue of their very attractiveness, have succeeded in drawing many people to them, and these people, with their unscientific farming methods, proceed to destroy the subsistence base of their own and their descendents' existence.

The dry serras have cattle raising as a secondary economic activity; they also serve as a refrigerio, or cool mountain retreat, after the

[23] Ibid., p. 32.

[24] Bernardes, "Estudo Sôbre a Utilização da Terra," p. 32.

cattle have grazed the straw and stubble of the harvested field crops. These serras, which lie at an elevation of less than 700 meters above sea level, reminded Bernardes of the polycultural agreste to the east of the sertão.[25]

The humid serras have much sugarcane, fruit, cotton, and coffee mixed in with maize and beans. The serra upon which Triunfo is located is a good example of a humid serra; it is also one of the most spectacular features of the landscape of Northeast Brazil.[26] It rises abruptly from the flat sertão surface of interior Pernambuco. One approaches it across the caatinga and notices the presence of fences made up of interwoven caatinga branches; this is part of the travessão that separates the dominantly livestock areas of the sertão lowlands from the mainly agricultural areas of the serra itself. One can look upward and see the roças on the upper slopes and note that the alignment of the serra is ideal for catching the humid, rain-producing winds from the east. Horses can be seen munching the remains of the cotton plants after the harvest. In the background are the wasting slopes, being eroded because of overcropping through countless decades.

The serra itself is all capoeira; it has long since been cut over and is intensively cultivated with maize, beans, manioc, and so on. This is an area where people carry umbrellas, a phenomenon rarely seen on the sertão. Some of the slopes are as steep as 30 degrees although they appear to be closer to 45 degrees. The feeling seems to be that if a man can remain upright and operate a hoe, he can cultivate a crop there. Many rocks are piled up in the fields to slow the erosion, but with little effect. The area has the aspect, to one coming from the dry sertão below, of being a Garden of Eden. It is densely populated, and the city of Triunfo itself has been a place of some importance and pretensions, at least in the past. Today its economic role has been captured by Flores and Serra Talhada, and the road to Triunfo has been bypassed by the modern east-west highway that remains on the sertão floor. Unless some source of economic revival is discovered, Triunfo will continue to languish while other cities prosper. The through bus services have been decreased, not increased as with the great majority of Brazilian cities today. It is a city in decline.

The serras are sometimes sites of agricultural innovations.[27] In Ceara, north of Crato, in a hilly area, I saw probably the first agave plantations there. It turned out that the agave farmer was from Paraíba and that he had moved westward to southern Ceará where he was one of the few people who understood how to cultivate and generally care for an agave plantation. He also knew how to operate the defibering machine; a local businessman was a partner in his venture, furnishing the needed capital. The agave morador worked 15 tarefas, of which 2 are worked for the landowner. The name of the place, interestingly enough, is Mata, some 6 kilometers east of Caririaçu (elevation 710 meters). The system there is to cut the capoeira, burn off the land, plant agave for two years, harvest it, let it lie fallow, and repeat the cycle on another area. One kilogram of agave fiber brings 200 cruzeiros, or 20 cents, and the morador works one day each week for 400 cruzeiros, or 40 cents. He plants pieces of agave one foot long; he will buy land later when he has saved some more money. In 1964, in that part of southern Ceará, there were the kinds of well-drained sandy soils and slopes in which agave would thrive, and of course the high market prices for agave fiber brought the rapid dispersal of the plant over much of Northeast Brazil. Since 1966, the fall in sisal fiber has had a depressing impact upon many places.

Another interesting serra is the Serra do

[25] Ibid., p. 35.

[26] Field notes, February 1964, p. 16.

[27] Ibid., p. 19.

Oratorio, upon which the town of Mata Virgem (Virgin Forest) is located, and to which I referred in chapter 3. The intriguing name of that town drew me to visit it—and the reason, of course, that forests existed there in the first place was the presence of this serra as an orographic barrier. Mata Virgem, though never as developed as Triunfo, has shared somewhat the same fate in that it is a town that, a hundred years ago, used to be the feira, or fair, for Surubim, but is now in decline. The consensus, when I passed through there, as to how many cars or trucks a day passed through Mata Virgem, was "four or five a week." Mata Virgem lies at an elevation of 646 meters above sea level, and was once covered by a dense, tall forest. One finds the remnants of that original virgin forest in the beams and ridge poles of the town's houses. The town itself, however, is generally dilapidated and does not have the vigor of most Brazilian towns. The presence of good soils is no guarantee that prosperity will continue if the access to markets and the presence of other diversified economic activities is not assured.

The land use of serras varies, as do the work relationships.[28] In Rio Grande do Norte, north of Currais Novos, a tenant farmer informed me that the whole north and south slope of the Serra de Santana was cultivated as recently as 1950 to 1955, and that maize, beans, and cotton were the economic base worked by the moradores. Manioc was the only crop that did well on the very top of the serra, probably because the summit soils are well drained and sandy, and manioc is known for its capacity to tolerate a wide variety of conditions, especially sandy, well-drained soils. The reason that agriculture was abandoned was that the fazendeiros wanted to be meeiros (sharecroppers) in all things, not just the cotton. It simply did not pay the moradores to operate on that basis, so by 1964 the area was devoted to open-range cattle raising.

Air photographs of the area show that the capoeira caatinga was about fifteen years old in 1964. One conclusion is that the caatinga yields subsistence crops readily if the rainfall is adequate. Interviews with two youths (eighteen and twenty years old) confirmed the story that all that area was cultivated around 1950; that the fazendeiros had plenty of land and simply did not want more moradores.[29]

There are also problems associated with living on the serras. While they may receive more rainfall than the drier sertão, at times the amount they receive is excessive.[30] One informant with a sizeable family (nine children, a wife, a ninety-five-year-old father, and an eighty-five-year-old mother-in-law) recounted with great clarity how, on the previous Sunday, May 3, it had rained for ten hours and fifty-five minutes and the result was the most of his maize, beans, and cotton were washed away. While people tend to think of the droughts as being the main hazard in the Northeast, there are considerable calamities caused by heavy rainfall; the year of my 1963-64 fieldwork was one of the rainiest on record. There were many instances, such as the foregoing, where people lost many of their crops. In this same area, during the droughts of 1934 and 1953, the local people peeled, roasted, and ate the mandacuru cactus plant, according to the informant. (I think it must have been the facheiro plant because of its rounded cross section.) My informant allowed that it "tasted something like macaxeira," which is the variety of manioc that can be boiled like a potato and is quite tasteless, although nonpoisonous—unlike the manioc utilissima, which has to be purged of its poisonous cyanic acid. In that particular area, people called the zone agreste. Life was generally better in the mid-1960s than it was before, because the government had helped during the droughts.

[28] Ibid., May 1964, p. 91.

[29] Ibid., p. 92.

[30] Ibid., p. 96.

In summary, the brejos and serras are truly significant in the physical and cultural landscape of Northeast Brazil. They tend to be the areas of certain rainfall, of dependable crops, in a section where there is much uncertainty. The fact that man has used and misused those agricultural oases for hundreds of years does not detract from their important roles as potentially promising areas for agricultural reforms and improvements. While some planners recommend relocating people in more remote states, it would be well to consider the possibilities closer to home. The brejos and serras have many as yet unrealized qualities that could go far in improving the standards of living in Northeast Brazil. Not enough attention has been drawn to their significance; they are small in area, but great in importance. They are generally located far from the capital cities, and far from the larger inland cities. One has to go out and find them, and when he arrives he finds large numbers of rural people; this is where the greater part of the basic food commodities come from that supply Northeast Brazil.

Chapter Nine
KEY INSTITUTIONAL AND OTHER FACTORS AFFECTING MAN-LAND RELATIONSHIPS

In this chapter we shall try to go beyond the air photograph and seek the answers to basic questions about Northeast Brazil in the operating reality of everyday life. In many instances we must rely upon the insights of students in other disciplines. However, the basic material presented here is from the local experts, namely the resident informants encountered in the field. The discriminating question, in terms of the subject matter in this chapter, is whether or not it is relevant to the interpretation of landscape; does it make sense out of the observable facts? In this section, then, we shall comment briefly upon a number of problems and cultural situations that, although not directly germane to the central theme of regional characterization, are nonetheless indirectly and inextricably involved in any understanding of the causal relationships and the cultural fabric of Northeast Brazil.

CAUSES AND CONSEQUENCES OF DIFFERENT FORMS OF LAND TENURE

In the foregoing regional discussions of the zona da mata, agreste, and sertão, we have looked at the historical development of different forms of work relationships. A number of themes have emerged—namely, that in most of the zona da mata and the sertão there is a strong patriarchal figure involved; in the sugar zone, the senhor de engenho; in the cattle fazenda, the coronel. There is no equivalent strong figure in the agreste as it is now. On the basis of field experience, it is suggested that a hierarchy of different forms of land tenure can be listed in order of decreasing independence, or decreasing control over one's life:

1. *The large landowner.* This is the characteristic latifundio of the sertão and is also the large sugarcane plantation of the zona da mata, whether it is owned by an individual (as in the former engenho days) or by a corporation (as the present-day usina). These large properties characteristically have abundant capital or access to capital, and their directors have traditionally been powerful political figures. These figures have been and are the elite and, as is common in many developing countries, they are at the top of the society, dominating the economic, social, political, military, and clerical realms. Most of these realms are linked by marriage and extended family relationships. On the establishments run by the large landowners, it can be said that the owner is very much within a money economy, but the workers are much less so, if at all. In the context of Northeast Brazil the workers on the fazendas and sugar plantations earn a wage that barely covers their subsistence needs. There is almost a guarantee that the worker will not be able to rise up out of his situation unless he leaves both it and the area. Many people do leave.

2. *The medium-sized landowner.* This category is relatively rare in Northeast Brazil. It shares with the social middle class of the cities the distinction of not comprising a sizable segment of the population. It is more characteristic of developed, industrialized countries. Generally, these farmers operate the same kind of establishment, on a smaller scale, as do the large landowners.

3. *The small landowner.* These individuals live, for the most part, close to the edge of survival. In the minifundio areas of the agreste, properties might have as little as 5 hectares or even less, and the standard of living supported by such a small property is not adequate although it is still better than that of the landless farmers. There is, moreover, a marked distinction in the degree to which the small landowner is part of the national money economy or, on the other hand, to which he is part of a low-level subsistence operation.

4. *The tenant.* This person does not own land but instead contracts for the use of it. The extent to which he can earn a living depends upon the ratio between the productivity of the land, his efficiency as a farmer, and the amount of rent he must pay. Of course, one difficulty common to all four categories mentioned thus far is the low technical competence and the small degree of investment in machinery, which mitigates against higher productivity per unit of land or per hour of labor. Men working with hoes simply cannot produce the yield per man-hour that a man with a machine can.

5. *The meeiro (parceiro).* This person is a sharecropper. There are many variations in this system ranging all the way from the parceiro (generic term for sharecropper) who is actually a meeiro, splitting half of his cotton crop with the landowner and keeping the subsistence food crops and fruits for himself, down to the less-fortunate quarteiro, who must give 75 percent of his produce to the owner and can keep only 25 percent for himself. It is possible, though rare, for a sharecropper to become a wealthy farmer. The great majority of them just scrape along.

6. *The day-wage worker.* At the bottom of the list is this individual who hires out—at low rates—to others. He may have some independence in that he may own a small house and a plot of land with a vegetable garden at the same time that he works for others for a dollar a day or less. Or he may work under a contract system, like the *cambão,* as a morador de sujeição, paying an exhorbitant "rent" for a small house and lot by giving the landowner two or three day's labor per week.

All the work systems are characterized by low productivity per unit of land and per unit of labor. In any discussion of the economy and society of Northeast Brazil, two things must be kept in mind: (1) the aggregate product of the various systems of production—that is, how much in total is produced under each system, and (2) the distribution pattern of the profits from the productive process. The weight of history in Northeast Brazil has always been on the side of the property owner. Although there may be a strong desire in the hearts of farmers to own land, the means or mechanisms (such as cooperatives, credit assistance, effective agricultural extension work adapted to small farming operations) for people to become independent farmers are not woven into the work relationships or the agrarian society. Any threat to the existing order has been traditionally repulsed. For example, the Ligas Camponesas was a threat in the early 1960s. It is a question of patience and time as to how long such a large segment of the population will remain unsatisfied. The outcome is not clear.

RURAL LIFE IN AN INFLATIONARY ECONOMY

Since World War II, Brazil has been on a roller coaster of varying rates of inflation. The rate of devaluation of the cruzeiro has varied all the way from 20 percent per year in 1956–57 to as high as 90 percent per year in 1963–64. Since the revolution of 1964 the military government has attempted, with some success, to slow the rate of inflation to 30 or 40 percent per year, and to even less in the 1970s.

However, the economic facts of life are very clear in an inflationary society. What it means is that to hold money in one's pocket is to lose it. The only things that retain their worth are *real* things, such as real estate, automobiles, refrigerators, television sets, or even an airplane ticket valid for one year. The resulting hunger to buy *things* has fueled the industrial machine of Brazil at the same time as—and precisely because—the cruzeiro has been devalued.

In the countryside, where there is little ready cash in the pockets of most working people, the effects of inflation are most serious. When the traditional symbols and measures of value and worth go out of balance, prudent people tend to revert to the basic forms of wealth, such as land. The rural poor are usually thrown back into subsistence activities in order to feed their families. The reason for this is that the prices paid for basic food commodities, such as manioc, maize, and beans, do not compensate the farmer for growing them commercially. It is an ironic and cruel fact that at the same time that rural man is trying to enter the money economy, the value of that money is vanishing.

One elderly fisherman, seventy-six years old, who lived 5 kilometers east of Açu, Rio Grande do Norte, was on what can be considered close to the bottom rung of the subsistence ladder.[1] He lived with his second wife and their young children in a three-room daub-wattle house. They ate only fish and manioc meal. He caught the fish in nearby ponds and they bought the manioc. The dirt-floor house was furnished with almost the smallest number of items imaginable. In one room there were three ham-

Seventy-six-year-old fisherman, his family, and his home. They eat only fish and backyard-grown manioc. His house had no chairs nor tables, and only one cup and saucer. Yet he feels that life for poor people is easier in rural areas than it is in the money-economy cities.

mocks, an old suitcase, and some empty bottles; the second room had some fish nets hanging up; in the back was the kitchen, meaning a place where a small fire could be built over which to place a cooking pot. There were no chairs nor any table. With characteristic Brazilian hospitality, he offered me a cafezinho. There was one cup and one saucer in the house (he drank out of the saucer, I drank from the cup). This man was complaining about the high cost of medicine, saying that poor people could not afford to be ill. When asked whether poor people found life easier in the city than in the rural areas, he replied that the rural areas were better for poor people because, with as little independence as they have, they can at least grow a few food plants around a shack that they can throw together beside a road, and which does not cost much to build except one's own sweat. In the city everything costs money, and the imagined advantages of higher wages soon proved illusory when people moved to Rio and São Paulo where they had to pay for everything.

Another informant was comparing 1940

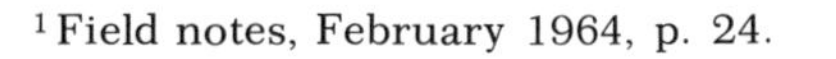

[1] Field notes, February 1964, p. 24.

with 1964 and observed that in 1940 farmers tried growing crops, but there was no price or market for them.[2] In the mid-1960s, everything cost more money but commodities also brought higher prices. He thought life was easier in the 1960s. Farmers worked more; they used the banks for financing. People who formerly worked one quadra of land now worked three quadras. A bicycle that cost 100 cruzeiros in 1936 or 1937 was something almost no one could afford, while although bicycles cost 20,000 to 30,000 cruzeiros ($20 to $30) in 1964, and $50 to $60 in 1973, some people could and can afford to buy them. These two instances illustrate only part of a wide variety of contexts that show how people's attitudes vary toward an inflationary society, and frequently the line between abject poverty and survival on a higher plane is a very narrow one. One has to learn how to survive an inflationary world.

DETERMINANTS AND CONSEQUENCES OF TAXES

One of the most underrated and important elements for Northeast Brazil is taxes of all types; land taxes, sales taxes, income taxes, and so forth. Taxes are one thing that have not experienced much inflation, and this is crucial to understanding the dire straits in which most municipal and state governments find themselves. As one travels through the backlands and talks with people, he encounters instances of how ridiculously low taxes are. For example, the prefeito in the town of Correntes, near Garanhuns Pernambuco, remarked in 1964 that the tax on the sale of 80 head of cattle (sold for 12,000 contos or $12,000) was only 800 cruzeiros or about 80 cents, or one cent per head.[3] And this is an area where a major source of municipal revenues is the sales tax!

The annual house taxes, paid by the woman owner on a large town house in the heart of Correntes, amounted to 240 cruzeiros, or 24 cents per year! People pay little and receive little in return in the way of municipal services.

Land taxes vary considerably according to the area and the quality of the land, but they are still extremely low. One man with a property of 500 hectares near Garanhuns paid 20,000 cruzeiros per year, which works out to about $10 per square mile per year.[4] This is agreste land, which yields not only cattle but also crops; it is not to be confused with the open sertão of generally low productivity.

Near Currais Novos, in the serido area of Rio Grande do Norte and one of the driest areas devoted to cattle and cotton, one informant allowed that he paid 4,900 cruzeiros per year on 1,000 hectares in 1963. This works out to about a dollar per square mile per year.[5] He then related with great indignation how the town fathers had raised his taxes to quadruple the 1963 rate, but in the end, he "gave a jeito" and "arrived at an understanding" with the tax people, and his tax was negotiated down to 11,000 cruzeiros; his taxes were raised from $1 per square mile to a little over $2.

An employee of the Coletor Federal and of the Coletor Estadual in Itabaiana provided the information that of the 17 million cruzeiros state taxes collected in that municipio, less than 500,000 came from the livestock sector, and livestock form the economic base of the municipio.[6] He said that the federal and state governments collected only about 1 percent of the money to which they were legally entitled. It is much easier to check up on merchants because they have visible assets, such as stocks and inventories that can be counted. He observed that in some towns the prefeito (mayor) can get the vereadores, or councilmen, who are fellow cattle raisers, to receipt expenditures in

[2] Ibid., May 1964, p. 131.
[3] Ibid., January 1964, p. 6.
[4] Ibid., p. 7.
[5] Ibid., May 1964, p. 87.
[6] Ibid., February 1964, p. 14.

the rural sector, but then they pocket the money. He benefits; they benefit. "Each hand washes the other." It is much more difficult to keep track of herds of cattle moving around the countryside from sellers to buyers than to keep an eye upon the owners of commercial establishments.

People in Northeast Brazil, and in many other countries as well, are quite accustomed to the mishandling of tax revenues. They are used to seeing money disappear into the pockets of elected officials and their friends, and they are somewhat less than enthusiastic about paying taxes when they see little good coming from it. On the other hand, all levels of government are obviously limited as to what they can achieve if they do not have the revenues to begin with. This is one of the wonders of developed societies, that people accept the notion of payment of taxes, and that one does not appreciate what can and is done with tax money until one lives in an area where there is very little public welfare because of the lack of the tradition of collecting and spending tax revenues.

On the other hand, one might cynically observe that inflation and the government's policy of fueling the economy by devaluating the currency constitutes an indirect and unavoidable tax. But it is also a discriminatory tax in that it hurts most of all those who are least equipped to live with it. The wealthy classes are those who have the facilities, mentality, and professional advice with which to live successfully with inflation.

INHERITANCE LAWS AND LAND FRAGMENTATION

The way in which land is divided among heirs is of almost as much importance as are taxes in indirectly shaping man-land relationships. The general custom in Northeast Brazil is that when the head of the family dies, after thirty days the entire property is divided, with half going to the widow and the remaining half split between the surviving children. Of course if all lands were actually divided in this manner, it would take only a few years for the entire area to be converted to minifundio. In actuality, the subdivision occurs much more slowly because one of the children often becomes the manager of the estate-fazenda and, being duly compensated, will administer it and pay out proportional shares of the profits to his mother, brothers, and sisters.

An agronomist in Esperança, north of Campina Grande, listed several causes for the decrease in property size, especially in the minifundio zones.[7] First in importance was division by inheritance, as already described. Second was the lack of financial resources and education with which to use land effectively. For example, in nearby Alagoa Roça the land will yield five tons of potatoes per hectare without any fertilizer; with fertilizer the yield shoots up to thirteen tons per hectare. But few people there use fertilizers. Third, the wages in the cities are around 2,000 cruzeiros per day ($2), whereas in the rural areas the wages are around 500 cruzeiros per day (50 cents). Around 90 percent of the farm owners live on their properties and most have one or two moradores. In this agronomist's opinion an average family of five or six persons can live adequately on five hectares of land around Esperança, if it is properly managed. The point is that when the land becomes divided to an extreme degree, it becomes uneconomic to operate because there are few economies of scale that can be effected. This becomes an added incentive for the sons and daughters to leave the farm and seek work and marriage in the city.

In Joazeirinho, Paraíba, a man who was twice mayor and twice councilman and also a judge recounted the case of an elderly town resident who had died recently at the age of 100 years, 10 months, and 29 days. He left fourteen chil-

[7] Ibid., April 1964, p. 47.

dren, sixty grandchildren, and fourteen great grandchildren. His 200 hectares had to be distributed among all the legal heirs. It becomes easy to understand how large families can result in a dilution of the subsistence base per family. The informant himself responded to the question of how many children he had with the traditional compound answer: He said, "thirteen boys, nine alive; and six girls, six alive." In other words, of nineteen children born, fifteen survived.[8]

In another instance, in São José da Mata, recounting the local history, an informant said that the original property of one João Miguel Leão was 500 hectares, which was a common-size property around 1900. But after distributions resulting from his death and that of his children, the average area left with each grandchild in 1964 was only around 25 hectares. Some of the descendents exchanged one piece of land for another; for example one daughter might be more interested in a smaller house-lot along the road to town while a male descendent might prefer her piece of varzea bottomland. In this manner the heirs sometimes trade properties for mutual benefit.

The important thing about the inheritance laws and procedures is that they appear to have little relevance to the economic use of land and the productivity of each producing area. One feature of the sugarcane zones is that the sugarcane property tends to become less divided because of its inherent character. As one man said emphatically, it is "indivisavel" (indivisible) because of the requirements, especially in the brejos area, for a *sugar* engenho to have a certain definite area from which to draw sugarcane to feed its machines. If that volume of cane supply is decreased by some land having been sold off, then the milling operation may become uneconomic. In the sertão the fazenda can be divided, but there must always be access to water. This is why the long strips of boundaries marked by aveloz hedgerows can be seen stretching across the countryside. The agreste is the area that has experienced the most fragmentation and in which the effects of minifundio are most acute.

[8] Ibid., p. 59.

THE PULL OF THE INDUSTRIAL CITIES OF THE SOUTH

The relative prosperity of eastern and southern Brazil culminating in the metropolises of Rio de Janeiro and São Paulo have had a dual impact upon the Northeast. They both attract and repel people. Rumors of high wages paid in those cities are passed along by truck and bus drivers, and by people who have been there. Many people have resolved to leave whatever situation they are in to try their luck in the city. Two studies, especially, have pointed out that most people do not move directly from the roça to the big city but move first to a larger local town or perhaps to the state capital; they may move to the South later.[9] In any event, it is a two-way movement. The distinction of who leaves for the South and who stays behind is interesting. Some students of developing areas claim that it is the vigorous, adventurous, and enterprising who are apt to leave for the areas of greater opportunity, and that the problems of the home area are compounded by their being left in the hands of the less imaginative and less competent. Many of the migrants to "modern Brazil" move into a complete money economy and find that their so-called higher wages do not buy what they had hoped they would. They have to pay the rent for a favela shack, pay the bus fare to and from work, pay for all food, and spend long hours commuting and waiting in lines. Many do not find work because there is less and less demand in the industrial South for unskilled

[9] Brazil, Instituto Joaquim Nabuco de Pesquisas Sociais, *As Migrações Para O Recife,* and Souza Barros, *Exodo e Fixação,* Ministerio de Agricultura, Rio de Janeiro, 1953.

labor. Many of them return, discouraged, to their home areas. Still, it is one solution to population pressure in the Northeast, as this massive, spontaneous migration of people far outweighs in magnitude the small numbers who have been moved by government-planned resettlement schemes. The way people move varies. Most travel by surface in buses or on paus de arara (trucks fitted with wooden benches), riding the dusty route all the way from Fortaleza or Recife or Crato to Rio de Janeiro.

ACCEPTANCE OF AND RESISTANCE TO TECHNOLOGICAL CHANGE

The traditional routines and ways in which things are done in farming and ranching are so common that the rare exception stands out. In Northeast Brazil, one finds a resistance to technological change, even when the change is in one's favor. The most modern fazenda visited during the 1963–64 year of field study was owned *and operated* by a man who had studied agronomy for two years at Louisiana State University. He was highly trained, but was functioning in a vacuum compared to his neighbors who practiced nineteenth-century ranching. He was practicing modern animal husbandry. This was the Fazenda Guanabara in Rocha Cavalcanti, Alagoas, and is a model fazenda specializing in the breeding of bulls of the Nelore breed.

Of course, one of the aspects of raising breeding cattle is to know well the genealogy of each animal. It came as a surprise that the two brothers who owned and operated Fazenda Guanabara knew the genealogy of practically all their 170 animals. In fact, they could look at an animal and recognize by its facial characteristics, as one might with a person, who its parents were. It was somewhat amusing, as well as impressive, to witness the discussions of the family trees. The arithmetic of cattle breeding is not common knowledge, but perhaps some notion of it can be appreciated from the data on this particular establishment. The average bull on Fazenda Guanabara sired fifty calves per year, and he had an average reproductive life of fifteen years. The bulls are enormous; a fat bull weighs as much as 1,000 kilograms. In 1964 a young bull of excellent quality sold for 300 contos, or $300. One bull, siring 750 calves during his lifetime, produces a sizable income for his owners.

Innovation and acceptance of technical change does not necessarily come by way of a university degree. One of the most impressive informants, José Acanta, used to be an ordinary morador, selling his services cheaply to landowners. By chance, however, he acquired a tinsmith's trade and there in the sertão of interior Paraiba he worked with his tin cans, cutting them and soldering them into new shapes and functions (kerosene lamps, watering cans, wash basins, strainers, drinking cups, pitchers) to serve the needs of the area.[10] The significant thing about José Acanta is that his skills as a tinsmith and sheet-metal worker are exactly the kind that Brazil and the Northeast needs today; they do not need more untrained farm laborers. José Acanta has all the work he can handle. People drive up, deliver half a dozen liter-sized empty oil cans, and leave an order for him to make some other utensils out of them to be picked up two days later. It was a source of wonder to watch this man successfully repair my leaking gas tank simply with solder and a soldering iron heated by a small charcoal fire. By 1973 José Acanta enjoyed a higher standard of living, due mainly to the expansion of his goat herd from one to thirty head.

It is perhaps for the psychologist and the psychiatrist to answer the questions of why people accept or resist technological change. But the answer to the question is important, because if there is one thing that characterizes the twentieth century and that is the reason that

[10] Field notes, April 1964, p. 68.

some countries are more economically developed than others, it is certainly the element of innovation, the employment of technological innovations, and their incorporation into the respective societies on a broad scale. It is the use of controlled inanimate power for the benefit of people that has put the developed areas ahead of all others. This is what separates São Paulo from Paraíba state. One does not have to go outside of Brazil to seek the models of development; some people, even Brazilians, fail to recognize the desirability of following national models of innovation and development.

THE COSTS OF TRADITION, INERTIA, AND IRRATIONAL BEHAVIOR

The costs of resistence to technological change cannot be easily computed, but they are high. The level of education in Brazil has been low, and is still low. Large landowners, fazendeiros, and senhores de engenho who have been dominant figures of society were not traditionally educated in a formal sense. Or if they had been to the university, especially before World War II, their education was more classical and bore little relationship to the needs of society or to the specific needs of gaining a livelihood.

It is in a developing country such as Brazil that one can observe the very rapid changes and improvements that result when an innovation is successfully applied. The opposite is also true. For example, when a town such as Acaú is cut off for lack of through roads, it becomes squalid and depressing. Acaú is a town that had one of the largest feiras of Paraíba state in the nineteenth century.[11] Its base was and is agriculture, but today it is located at the end of a deadend road. On the other hand, one can spot innovation in simple ways. For example, in Rio Grande do Norte, a large plot of crop land 300 by 1,000 meters was observed that belonged to four or five owners but was enclosed by only one fence.[12] This is an example of how farmers can work together, but it is not at all common in the Northeast. The several owners put their moradores (four or five working for each owner) on the job of clearing the large tract, burning it, and building the large single enclosure. Within that large field, each owner's portion was identified with stakes. In this way, some economies of scale were realized, there was a smaller investment in fencing, and less land was wasted by being occupied or shaded by a fence. Sometimes these simple, small-scale innovations are more impressive and successful than the more ambitious ones attempted through government or institutional incentive. Simplicity can sometimes be a virtue.

CONSEQUENCES OF CLASS AND SOCIAL ATTITUDES ON RURAL WELFARE

Again, it is difficult for me to weigh the influences of class and group attitudes; that is the task of anthropologists and sociologists, and some have done it.[13] It is difficult to document the ideas that people have toward classes, toward certain kinds of work, toward manual labor, but one fact is certain; the gulf between landowners and workers is widening. When there is a stagnation in the rural sector among the working-class living levels, and when at the same time there is an improvement in the wealthy-class living levels, the distance between the two levels is bound to increase, as does the dissatisfaction of the workers. In this day of radio and television, rural workers have a clearer idea of what the world could give them, and of what other more fortunate people are enjoying. It is imperative that something be done to improve the lot of the rural worker in Northeast Brazil.

[11] Ibid., May 1964, p. 116.

[12] Ibid., February 1964, p. 22.

[13] See, for example, Charles Wagley (ed.), *Race and Class in Rural Brazil*, UNESCO, Paris, 1952.

LOCAL AND FEDERAL GOVERNMENT: THEORY AND PRACTICE IN RURAL AREAS

Here we see the evidence of the great gap between plans and reality, between dreams and achievement. The nature of Brazilian society is one of groups helping their members and of members helping other members. The extended family is not only a cultural institution, it is also an economic and social institution, and members of a family depend upon each other from one end of the country to the other—to a far greater extent than occurs in, for example, the United States, where the nuclear family is the main interdependent unit. The caboclo farmer is understandably cynical of national pronouncements of help for him. He has a history of cynicism regarding the federal government. The main reasons for failure of government plans are the lack of follow-through or of real commitment to the projects. José Guimarães Duque, in a personal conversation in 1964, cited the importance of this factor—the lack of articulation between plans and functioning—in those early aid programs for the Northeast in this century.

There have been government programs (such as that of the Grupo de Trabalho de Garanhuns) set up for loans to cattle raisers who know that they need help but who do not have a professional's view of their own needs.[14] The fazendeiro is visited by a team composed of a veterinarian, agronomist, and engineer; questionnaires are filled out, and a plan for spending the loan is worked out. The average loan is not large—perhaps 200 contos, or $200 each. The interesting, but not really surprising, thing is that there were no defaults in the eighteen loans made in the two years preceding 1963.

Other financial institutions, such as the Banco do Nordeste do Brasil and SUDENE, have had a sizable although indirect impact.[15] There is considerable evidence that their loan programs, where imaginatively applied, have shown generally good results. A regional development bank, such as the Banco do Nordeste, can achieve quite a lot, although it is usually the more solvent middle- and larger-property owner who knows how to secure a loan. In other words, "to those who have, it shall be given."

In an interview with a man from Gloria de Goitá it turned out that he had bought four quadras of land in 1958 for 65,000 cruzeiros (about $800 at that time) and had just paid off 115,000 cruzeiros ($115 in 1964) against a loan he had with the Banco de Brazil.[16] He had a very small farm but it is a hopeful development if loans are being extended increasingly to the smaller farmer-operators.

TRENDS OF DEPENDENCE AND INDEPENDENCE OF THE RURAL MAN

Is the rural Northeasterner becoming more or less independent? The evidence of this study shows the cane worker of the zona da mata becoming more dependent, and the person of the agreste becoming more independent. The sertanejo's situation is unclear; the evidence is inconclusive. There has been great selectivity in the manner in which benefits have flowed from the industrializing society. Some people are worse off, as we have seen in the varzeas of the "sugar rivers" of the zona da mata; these are the people who have lost their backyard subsistence garden plots to the engulfing sea of sugarcane. They are paid more but their diet is worse.

The small independent farmer in the agreste can afford to buy a bicycle and to maintain a reasonable standard of living provided some of his children leave the farm and can get jobs in the city. There are some encouraging signs, such as the installation of small industries, as at Canhotinho where a fruit-canning plant employs about seventy people from that agreste

[14] Field notes, January 1964, p. 10.

[15] See Stefan Robock, *Brazil's Developing Northeast: A Study of Regional Planning and Foreign Aid.*

[16] Field notes, May 1964, p. 134.

area.[17] These workers, mostly women, were paid more than the 12,000 cruzeiros ($12) minimum wage for that zone. For them, there was a choice of employment. In an area where job opportunities are practically nonexistent, except for work as a domestic, the presence of job options is rare and appreciated.

In the agreste, one informant thought that the trend there was away from moradores, who received a house and a small garden plot in exchange for three days of work each week for the landowner, to ownership of a small house with a half or whole quadra of land on which to raise subsistence crops, and day wages of 600 cruzeiros per day (60 cents). He felt that everyone was happier and more independent under this system, which, under the circumstances, was probably true. On the other hand, another informant of the mata zone was definitely worse off in 1964 than he had been fifteen years earlier.[18] Earlier, he and his family had had food, but in 1964 the usineiro wanted to grow cane in all the best areas, including that in which the informant's house and garden were located.

[17] Ibid., January 1964, p. 6.

[18] Ibid., May 1964, p. 135.

Chapter Ten
CONCLUSIONS

The principal conclusions of this study may be grouped under two broad headings: those dealing with the study area of Northeast Brazil itself, and those relating to the method of study that was used, namely the concept of landscape evolution.

NORTHEAST BRAZIL

1. The age-old and widespread poverty of Northeast Brazil is not primarily a result of environmental heritage but is rather the product of a complex association of social and cultural factors that have conspired over the centuries to leave most Northeasterners with a very low standard of living, and subject to a social system of gross inequities. The fact that there is a *coincidental* relationship between the drought area of Northeast Brazil and the area of greatest poverty does not mean that there is a *causal* relationship between them. The actual causes of poverty have more to do with antiquated land-tax structures, inheritance patterns, types of land tenure, and the ideas of the socio-economic-political elite groups than they do with climatic drought and soil infertility.

2. The humid coastal forested zone and the dry sertão are relatively homogeneous regions whose distinctive personalities derive mainly from physical characteristics, whereas the transitional agreste zone, borrowing physical characteristics from both the adjacent mata and sertão, is largely a cultural or man-made invention of the nineteenth and twentieth centuries. All three regions, along with the brejos and serras, are classic geographic examples where a region is defined as "an area of any size which is homogeneous with respect to certain specific criteria."[1] The significant distinguishing criteria differ from one region of Northeast Brazil to another. The agreste, then, emerges as a cultural region, based upon cultural criteria.

3. The agreste is the last frontier of pioneer settlement by small farmers in Northeast Brazil. The sugarcane zona da mata was the first pioneer zone of the Northeast; the sertão, with its ranching, was the second; but it was not until around 1900 that the agreste came to evolve its own particular character. And it was settled by people from the sertão to the west and from the zona da mata (and brejos) to the east.

4. The boundaries separating the zona da mata, agreste, and sertão have shifted geographically. As these boundaries have shifted, generally eastward, at the same time the very character of each zone has also changed. It is this dynamic character of evolving regions—which in themselves have boundaries that are shifting spatially through time—that makes a dynamic method of landscape interpretation essential. There is nothing static about Northeast Brazil, and static methods of analysis are irrelevant to an area that is changing so selectively and rapidly.

[1] Preston E. James, and Clarence F. Jones, *American Geography: Inventory and Prospect* (Syracuse, N.Y.: Syracuse University Press, 1954), p. 30.

5. The social health of the rural zones of Northeast Brazil can be ranked in a hierarchy of decreasing order. This study finds that, from most healthy to least healthy, in social terms, the regions of the study area would fall in the following order: agreste, brejos and serras, sertão, and zona da mata.

6. Within Northeast Brazil there is a wide range of tolerance by the physical habitat to man's actions. In such a ranking, the hierarchy from high tolerance to low tolerance would be as follows: zona da mata, sertão, agreste, brejos and serras. The implication of this is that the provision and adoption of sound land-management techniques is going to be necessary if the healthiest areas, in social terms, are not to disappear. The reasons for the differing tolerance levels are complex, but the areas of high tolerance, such as the zona da mata, *are* so mainly because of the high water retention of soils there, and their resistance to erosion; the brejos and serras are subjected to intense erosion because of their slopes; the sertão has shown low susceptibility if only because of low population densities, although the decimation of the catinga is already evident. The agreste is in a difficult situation because it is transitional in that it receives enough rainfall for crops, but does not have the appropriate vegetation and soil cover to prevent widespread erosion, yet it is the agreste that has attracted more and more people.

THE METHODOLOGY OF LANDSCAPE EVOLUTION AND ITS IMPLICATIONS

1. The traditional "regional study" and its static descriptions of area content is less valid than an evolutionary interpretation of landscape changes that emphasizes the interaction of cultural and physical processes through time. The concept of landscape evolution holds that: *the cultural and physical processes that shape any landscape interact with each other continuously, in varying degrees of intensity, and also with the earth's surface; this surface becomes altered, thereby presenting a continuously changing base upon which subsequent interactions occur.* Within the highly diversified ecological and social laboratory of Northeast Brazil, the fast-moving developments of the twentieth century lend themselves ideally to dynamic interpretation of processes, regions, and shifting boundary zones that have had different significance at different times.

2. The comprehensive view of a problem area, or of an area's problem, is much more important than the narrow specialist's view in determining how the component parts of the problem area and its solutions may or may not fit together. In its dealings with other nations, the United States has been notably more successful in providing "technical assistance" than in solving comprehensive problems. One reason is that learning is a topical and not a regional matter, whereas area problems or even urban problems are by definition comprehensive regional matters that cannot be dissected without a sound understanding of the whole. The lack of an understanding of a "whole problem," such as Northeast Brazil's poverty, can degenerate into a fascination by tecnicos with manipulative approaches on a limited basis, "crash programs" and "impact programs" that have more onomatopoetic and semantic effect than true substance.

3. The evolutionary approach to area study and area problems has the advantage of being able to look ahead and predict outcomes and future landscapes. A projection of settlement and land-use trends in Northeast Brazil is disturbing because it shows that the final decades of this century will bring an accelerated destruction of the environment and resource base in precisely those areas (agreste, brejos and serras) that are the most desirable for the average farmer and that are the healthiest areas socially. Brazilian farmers have traditionally tended to destroy the very areas to which they

have been attracted. The corollary of this is that the more "developed" a society becomes, the less apparent control it can exert over the ecological balances of its living space. In view of the difficulties that "developed" industrialized countries are having with problems of air and water pollution, of pesticide overapplication, and of urban blight and traffic congestion, it is not encouraging to anticipate how developing countries such as Brazil, and especially the Northeast, can face such challenges with their limited financial, technological, and institutional resources.

Finally, this book has tried to be relevant to several themes: population pressure on resources, man-land relationships, a technique of landscape interpretation, and a philosophy of geography. It has tried to treat these topics by focusing on an actual landscape and watching how and why it has become what it has. Direct observation and use of primary sources such as aerial photographs and field interviews help to reduce the possibility of factual errors and thereby of misinterpretations. The more one becomes removed from the basic data, the greater the chances that an ethnocentric bias may creep into the interpretation. Possibly one of the most valuable educational experiences for someone nurtured in the cradle of our "rational, industrial society" is to understand and believe that a rational view of one's life, activities, and habitat is not necessarily an integral part of the cultural baggage of all societies. Unless we are sensitive to these "indeterminate" factors as well as to the "more determinate" factors, our interpretations and portrayal of the geographic facts of life may be wrong and misleading.

Epilogue: THE NORTHEAST IN THE MID-1970s

One of my clearest impressions of Brazil, after observing it over a fairly long period, is that it is a giant, complex time-space machine. Return, after an absence of over six years from a country with which one has been deeply involved for almost twenty years, is bound to provoke some strong reactions.

My return, in May and June of 1973, to old haunts where I had spent a year doing geographical field work in 1963–64, wrenched my senses forward and backward from earlier projected reference data lines. The analogy and image of a Brazilian time-space machine appeared as I came to realize how some sectors of society and areas of the country had progressed well into the last third of the twentieth century while others had remained relatively static. It was also apparent that still others had regressed, or moved backward in relation to the average evolutionary rates of development in Brazil.

What is the overall context within which the analogy of a Brazilian time-space machine can be presented? In the mid-1970s the population is growing at the rapid rate of around 2.9 percent per year and, in an economic boom, the gross national product is growing by around 10 percent per year. Yet at least half of the total population of around 100 million people is suffering a decline in real income. As one informant put it, "The country is getting richer and the people are getting poorer."

Another general trend since the mid-1960s has been the take-over of small businesses by larger ones—both national and foreign—through the assimilation or elimination of less productive, and therefore less competitive, enterprises by more efficient ones.

Another component of Brazilian life in the mid-1970s is the Law of the Rural Worker, in which social security provisions have been extended by law, and in some cases even in fact, to the agricultural laborer. I had the unique experience of interviewing and photographing a lower-class, retired farmer, a former sugarcane worker, near Santa Rita, Paraíba, who had received 260 cruzeiros ($65 at the May 1973 exchange rate of 6 cruzeiros per United States dollar) per month, beginning in March 1973, as a result of this new law.

In broadest outline the preliminary conclusion can be summarized as follows.

1. The so-called Brazilian miracle of economic growth since 1964 is an undeniable achievement, but it is equally undeniable that the resulting improvements to the country have been highly selective. Most of the evidence of the "miracle" is to be found in and around the larger cities and in the improved material well-being of the middle and upper classes.

2. More systematization has been introduced into the functioning of Brazilian economic and social life. There is more specialization of functions. But the greater regularity of supply and flow of commodities also means there are fewer opportunities for windfalls and speculative gain, compared to the pre-1964 period.

3. There are more innovations, more new

elements and procedures on the landscape. These innovations can be viewed as successive waves passing over the national territory, waves that tend to carry with them the more bouyant (adaptive, capable, and modernized) elements of the society while the more backward or traditional elements tend to be swamped and left behind.

4. An extremely high rate of valorization has occurred in the professions, among skilled labor, and in areas which increase productivity. Many of those activities, zones, individuals, institutions, or groups which have contributed to productivity have been highly rewarded. Those which have not been, have been left behind. There is increasing pressure for every individual and every organization to become more productive and to become part of the economically effective national territory.

PROGRESSIVE OR FORWARD-MOVING SECTORS AND AREAS

Education, research, and literacy are highly valued in Brazil in this decade of the 1970s. The value of an education and specialized skills are more widely appreciated now than ever before, and there are many incentives for Brazilians to further their educations. For example, many domestic servants are going to night school to learn basic reading and writing skills, while in the universities more and more young instructors are aiming toward a doctorate.

Scientific research and area inventory studies are recognized as essential to the national and regional planning efforts. Hence, we observe a greatly expanded network of meteorological stations over Northeast Brazil, installed under the auspices of SUDENE. In addition to the earlier instruments that measured temperature, rainfall, atmospheric pressure, and sunshine duration, there are now anemometers that measure wind velocity both near the ground and at 10 meters elevation as well as evaporimeters and thermographs that measure soil temperatures.

The work of agricultural experiment stations is becoming more effectively integrated into the real world of the farmer. The Banco do Nordeste is actually installing experimental plots, at its own expense, on the farmer's land. In the old days, experimental farms in the Northeast were places to which visiting dignitaries would go but with which neighboring farmers had very little contact.

Surface communication has been greatly increased and the economic growth of all areas of Brazil has been aided by the national highway-building program. This program has had a tremendous impact in Northeast Brazil. The existence of a paved highway all the way along the coast from Salvador northward to Fortaleza has diverted some of the economic growth from Campina Grande to João Pessoa, the state capital of Paraíba.

The character of urban life has changed most radically for the middle and upper classes. An increasing proportion of shopping is done in supermarkets instead of in small neighborhood shops and fairs, and the five-day work week has become more common—there are few offices that remain open on Saturdays.

To the casual observer most of the visible change in Brazil has occurred in and around the larger cities and has accrued mainly to those who belong to what I would call the "car culture"—to those members of the middle and upper classes whose skills, professions, and family situations enable them to own automobiles. Owning a car, even in the middle 1960s was a definite status symbol, whereas in the mid-1970s a Volkswagen is a fairly common accoutrement of middle-class families, and for the lower classes, owning a car has provided a livelihood for the families of many taxi drivers.

Of course, the greatest single cause of the economic leap forward is the rapid expansion of industrial production which Brazil has experienced since the middle 1950s and especially since the middle 1960s. Most industrial production occurs in or near the large cities which supply both the labor force and the markets for the products. Historically, most industry has been located in central and south Brazil, mainly in the state of São Paulo, and especially in and near the state capital of São Paulo City. In the early 1960s Northeast Brazil became the focus of special efforts to promote industrial growth, and tax incentives to encourage investment in new industries there have produced tangible results. Most of these can be seen in the industrial parks located outside the capitals of the Northeastern cities.

A progressive practice in the rural zones has been the widening use of planted pastures. This practice gives the rancher greater control over the quality of his livestock and greatly increases his productivity. A further progressive element, mentioned before, has been the inclusion (in 1973) of the rural worker, at least by law if not in widespread practice, under the protection of social security, INPS (Instituto Nacional da Previdencia Social). This is a fundamental departure from the past, in which rural sectors have been low on the list of national priorities and the rural worker has been almost totally neglected in comparison with the urban worker.

There are even some aspects that tend to move Brazil out of the present and into the future. One is the development of microwave long-distance telephone communication. Another is urban planning, and the execution and realization of that planning. Decisions are made which are not subject to alteration or consideration of opposing views. Planners can therefore anticipate and respond to needs quickly without delay. What other country could relocate its capital hundreds of miles away in the middle of nowhere the way Brasília was?

The gathering of data and observations concerning the national territory is proceeding at a tremendous rate. One example of this is the RADAM project which involves radar mapping of the northern half of Brazil. This, in turn, will provide extremely important information to assist in the planning for and utilization of those areas for a number of different objectives.

One of the most impressive and progressive achievements has been the planning and installation of a network of giant, basic-food supply centers (CEASA—Centrais de Abastecimento) outside of seventeen of Brazil's largest cities (São Paulo, Brasília, Fortaleza, Recife, Aracajú, Salvador, Manaus, Belem, São Luis, João Pessõa, Belo Horizonte, Campina Grande, Campinas, Goiania, Curitiba, Porto Alegre, and Niteroi). Having designed and carried out the first studies of urban basic-food supply in Brazil,[1] I was gratified to see such striking results from those 1950s geographical research methodologies. The Bank of the Northeast and its chief economist, Rubens Costa, had, in 1957, commissioned a study of Fortaleza's basic-food supply. With the help of other Brazilian colleagues (Juarez Farias and Pedro Sisnando Leite) we applied a geographical methodology of food-supply systems of the city, and it was this methodology that was subsequently applied by my colleagues in the Bank of the Northeast, to all the major cities of Northeast Brazil. They proceeded to improve and expand the scope of the studies until there existed in the Northeast more detailed knowledge of food-supply distribution and marketing systems than there did in any other large area of Latin America. SUDENE further elaborated these and other studies on food supply and specific commodities, such as the markets for chickens, eggs, and so on.

What has resulted is that the Centrais de Abastecimento, or Food Supply Centers, are a functioning reality in the first phase of a twenty-year program whose impact has yet to be measured or fully appreciated. The central marketing systems of CEASA already exist in

[1] Webb, *Suprimento dos Generos Alimenticios Basicos para a Cidade de Fortaleza,* and Webb, *Geography of Food Supply in Central Minas Gerais.*

São Paulo, Brasília, and Niteroi (across Guanabara Bay from Rio de Janeiro), but in the Northeast they are relatively new. During my visit of May-June 1973, I was fortunate enough to be able to visit the CEASAs of Fortaleza (inaugurated September 1972), Recife (October 1972), Aracajú (March 1973), and Salvador (April 1973).

These central wholesaling and redistribution centers are revolutionizing not only the Brazilian food-marketing mechanisms by essentially eliminating most of the middlemen, but in the interior of the country they are having a direct salutory impact upon the individual producer. The CEASA in Recife is the oldest in the Northeast and has been operating at increasing levels of activity for almost six years. I shall cite some details of its operations which are particularly significant and which are representative of probable future developments in the more recent CEASAs.

Primarily, CEASA achieves a higher degree of specialization in food wholesaling than was possible before. Whereas formerly there were sometimes five, six, or even ten intermediaries between the producer and the ultimate consumer, now there are only three, two, or sometimes one. No fruits or vegetables entering Recife for sale to retailers may be unloaded anywhere except at CEASA, under an enforced penalty of fines. The individual farmer or cooperative agent may sell his truckload directly to a wholesaler at CEASA and drive away with cash or a check in his pocket, or for 5 cruzeiros per day (about 85 cents) he can rent a space of 7 square meters (2 by 3.5 meters) and sell directly to the retailer. CEASA does not set or otherwise interfere with prices. It provides a structured, sanitary setting in which producers and principal intermediaries dealing with these commodities present their produce to bulk buyers (retailers), who then resell to the consumer.

The production of carrots was stimulated by CEASA because the method of packing them in boxes decreased their perishability. Initially, only two suppliers shipped their carrots in wooden cases; now over thirty suppliers pack their carrots in this way. The improved preservation has, in turn, expanded the market for carrots and stimulated greater production. Oranges are mechanically washed and sorted by size in the Recife CEASA, but there is room for improvement in their handling before they arrive there. Most oranges are still thrown loose into a stake-truck body where they crush and rot easily instead of being protected.

Within the 15 acres that CEASA occupies in Recife, there is a large, wholesale section segregated according to commodity, with protected and ventilated storage facilities, a large retail section, a large modern market resembling a Safeway supermarket, a bank offering credit lines for financing wholesalers' purchases, and a restaurant and packing space. Plans are afoot to eventually include the basic "cereals," such as maize, beans, manioc meal, and rice in CEASA's operations.

Communications are highly important to CEASA's efficiency. For example, by 9:45 every morning the wholesale prices of all basic-food commodities from every major Brazilian city are sent by telex to Brasilia. By 2:45 P.M. on the same day, Brasilia transmits back a list of all the wholesale prices from all of those sending cities. Therefore, if carrots are selling for 5 cruzeiros per kilogram in Recife, and for 7 cruzeiros in Salvador, the individual entrepreneur does not need a computer to figure out that he can make a profit by shipping his carrots even an extra five hundred miles in fourteen hours to Salvador if his transport costs him only 2 cruzeiros per box of 23 kilograms. There are no longer any food price secrets in Brazil, which is a very different situation than prevailed before CEASA, when monopolistic practices and speculative windfalls were common. Now there is a full and open availability of price information.

The farmer in the interior of Pernambuco

hears food market prices by radio at 5 A.M. on his local station and at 6 A.M. on the powerful Recife station. Prices are also posted biweekly in the interior towns, and are published locally. The farmer may be selling locally for 22.50 cruzeiros per arroba of 15 kilograms of onions, which are then sold in Recife to the wholesaler for 50 cruzeiros per arroba. Knowing this, the farmer can then decide whether it would be worth his time to take his onions to Recife in his own or a hired truck to sell them himself at CEASA.

Interviews in Salvador revealed that the original financing for CEASA comes roughly half from federal and half from state sources, and that, after this original installation, maintenance is supposed to be covered by the fees paid for services provided. The aim of the entire system of supply centrals is to provide a fair market for both producer and consumer, which is viewed in Brazil as an essential element of true agrarian reform. What good does it do a farmer to have free land distributed to him if there is no fair and efficient market for him to sell his produce? The philosophy underlying this agrarian reform is predicated upon the existence of an integrated highway system, the physical facilities of the CEASA installations, and an efficient communication system through radio and newspapers where prices are widely and frequently disseminated. This is certainly a far cry from the food supply situation I observed in the mid-1950s when the infrastructure of good roads, communications, and storage facilities were lacking, and food production was a far more speculative activity.

One of the aims of CEASA is to stimulate the growth of cooperatives. These cooperatives are the producer equivalents to CEASA in that economies of scale can be achieved by farmers working and selling together. It is anticipated that in the future the existence of this nationally integrated network will result in much more intranational movement of food commodities between, for example, northern and southern Brazil, in much the same way as specialty foods move from California and Florida to the northeastern United States during the winter.

In general, the geographical areas in which progressive tendencies are most clearly in evidence are those of the industrialized center and south, which have participated most in the economic boom. These areas, in combination, refer to the zone to the south of, and including, Belo Horizonte, capital of Minas Gerais state; the states of Minas Gerais, Rio de Janeiro, Guanabara, São Paulo, Paraná, Santa Catarina, and Rio Grande do Sul, are probably the most modernized in Brazil.

The central business districts of all urban centers exhibit a changing morphology which reflects their rising rent values, and these districts have their counterparts in the rapidly expanding residential areas of upper- and middle-class population. The metropolitan fringes generally encompass the industrial parks, but also the favelas, or slums.

Brasilia occupies a special place in the process of urban development and is, in the minds of many people, a city of the twenty-first century. It is a part of Brazil, yet it is also apart from it. It is the head of the country and in many ways it tries to lead the rest of the country in its direction—even literally, by being the destination for radial highways from the coastal cities. To its full professors, the University of Brasilia pays the highest teaching salaries in all of Brazil, up to around 8,500 cruzeiros ($1,400) per month. The university is a sort of an intellectual island where the silence of the vast planalto spaces permeates the library, and students study in what must be the most tranquil university setting in all of Latin America. It is easy to study in Brasilia because there are fewer distractions—such as beaches, movies, and families—of the type one finds in other cities.

In Brasilia, however, one misses the jostle of human contact which is the rule in other Brazilian cities. One must plan his social encounters—as well as his personal transportation, because without a car there, life is difficult. Brasilia is also unusual in 1973 in that there is a mild labor shortage compared to the past. In the 1960s there were sometimes a hundred applicants for a construction laborer's job. Now there is a scarcity of construction laborers. This means that people have other, more attractive, employment opportunities—a highly unusual situation in Brazil.

In the Northeast of Brazil the areas experiencing the most progressive change include the tabuleiros (flat, sandy, coastal plateaus) of Alagoas zona da mata, where more mechanized and modernized sugarcane production is being carried out on recently cleared forested land. Some of the last remaining forests in the Northeast can still be seen south of São Miguel dos Campos. This is in contrast to the traditional valley (varzea) production of sugarcane in Pernambuco and Paraíba. Mention has already been made of the planted pastures of the agrests, observed especially in Paraíba state. In the sertão there are small but economically important areas of intensive crop production, such as the tomato plantations at Boqueirão in Paraíba state, and the new peanut and cashew plantations in Ceará state.

STATIC SECTORS AND AREAS

The main sector, or group, which can be characterized as static within Northeastern Brazil is that group of farmers who own less than 5 hectares of land. These farmers' subsistence base is not large enough to give them any economies of scale. However, their production allows them to feed themselves and to keep up with the national inflation rates at more or less the same standard of living.

An equivalent sector is the better-trained salaried workers of the cities, including members of the lower-middle-class workers whose specialized skills have enabled them to earn rising incomes with a purchasing power which has kept even with the rising cost of living. In real terms, these people, like the aforementioned farmers, have occupied a relatively static position within Brazilian economic life.

The standard of living, however, amounts to much more than simply the goods and services that incomes will buy. In many instances there is an improvement in the living standard owing to increased access to educational and health facilities; in other words, people now have access to these services which often cost little or nothing and which were previously unavailable to them.

The areas which could be characterized as static would also include most of the mountain fastnesses, or serras, such as the Serra do Baturité in Ceará or the Serra de Triunfo in Pernambuco state. These are relatively remote areas which have always been difficult of access and, in most instances, the serras, although they continue to be oases of fruit and vegetable production for the cities, still have not experienced a pronounced economic growth. I was surprised to see that the roads over the Serra da Baturité had not been improved since I had been there in 1957. Triunfo, which is the most highly elevated city in Northeast Brazil (1,060 meters), is relatively less accessible now than it was in the nineteenth century when it lay along the main road from Ceará to Recife and was an important regional market town. As with most places which have historically been difficult of access, the development of those which continue to be inaccessible tends to remain static.

REGRESSIVE OR BACKWARD-MOVING SECTORS AND AREAS

Some aspects of Brazilian life represent, in my opinion, a step backward. Most of these aspects are not unique to Northeast Brazil, although others are. Pollution, certainly, has no nationality.

First of all, the quality of urban air and of

noise level have deteriorated, and although the quality of drinking water may have improved, owing to installation of more treatment plants, the quality of other water near the cities has certainly deteriorated. Industry and the lack of adequate sewerage have increased water pollution tremendously. Rio de Janeiro and São Paulo have a level of air pollution comparable to that of Mexico City where, in January 1971, it was impossible to see the snow-capped volcanoes of Popocateptl and Ixtacihuatl, which were clearly visible in 1955 and 1959, and the Paseo de la Reforma was intolerable at times because of the noxious, polluted air. In May 1973, Sugarloaf Mountain was barely visible from Santos Dumont Airport in downtown Rio de Janeiro. There is an unmistakable deterioration of the air in Brazil's cities as the rates of industrial production and car ownership increase without adequate antipollution enforcement.

The Brazilian automotive industry has grown fantastically from a production of practically nothing in 1956 to one of around half a million vehicles per year in 1973. While the highway program has provided the means for national integration by which many Brazilians are coming to know their country it is obvious that the street plans have not been altered to handle this burgeoning number of automobiles. One notes that Europeans are contemplating closing certain areas of their cities to vehicular traffic, and Brazil may have to choose that route also. It is ironic that progress in certain sectors (car production) brings such misery in others (urban traffic). In Salvador, for example, not only do cars now clog the ancient, steep streets which were built to accommodate animal-drawn conveyances, but the construction of a new sewer system has further compounded the problem. Salvador, long remembered as a romantic, sleepy, colonial city, has become one prolonged traffic jam. Traffic jams are also the rule in Rio, São Paulo, Belo Horizonte, and so on.

The man in the street in Brazil will tell you that the fixed-wage worker is falling behind in the face of the rising cost of living. I met sugarcane workers in Pernambuco who were earning 7.120 cruzeiros a day, or about $1.20, yet meat costs 8 to 10 cruzeiros a kilogram and beans cost 4.50 cruzeiros, and on top of all this, a further anxiety to these workers is the fact that their jobs are being taken away by machines. In other words, while the sugar industry becomes more efficient, the people who work in it get displaced. A recent statement[2] by a group of prominent Northeastern priests documented some of these inequities. The pamphlet merited an editorial in the *New York Times* but could not be openly circulated in Brazil.

Urban crime is on the increase, as is most apparent in those cities which have experienced the most economic and social transformations—namely, São Paulo and Rio de Janeiro.

There has also been a relaxation in the enforcement of child labor laws, especially in the industrial South, so that a minor between twelve and eighteen years of age may now be paid at half to two-thirds of the former rate for some jobs—even skilled jobs. The relaxation is not in the fact that minors are allowed to work, which is frequently the only livelihood for a family, but in that they are now allowed to be paid less than their work is worth because they are minors.

Brazilians are bemoaning the demise of the free, easy-going Cariocan spirit in Rio; the man who shines shoes is earning more money but is apparently enjoying it less. A taciturn demeanor has, in at least some instances, replaced the earlier talkative, jovial air.

The quality of Indian life continues to deteriorate. One anthropologist related that the relocation of Indian tribes during the opening of the trans-Amazon Highway, done supposedly

[2] *Eu Ouvi os Clamores do Meu Povo,* Documento de Bispos e Superiores Religiosos do Nordeste, May 6, 1973. Editora Beneditina Ltda. Salvador, Bahia.

to protect them, has instead had extremely debilitating repercussions. The reason is that the natural habitat of a tribe, its environmental locus and the field of its activity, is very important. Certain natural features, such as unusual rock formations or waterfalls, often have a personal or religious significance to tribal members. To pick that tribe up and move it elsewhere is to strip it of its religious reference points and parameters and thus hasten the process of deculturation.

The areas affected by the displacement of Indians are of course vast, even though the densities of population are small. The Indian population of Brazil has dropped from around 2 million at the time of the European conquest to about 100,000 in 1973. The areas where the Indian live are the states of Goías, Mato Grosso, and all states and territories to the north of these, including the Amazon Basin. These are the areas where religious symbols are essentially obliterated if the tribes are relocated. One proposed solution has been to preserve tribal areas as reserves, but so far this plan has not been successful.

Other places or areas that are regressing are towns which have been bypassed by the new highways. While it is easy to talk about Brazil in terms of forward movement, a little-realized fact is that, with the extension of highways, quite a few small towns have been cut off from easy access to the outside world. The towns of Acaú (Paraíba), Mata Virgem (Pernambuco), and Triunfo (Pernambuco), were all isolated. Triunfo was isolated in the 1920s when the road-building programs of the Federal Inspectorate of Works against the Droughts linked the interior of the Pernambuco sertão directly to Recife. The 1920s federal intervention to fight the droughts had deleterious effects upon many nondrought areas. Triunfo, for example, being a moist highland oasis (serra), was not eligible for drought-relief funds, so that it, together with the wetter coastal zona da mata, tended to be discriminated against by federal spending programs.

Forested areas are also regressing, whether they are the coastal zona da mata, the agreste, or the dry sertão. The history of Brazil can be written in terms of the quest for forested land in which to open farming areas. In the Northeast in particular, the new highways have made the acceleration of deforestation possible so that more charcoal can be produced to fuel the urban cooking hearths. Effective, large-scale reforestation is still an unrealized dream in Brazil.

INNOVATIONS AND THEIR SIGNIFICANCE

We can observe more system and more rationale in the functioning of the Brazilian society and economy, and this has meant less opportunity for speculation and more opportunity for the specialization of functions. There are currently more new elements and innovations in the Brazilian society. Planted pastures, more contour farming, and the already mentioned revolution in food-supply systems all contribute to the newly evolving landscape of Brazil.

Brief mention should also be made of two strikingly new potential food sources not only for the Northeast but also for the rest of Brazil. One is the prospect of fish farming, which is essentially the transfer of ancient Asian fish-farming practices to South America. Possibly the most modern fish-farming research facility on the continent is located in Pentecoste,[3] near Fortaleza, Ceará.

Fish farming, in essence, consists of growing fish in small ponds as an important protein supplement to the diet. Northeasterners have traditionally fished in fresh-water reservoirs and farm ponds, and the ocean, but the quantity and size of fish caught has always been small. Under

[3] The DPAN agreement is a project jointly supported by SUDENE, DNOCS, and USAID, and is directed by Dr. Leonard Lovshin.

the system now being tested, fish can be harvested by tons per acre per year, just like an agricultural crop. For example, the hybrid Tilapia raised at Pentecoste are placed in the ponds at six weeks of age and remain there seven months, by which time they have attained a respectable weight of 180 grams. More impressive are the enormous tambaqui fish of the genus *colosomas,* which at three years of age weigh 6 kilograms, and in their source region of the Amazon, from which they were introduced, grow to around 20 kilograms (50 pounds). The scientific growing of fish involves stocking ponds with fish which will eat the zooplankton, or small crustacean such as fresh-water shrimp, and also phytoplankton or algae. The Chinese have always stocked different varieties of fish in the same pond so that all the food sources there will be fully consumed. Different fish feed over a broader range of the biomass available to them in the same pond. It may be that placing experimental ponds on individual farms, as the Bank of the Northeast has done with agricultural experimental plants, will, hopefully, produce outstanding results.

Another key potential food source is the sorghum and millets with which experiments are currently being carried out in Northeast Brazil. Sorghum and millets are crops related to maize and which are basic food crops in Asia and Africa. Sorghum can grow in temperatures between 15°C and 34°C and requires up to a hundred days to mature, with a minimum of 500 millimeters of water within four months, although as little as 400 millimeters of rain will produce a satisfactory crop—depending upon the timing of the rain. Millets will grow at temperatures between 15°C and 38°C and can produce a crop within as little as seventy days. They are even more drought-resistant, requiring as little as 200 or 300 millimeters of rain during the growing season. Millets are also unusually tolerant of flood conditions. In India, for example, millet fields stood under water for as long as two weeks and then recovered to produce a crop. An Egyptian plant geneticist, Mohammed Faris, has initiated extremely significant experiments with IPA (Institute de Pesquisas Agronomicas) in Pernambuco in his capacity as a Ford Foundation consultant. The point is that the driest areas of Northeast Brazil get more water than the minimum required by millets.

Sorghum and millets represent, therefore, not only new crops on the grocery list of Northeast Brazil, but also a new food resource in a new area, namely the dry sertão which has traditionally been devoted by default to cattle raising. Sorghum can be grown in grain varieties and used in bread and similar products, and the forage sorghum can be ground up as cattle feed. This is a highly significant innovation, and if these crops can be grown successfully within the physical conditions of Northeast Brazil, then the main subsequent challenge will be how best to introduce them to the Brazilian farmer. Possibly social reforms can be linked with the introduction of these new crops.

One of the study's conclusions involves the changing perceptions of areas and problems in Brazil. One person stated that the drought no longer exists in the Northeast. In the past, many of that region's problems were blamed upon the droughts when in fact poverty can be more directly tied to a web of historical and social factors. There are certainly drier areas in the world than Northeast Brazil, such as Israel or Arizona and New Mexico, all of which are more prosperous; conversely, there are wet areas such as Maranhão which are poorer than most areas of the Northeast. In other words, the perception of the droughts is changing as man is gaining more control over his physical habitat.

The notion of productivity is in ascendancy now. People are understanding that those who produce are being rewarded to a greater and greater degree. But the crucial problem is that of dependency, and the main challenge is to break the old dependency bonds, namely those of the sharecropper, morador, sweatshop worker, and domestic servant. These are people who live in a strongly dependent relationship with their employers. Recent changes in and enforcement of labor and social legislation are slowly changing this situation.

The most important and promising considerations for Northeast Brazil in the future, then, are (1) the existence and development of the new food sources of sorghum, millets, and fish farming, and (2) the new food-supply system embodied in CEASA.

There is now in Brazil competition among all these innovations. This competition involves (1) plans for irrigation systems, as installed in Bebedouro on the São Francisco River and at Serra Talhada (Pernambuco); (2) schemes for new colonization, involving the relocation of farmers to new areas such as Maranhão and the Amazon; (3) plans for implantation of new crops into already settled areas; and (4) the introduction of fish farming.

Evidence available thus far favors "dry-farming" techniques—involving the introduction of sorghum and millets in the dry areas of Northeast Brazil—over the highly specialized and technologically sophisticated techniques of irrigation farming. For example, even the twenty-five chosen farmer-colonists of DNOCS's irrigation scheme were not allowed to drive tractors on their own land. The DNOCS tractor-drivers' employees had to do that job. Irrigation schemes seem highly artificial except for special crops, such as certain high-value fruits and vegetables, and export items, such as peppers and tomatoes to satisfy French winter markets. But to achieve the greatest leverage in improving the livelihood of the maximum number of people, I believe one must introduce a crop which will be disseminated readily and without the difficult barriers of technology, financing, and the like. The history of the revolutionizing of livestock feeding in Texas over the past thirty years—using sorghum—is an impressive precedent. Brazil is headed for a beef boom, and the Northeasterns, with their sertão and forage sorghum, would be in a position to take giant steps in new areas in new ways.

CONCLUSIONS AND THEIR IMPLICATIONS FOR THE FUTURE

In the mid-1970s, it seems that those people who own a means of production, whether it be a taxi or a few hectares of land or a small household industry or a business, are able to cope with the rising cost of living. On the other hand, those on fixed incomes and salaries, who have only their unskilled labor to sell, are moving continually backward. The minimum wage of 6 cruzeiros, or a dollar a day, is the same as it was ten years ago, but it buys much less. Moreover, rarely does an employer pay the minimum wage. In the interior, employers pay 4 or 5 cruzeiros per day. In Aracajú, the capital of Sergipe, a manual laborer earns 128 cruzeiros a month, or 4 cruzeiros (66 cents) a day. A skilled carpenter or mason earns $3 per day and a skilled linotype operator earns $50 a month! And if a rural worker *is* paid the minimum wage of 6 cruzeiros a day, he is commonly paid that for only three of four days each week.

In summary, the forward part of the country is pulling away strongly, as can be seen in the technocratic, industrial and professional sectors of the society which are manned by the educated upper and middle classes of Brazil. At the same time, the tail end of the country, with its poorer half of the population which has not participated in the economic miracle, is left behind. The crucial question is whether Brazil can withstand the strains that are being built up in such a manner.

No one can deny Brazil's tremendous accomplishments over the past decade. Probably in the mid-1970s there is no country in the world that has greater self-confidence than Brazil. It is a country where success is a fact; there is a "can do" attitude such as characterized the United States before the mid-1960s.

The implications for the future are that the Brazilians are taking a more assertive and confident role in shaping and building their country. They think of themselves not only as a hemispheric power but as a world power. With respect to environmental issues, they have the capability to deal effectively with burgeoning problems because of the recency of their industrial revolution which has brought a tremendous capacity for movement and for the implementation of plans. The crucial question now is whether the basic decision will be made to simply preserve the impressive nation they have already built, or to continue to move ahead. Judging by the performance of the past decade, I believe that Brazil is capable of passing over several of the phases that other industrial nations have had to go through. If the Brazilians decide to, they can create a showplace for the rest of the world, demonstrating how even the most challenging environmental problems can be solved.

It is ironic, perhaps, that this recent decade of most impressive national economic growth and institution building has occurred during a period when open political processes were curtailed. It has been a period of economic intervention combined with political restriction which will ultimately carry some political price, although no one can measure what that price will be. What few people in the United States seem to realize is that the great majority of Brazilians appear satisfied with their government.

The main challenge to the Brazilian time-space machine in the mid-1970s remains that of whether the structure and fabric of the society can withstand the tremendous stresses resulting from the unequal rates of change between different social segments within the country. In any event, the rest of the world is going to learn a lot from Brazil during the remainder of this century.

GLOSSARY

Açudes reservoirs
Agave see *sisal*
Agregados tenants who pay rent by working for the landowner one or more days a week
Agreste transitional zone of reliable rainfall between the moist zone of mata along the Atlantic Coast and the dry sertão interior
Aliseos prevailing easterly winds
Altos upper slopes
Araucaria pinus angustifolia, evergreen coniferous softwood tree found mainly in southern Brazil; a source of construction lumber
Areiusco sterile, drained soil of the Açu basin, lacking organic material
Arisco variety of caatinga vegetation
Aveloz prominent evergreen shrub that grows as high as 7 meters and makes a dense fence or hedgerow, especially in the agreste and sertão
Bagasse sugarcane pressed until it is dry enough to burn in the boilers of the sugar mill
Baixios lower slopes
Bajadas, baixadas basins of interior drainage
Bangues places where cane is squeezed and the juice boiled down to sugar
Barlavento windward slopes that receive moist ocean breezes
Barreiras recent sandy Piocene sediments fringing the Atlantic coast of Northeast Brazil
Barro heavy, sticky clay soils
Boiadas cattle herds; cattle drives
Boqueirão water gap in a mountain ridge created by antecedent stream superposition
Borborema plateau; broad crystalline mountain system of 1,000 meters elevation (maximum) dominating eastern Northeast Brazil (Paraíba and Pernambuco)
Brejos moist areas
Caapueras old orthography for capoeira, meaning second-growth vegetation
Caatinga drought-resistant, cactus-infested vegetation of interior Northeast Brazil; (1) *baixa,* low; (2) *alta,* high; (3) *verdadeira,* true caatinga, also referred to as sertão; (4) *arejada,* open or sparse
Caatingão dense caatinga or thorn-scrub forest of dry interior Northeast Brazil
Caatingueiros rural people from the dry sertão zones
Caboclo subsistence backwoods farmer
Cactaceas cactus plants as a group; *cactus inerme,* spineless cactus used for cattle forage
Caju cashew nuts
Cambão wage worker
Campo cerrado savanna vegetation; i.e., grasslands with scattered trees; *campos* grasslands, fields
Cana Amarela type of cane planted before 1940
Cana damerara type of cane planted after 1940
Capão scanty remains of true, dense mata
Capim local grasses
Capoeira secondary vegetation growth; *capoeira brejada,* moist second-growth vegetation
Capoeirão dense second-growth forest vegetation
Carices local name of tabuleiro (flat plateaus) near Goiana, Pernambuco
Cariri Indians who fomerly inhabited Northeast Brazil
Cariris Velhos of Paraíba example of a vast ero-

sion surface 500 to 600 meters in elevation. Name derived from Cariri Indians who formerly inhabited the area

Carnaúba palm tree whose leaves yield a hard wax used for car and floor polish

Carne seca see *charque*

Carrasco vegetation characteristic of land that is sterile, stony; xerophilous grasses and cactus plants

Carrisco brambly variety of the xerophytic caatinga vegetation

Casa grande big house of the sugar mill complex in preusina days

Chã local word for tabuleiro or flat, sandy, low plateau, too porous for crops

Chapada de Araripe 1,000-meter-high porous sandstone cap rock covering Ceará-Pernambuco boundary; an important aquifer

Carne do Ceará Ceara meat; beef with all moisture removed, very light and tasty, and ideal for frontier life where mobility and storing qualities are essential

Charque dried beef, jerky; see also *carne do Ceará*

Chuvas de caju critical rains on the eastern coast of Brazil (cashew rains)

Chuvas de verão summer rains (November through March)

Ciclo dos bangues engenho cycle of sugarcane production before the modern usina (sugar mill)

Coronel Colonel, local politically powerful individual, usually a large landowner

Cruzeiros Brazilian currency unit—1,000 worth $15 in 1957; 1,000 worth $1 in 1964; 1 new cruzeiro (equal to 1,000 old cruzeiros) worth 17 cents in 1973

Cuestas ridges of dipping sedimentary rock formations

Desbravador colonial frontiersman or bushwacker

Devastação das matas deforestation

Dizimo one-tenth

Doação document or letter of land grant

Donatories individuals who received large grants of land from the Portuguese Crown

Embaúba tree of the mata zone, usually indicative of second growth in a fertile area

Engenho, engenho simple preindustrial sugar mill

Facheiro tall, treelike, cactus-plant species of the caatinga

Farinha de mandioca manioc meal; *farofa,* manioc meal toasted in lard with bits of meat added

Faveleiro tall cactus plant of the sertão

Fazendas farms, usually large cattle ranches; *fazenda de gado,* cattle ranch

Fazendeiros farmers

Feitorias factories

Flagellados drought refugees, literally "the beaten ones"

Foreiro landless worker

Gerais grassy wastelands; contractions of *campos gerais,* which means literally general fields

Goiaba a fruit used to make a sweet, paste dessert

Grandes secas extreme droughts, such as those that occurred in 1877 and 1932

Herbaceo herbaceous cotton

Humus topsoil horizon rich in organic materials

Inverno literally winter, but the connotation in Northeast Brazil is the time of the rainy season—in the winter along the coast and during the fall in the interior

Juiz Conservador das Matas Forest conservation judge

Latifundios large land-holding

Lavouras secas dry crops not requiring artificially applied water

Lenha firewood; *lenhador,* woodsman who gathers firewood, sometimes for making charcoal

Ligas Camponesas Peasant Leagues

Maçaranduba tall tree common in the original forests of the mata and agreste zones

Mandacaru cactus used as cattle fodder during drought and after the cactus spines are burned off

Massapé heavy, clayey, impermeable soils commonly drained for sugarcane growing

GLOSSARY

Mata forest, connoting moist, fertile conditions found in forest soils
Mata virgem virgin forest
Mattas true forest
Meeiro sharecropper
Meia one-half
Metropole mother country; i.e., Portugal
Mil Reis old currency denomination; literally "one thousand kings," which equaled one old cruzeiro—worth 1½ cents in 1957; 300 cruzeiros a year is the same as 300 mil reis a year
Minifundio small land-holding ranging from about 1 hectare in the agreste to 10 hectares in the sertão
Mocó arboreal cotton
Moradores sharecroppers
Moradores de sujeição "residents of subjection"; dependent sharecroppers
Municipio equivalent of county
New cariri area of southern Ceará to which the refugee Cariri Indians of Paraíba fled in the colonial period
Nordestinos people native to Northeast Brazil
Oficinas charque-making establishments
Palma spineless cactus used as cattle forage in the Northeast during droughts
Palma da corte or *aputia ficus-indica* great palma
Parceiro meeiro sharecropper
Pau Brasil Brazilwood
Pé da serra most piedmont areas
Planalto plateau
Palmares palm trees; the humbler *buriti* palm is used for roofing
Quintal backyard
Quinto one-fifth
Rapadura block of dark brown sugar
Retirantes refugees
Ria drowned river mouths along Northeast Brazil
Rios do açucar sugar rivers; felicitous descriptive expression applied to the sugarcane monoculture that fringes the lower courses of rivers emptying into the Atlantic Ocean south of Natal in Rio Grande do Norte
Roça fields, or farm plot of cultivated land; *roçadas,* farm plots; *roça farming,* slash-and-burn farming; land rotation
Salão alkaline, impermeable soil with high salt content used for cotton and pasture
Seismarias colonial land-grant subdivisions
Senhores de engenhoes sugar-mill owners and dominant social figures in Brazil's history
Seridó driest areas of Rio Grande do Norte and Paraíba, where cotton thrives
Serrano montane
Serras mountains
Sertanejos inhabitants of the dry interior of Northeast Brazil; those who live in the sertão (also *sertanistas*)
Sertão dry, sparsely settled interior of Northeast Brazil; *sertão baixo,* interior Paraiba immediately west of Campina Grande; *sertão de dentro,* inner sertãos
Sertões high sertões, deep interior backlands; *sertões de fora,* outer sertões
Sisal crop also called agave that produces fiber used for baling twine and rope; cellulose waste is used as fertilizer; grows well in agreste zone
Sitiantes small, independent farmers who own their land
Sitios small farm plot
Solto open-range cattle raising
Sorte "luck" system of paying a cowboy with one of every four calves born in his herd
Sotavento leeward slope of a summit divide that receives less rain than the windward slope (see *barlavento*)
Tabuleiros broad, flat, sedimentary surfaces between stream valleys
Técnico person with specialized technical knowledge
Terça one-third
Terracettes cattle paths, on slopes, not quite parallel to the contour; caused by trampling cattle hooves that aggravate erosion
Travessão regional divide composed of barbed wire, stones, or a trench separating essentially grazing areas from cultivated areas; *travessões,* fences

Travessias fording places and passes
Usinas sugar factories; *usina central,* large central sugar factory
Usineiros sugar-mill owners
Vaqueiros cowboys or ranch hands; *vaqueiros sertanejo,* backland cattlemen
Varzeas river floodplains characterized by moist, fertile soils
Vazante floodplain farming
Vintena one-twentieth
Xerophytic adjective referring to drought-resistant or drought-tolerant vegetation
Xique-xique low, rambling cactus plant
Zona da mata humid coastal zone of Northeast Brazil

BIBLIOGRAPHY

Abreu, Capistrano de. *Caminhos Antigos e Povoamento do Brasil.* Rio de Janeiro: 1930.

Ab'Saber, Aziz Nacib. "Relevo, Estrutura, e Rede Hidrográfica do Brasil." *Boletim Geografico* 21 (1963): 173.

Adonias, Isa. *Catálogo de Plantas e Mapas da Cidade do Rio de Janeiro.* Ministério das Relações Exteriores, Divisão da Documentação Mapoteca. Secção de Publicações, Rio de Janeiro: 1966.

Alberto, Joaquin. "Coloquio IV Internacional de Estudos Luso-Brasileiros *Inventario Geral de Cartografía Brasileira existente no Arquivo História Ultramarino.*" IRIA, 1966.

Almeida, Eduardo de Castro e. "Inventaria dos documentos relativos ao Brasil existentes no Archivo de Marinha e Ultramar de Lisboa organizado para a Biblioteca Nacional do Rio de Janeiro." Rio de Janeiro: 1913–21.

Almeida, Elpídio de. *História de Campina Grande.* Campina Grande: Livraria Pedrosa, 1962.

Andrade, Gilberto Osório de, and Lins, Rachel Caldas. "O Brejo da Serra das Varas." *Boletim do Instituto Joaquim Nabuco de Pesquisas Sociais,* 1963, pp. 5–22.

Andrade, Manuel Correia de. *A Terra e o Homen no Nordeste.* Rio de Janeiro: Editôra Brasiliense, 1963.

———. *Economia Pernambucana no Seculo XVI.* Recife: Arquivo Publico Estadual, 1962.

———. *A Pecuaria no Agreste Pernambucano.* Recife: 1961.

———. *O Vale do Siriji: Um Estudo de Geografia Regional.* Recife: 1958.

Antonil, André João. *Cultura e Opulencia do Brasil e suas Drogas e Minas.* São Paulo: 1963.

Azevedo, João Lucio de. "Algums documentos novos para a historia de restauração pernambucana" *Revista do Instituto Histórico e Geográfico Brasileiro,* 78 (1913): 285-329.

Azevedo, Pedro de. "Emprestina de 1631 destinado à recuperação de Pernambuco." *Revista de História,* 3 (1912), pp. 179–83.

Barbosa, Orris. *Secca de 32.* Rio de Janeiro: Adersen-Editores, 1935.

Barlaei, Casparis. *Rerum per Octennium in Brasilia.* Amsterdam: 1647.

Barrios, Linton Ferreira de. "Contribuiçao ao Estudo das Massas de Ar da Bacia do São Francisco." *Revista Brasileira de Geografia,* 3 (1957), 301–40.

Bello, Julio. *Memórias de um Senhor de Engenho.* Coleção Documentos Brasileiros, Livraria José Olympio, Rio de Janeiro: 1948.

Bernardes, Nilo. "Estudo Sôbre a Utilização da Terra no Nordeste." Paper prepared for the Banco do Nordeste do Brasil, 1965. (Mimeo).

Boxer, Charles R. *The Dutch in Brazil, 1624–1654.* Oxford: Clarendon Press, 1957.

Braidwood, Robert J., and Willey, Gordon R., eds. *Courses toward Urban Life: Archeological Considerations of Some Cultural Alternatives.* Viking Fund Publications in Anthropology, no. 32. New York: 1962.

Brazil, Conselho Nacional de Geografia. *Grandes Regiões: Meio-Norte e Nordeste.* Organizado por Maria da Glória Campos Hereda and Alfredo José Pôrto Domingues. Rio de Janeiro: 1962.

Brazil. *As Migrações para O Recife.* 4 vols. Instituto Joaquim Nabuco de Pesquisas Sociais. Recife: 1961.

Brazil, Thomaz Pompeo de Sousa. *O Ceará no Centenario da Independencia do Brasil. 2 vols. Fortaleza: 1922.*

Cascudo, Luis da Camara. *Geografia do Brasil Holandes.* Rio de Janeiro: Livraria José Olympio Editôra, 1956.

———. *Tradições Populares da Pecuaria Nordestina.* Ministério da Agricultura, Serviço de Informação Agrícola, 1956.

Cortesão, Jaime. *História da Expansão Portuguesa no Mundo.* Vol. 3. Lisboa: 1940.

———. *História do Brasil nos Velhos Mapas.* Vol. I. Rio de Janeiro: Instituto Rio Branco, 1965.

Cunha, Euclides da. *Rebellion in the Backlands.* Translated by Samuel Putnan. Chicago: Alfred A. Knopf, 1944.

Czajka, Willi. "Estudos Geomorfológicos no Nordeste Brasileiro." *Revista Brasileira de Geografia,* Vol. 20, no. 2 (1958), pp. 3–48.

De la Rüe, E. Aubert. *Brésil Aride (La Vie dans la Caatinga).* 3d. ed. Paris: Gallimard, 1957.

Deerr, Noel. *The History of Sugar.* 2 vols. London: Chapman & Hall, 1949.

Diegues, Jr., Manuel. *O Engenho de Açúcar no Nordeste.* Rio de Janeiro: Ministério de Agricultura, Serviço de Informação Agricola, 1952.

Domingues, Octavio. *Origem e Introdução da Palma Forrageira no Nordeste.* Recife: Instituto Joaquim Nabuco de Pesquisas Sociais, Ministério de Educacão e Cultura, 1963.

Duque, José Guimarãoes. *O Nordeste e os Lavouras Xeröfilas.* ETENE, Fortaleza: Banco do Nordeste do Brasil, 1964.

———. *Solo e Agua no Polígono das Secas.* 3d ed. Ministério da Viação e Obras Publicas, Departamento Nacional de Obras Contra as Secas, Serviço Agro-Industrial. Publ. No. 154, Series I-A, Fortaleza, Ceará, 1953.

Fisher, David, F. "The Influence of the Agrarian Reform on the Mexican Sugar Industry." Master's thesis, Columbia University School of Business, 1966.

Freyre, Gilberto. *The Mansions and the Shanties: The Making of Modern Brazil.* Translated and edited by Harriet de Onís. New York: Alfred A. Knopf, 1963.

———. *New World in the Tropics: The Culture of Modern Brazil.* New York: Alfred A. Knopf, 1959.

———. *The Masters and the Slaves: A Study in the Development of Brazilian Civilization.* New York: Alfred A. Knopf, 1956.

Galloway, John H. "Pernambuco 1770–1920: An Historical Geography." Ph.D. dissertation, University of London, 1965.

Gomez, Pimentel. "Agua no Nordeste." *Revista Brasileira de Geografia.* Vol. 22, no. 3 (1960), pp. 23–60.

Guenther, Konrad. *A Naturalist in Brazil.* London: 1931.

Guerra, Flavio. *Pernambuco e a Comarca do São Francisco.* Directoria de Documentacão e Cultura, Prefeitura Municipal do Recife, 1951.

Harris, Marvin. *Town and Country in Brazil.* New York: Columbia University Press, 1956.

Haynes, James L. "Estimates of Physical Resources for Agricultural Production in Pernambuco and Opinions Regarding Possibilities for Increasing Their Productive Use." Prepared for Instituto de Pesquisas Agronômicas, Secretaria de Agricultura, Industria e Comércio, Estado de Pernambuco, 1960. (Mimeo.)

IBGE. CNG. *Estudos da Zona de Influencia da Cachoeira de Paulo Afonso.* Rio de Janeiro: IBGE, 1952.

Iria, Joaquin Alberto. "Inventaria Geral dos Codices do Arquivo Histórico Ultramarino Apenas Referentes do Brasil." *Studie,* no. 18 (1966), pp. 41–191.

James, Preston E. *Latin America.* 3d ed. New York: Odyssey Press, 1959.

Koster, Henry. *Travels in Brazil.* London: 1816.

Lins, Rachel Caldas, and Andrade, Gilberto Osorio de. "Diferentes Combinações do Meio

Natural da Zona da Mata Nordestina." *Cadernos da Faculdade de Filosofia de Pernambuco,* University of Recife, no. 9, Serie VI-6, Department of Geography. 2 Facs. XXC Geografia Regional, October 1963.

Loefgren, Alberto. *Contribuições para a Questão Florestal da Região do Nordeste do Brasil,* Ministério do Viação e Obras Contra as Seccas, Publ. No. 18, Serie I-A. *Investigações Botanicas,* 2d ed. 1923.

———. *Notas Botânicas* (Ceará), Ministério de Viacão e Obras Publicas, Inspectoría de Obras Contra as Seccas, Publ. No. 2, Serie I-A. *Investigações Botanicas,* 2d ed., Imprensa Ingleza: 1923.

Luetzelburg, Philipp von. *Estudo Botânico do Nordeste.* 3 vols. IFOCS Publ. No. 57, Serie I-A. Rio de Janeiro: 1924.

Magnanini, Alceu. "Aspectos Fitogeográficos do Brasil," *Revista Brasileira de Geografia.* Vol. 23, no. 4 (1961), pp. 93–102.

Maksoud, Henry. "O Estado Atual dos Conhecimentos Sôbre os Recursos de Agua do Nordeste." *Revista Brasileira de Geografia.* Vol. 23, no. 1 (1961), pp. 3–119.

Marcgrav, Georg. *História Natural do Brasil.* Translated by José Procopio de Magalhães, São Paulo: Imprensa Oficial do Estado, 1942. Facsimile edition of the original volume with critical comments and evaluations. Original Latin version: Marcgrav, Georg (de Liebstad) *Historiae Rerum Naturalieus Brasiliae.* Amsterdam: 1648.

Martin, Gene. "Land Division in Central Chile." Ph.D. dissertation, Syracuse University, 1955.

Melo, Mario Lacerda de. "The Humid Zone of Pernambuco." Paper read at the AGB, 14 March 1964, Recife, Pernambuco.

———. *Northeast Excursion Guidebook.* No. 7. Rio de Janeiro: IGU, 1956.

———. "Aspectos da Geografia do Açucar no Brasil." *Revista Brasileira de Geografia,* Vol. 16, no. 3 (1954), p. 157.

Meneses, Djacir. *O Outro Nordeste: Formação Social do Nordeste.* Rio de Janeiro: José Olympo Editôres, 1937.

Meneses, José Cezar de. "Idéa da população da Capitania de Pernambuco e das suas annexas, extenção de suas costas, rios, e povoações notaveis, agricultura, número dos engenhos, contractos, e rendimentos reaes, augmento que estes tem tido, etc. desde o anno de 1774 em que tomou posse do Governo das mesmas Capitanias o Governador e Capitão General José Cezar de Menezes." *Annaes da Biblioteca Nacional do Rio de Janeiro,* Rio de Janeiro, 1918, vol. 40 (1923) pp. 1–111.

Moraes, Major João de Mello. *Aspectos da Região Litoranea do Nordeste.* Rio de Janeiro: Serviço Geografico do Exercito, 1948.

Moreira, José de Medonça de Mattos. "As Matas das Alagoas: Providencias Acerca dellas e sua Descripção." Written from Porto de Pedras, August 2, 1797. *Revista Trimensal do Instituto Histórico Geográfico e Ethnographico do Brasil,* vol. 22, 1859.

Nobrega, Humberto. *O Meio e o Homen da Paraíba.* João Pessoa: Departamento de Publicidad, 1950.

Pereira da Costa, Francisco Augusto. *Anais Pernambucanos, 1493–1590.* 6 vols. Recife: Arquivo Público Estadual, 1951–54.

Prost, Gerard. "Dans le Nord-Est du Brasil." *Les Cahiers d' Outre-Mer,* 22 (1967): 367–93; 21 (1968): 78–102. Also Extract (reprint) of above.

Risonis, Guehelmi, M.D. *De Medicina Brasiliensi.* Amsterdam: Libri Quatuor, 1648.

Robock, Stefan, *Brazil's Developing Northeast: A Study of Regional Planning and Foreign Aid.* Washington, D.C.: Brookings Institute, 1963.

Sampaio, Theodoro. *O Rio Sõ Francisco e a Chapada Diamantinas.* 2d ed. Bahia: Livraria Progresso Editôra, 1955.

Schlesinger, Hugo *Geografia Industrial do Brasil.* 2d ed. São Paulo: Atlas, 1958.

Soares, Maria Therezinha de Segados. "Fisionomia e Estrutura de Rio de Janeiro." *Revista*

Brasileira de Geografia, vol. 27, no. 3 (1965), pp. 329–87.

Sobrinho, Vasconcelos. As Regioes Naturais de *Pernambuco o Meio e a Civilização.* Livraria Freitas Bastos. No. 2. Rio de Janeiro, São Paulo: Instituto de Pesquisas Agronômicas, 1950.

Sodré, Nelson Werneck. *Formação Histórica do Brasil.* Rio de Janeiro: Editôra Brasiliense, 1963.

———. *O que se deve ler para conhecer o Brasil.* Centro Brasileiro de Pesquisas Educaçionais, INEP. Rio de Janeiro: Ministério da Educação e Cultura, 1960.

Sousa, Gabriel Soares de. *Tratado Descriptivo do Brasil em 1587.* 3d ed. Series 5a, vol. 117. Brasiliense: 1938.

Sousa, Pero Lopes de. *Diario da Navegação* 1530–1532. Vol. I, Rio de Janeiro: 1927.

Sousa, Pernardino José de. *Diccionario da Terra e da Gente do Brasil.* Brasiliense, Serie 5a, vol. 164. Rio de Janeiro: Companhia Editora Nacional, 1939.

Tavares, João de Lyra. *Apontamentos para a História Territorial de Parahyba.* Vol. 1, 1909. Parahyba: Imprensa Oficial, 1910.

Theofilo, Rodolpho. *História da Secca do Ceará (1877–1880).* Rio de Janeiro: Imprensa Ingleza, 1922.

Valverde, Orlando. "O Noroeste da Mata Pernambuco." *Boletim Carioca de Geografia,* vol. 13 (1960), nos. 1, 2, pp. 6–68.

Varzea, Alfonso. *Geografia do Açucar no Leste do Brasil.* Rio de Janeiro: 1943.

Vasconcellos Galvão, Dr. Sebastião de. *Diccionario Chorographico, Histórico, e Estatístico de Pernambuco.* Rio de Janeiro: Imprensa Nacional, 1921.

Wadsted, Otto Gustavo. "On the Structure of Regional Economic Differentials: Brazil's Northeast and Italy's Mezzogiorno." Master's thesis, M.I.T., n.d.

Webb, Kempton E. "The Climates of Northeast Brazil According to the Thornthwaite Climatic Classification." *Comptes Rendus do XVIII Congres International de Geographie,* 2 (1956), 609–12. Travaux des Sections I, II, et III, Comite Nacional du Brèsil. Rio de Janeiro: 1959.

———. *Geography of Food Supply in Central Minas Gerais.* Washington, D.C.: National Academy of Science-National Research Council, 1959.

———. "Origins and Development of a Food Economy in Central Minas Gerais." *Annals of the Association of American Geographers,* December 1959.

———. *Suprimento dos Generos Alimenticios Básicos para a Cidade de Fortaleza.* ETENE, Banco do Nordeste do Brasil, Fortaleza, Ceará, 1957.

INDEX

INDEX

INDEX

INDEX

INDEX